FRANÇOIS TRUFFAUT AND FRIENDS

FRANÇOIS TRUFFAUT AND FRIENDS

MODERNISM, SEXUALITY, AND FILM ADAPTATION

· *ROBERT STAM*

RUTGERS UNIVERSITY PRESS

NEW BRUNSWICK, NEW JERSEY, AND LONDON

LIBRARY OF CONGRESS CATALOGING-IN-PUBLICATION DATA

Stam, Robert, 1941–

François Truffaut and friends : modernism, sexuality, and film adaptation / Robert Stam.

p. cm.

Includes bibliographical references and index.

ISBN-13: 978–0–8135–3724–5 (alk. paper)

ISBN-13: 978–0–8135–3725–2 (pbk. : alk. paper)

1. Truffaut, François—History and criticism. 2. Roché, Henri Pierre, 1879–1959. Jules et Jim. 3. Roché, Henri Pierre, 1879–1959. Deux Anglaises et le continent. 4. Jules et Jim (Motion picture) 5. Deux Anglaises et le continent (Motion picture) I. Title.

PN1998.3.T78S74 2006

791.4302′33′092—dc22

2005011271

A British Cataloging-in-Publication record for this book is available from the British Library.

MANUFACTURED IN THE UNITED STATES OF AMERICA

CONTENTS

LIST OF ILLUSTRATIONS

PRELUDE

I T IS BY NOW a well-known fact that Truffaut's *Jules and Jim*—perhaps one of the most poignantly memorable films ever made—was an adaptation of a book by the French novelist Henri-Pierre Roché. The very mention of the film's title conjures up indelible images of the famous love triangle of Catherine and Jules and Jim. The characters and events of the film, we now know, were based on a real-life ménage à trois, to wit, the romantic triangle, begun in the summer of 1920, that involved Roché himself (the model for "Jim"), along with the German-Jewish writer Franz Hessel ("Jules") and his wife, the journalist Helen Grund ("Kathé" in the novel, "Catherine" in the film). Their lives, it turns out, were even more audaciously experimental than those depicted either in the novel or in the film. The story of the ménage is featured not only in the Roché novel and the Truffaut film but also in a larger transtextual diaspora that includes other novels and books by Roché and by Hessel, along with the intimate diaries of Roché and Helen Grund Hessel, published in 1990 and 1991, respectively. The diaries, together with these other materials, form part of a vast intertextual circuit. Each textual "stratum" offers still another layer of information relevant to the complex interplay of four distinct sensibilities, all mulling over the same nucleus of feelings and events. Although each text is on one level autonomous and self-contained, on another level each forms part of the *transtext* of this larger body of work.

It is this larger transtext that forms the subject of *François Truffaut and Friends: Modernism, Sexuality, and Film Adaptation*. The book addresses the multifaceted relation, at once personal and artistic, between François Truffaut and Henri-Pierre Roché and, through and beyond them, the work and lives of many others, especially Franz Hessel and Helen Grund. Along with *Jules and Jim* I study another Roché novel adapted by Truffaut—*Two English Girls*—and *The Man Who Loved Women* in the much broader intertext of a proliferating and variegated spectrum of texts generated by the three principals, all of whom were prolific writers and all of whom wrote about the ménage itself.

Although the book focuses primarily on the four figures already mentioned, it also touches on the people and movements to which they were connected. Thus the story of their lives and writings leads us to Franz Hessel's friendship with Walter Benjamin, to Roché's with Marcel Duchamp, and to Helen Grund's with Charlotte Wolff. These corollary figures lead us still farther, to the various movements in which these artists and writers were enmeshed, to Old World flânerie and the arcades of Berlin and Paris, to "New York Dada," and to the transnational worlds of bohemian sexuality—what has sometimes been called *sexual modernism*—in all these metropolises.[1]

Our discussion of these texts and relationships takes place against the backdrop of the sexual politics of bohemia during no less than four moments and sites of artistic efflorescence: the turn-of-the-century Belle Époque (the period of Roché's affair with the Hart sisters, which generated his novel *Two English Girls* and Roché's first meeting with Hessel); the period of World War I and the exile art of "New York Dada"; the *entre-deux-guerres* period of the "historical avant-gardes," an epoch of relative freedom and creativity in both France and Weimar Germany (the period of the ménage that generated *Jules and Jim*; and the postwar period of the French New Wave, existentialism, and the nascent international counterculture (the period of the Truffaut films). Since the three principals lived at the epicenters of various avant-gardes, located in some of the capitals of modernity (Paris, Berlin, Munich, and New York), I hope to illuminate in this study some of the lesser-known corners of artistic modernism.

In terms of Paris, specifically, we find that each epoch had its bohemia and even its favored neighborhoods. In the time of La Belle Époque, the period of the events portrayed in *Two English Girls*, the Butte de Montmartre and the "Lapin Agile" were the center of a vibrant avant-garde, where Apollinaire, Picasso, and Braque reigned supreme. (All three, as it happens, were friends of the gregariously ubiquitous Roché.) In the 1920s the center of gravity shifted to Montparnasse, and cafés like Le Dome, La Coupole, Le Select, La Rotonde, and La Closerie des Lilas, where figures like Sergei Diaghilev and Jean Cocteau dominated the scene, and where the members of the ménage first met. Montparnasse was home to Marc Chagall, Henri Matisse, Picasso, and Max Ernst, all friends, once again, of Roché. The French New Wave, finally, inherited the postwar bohemia of St. Germain des Prés, where figures like Juliette Gréco and Boris Vian, Jean-Paul Sartre and Simone de Beauvoir held court in cafés like Café de Flore, Deux Magots, and Brasserie Lipp. And although Truffaut was not in any way an official member of the 1960s counterculture, he indirectly helped shape its sensibility. In some ways a conservative figure, Truffaut was influenced, nevertheless, by the "historical avant-garde" of Jean Vigo and Luis Buñuel, and he knew and befriended Jean Cocteau, opposed the war in Algeria and the firing of film historian Henri Langlois from the post of director of the Cinémathèque Française, and protested the banning of the Maoist newspaper *La Cause du peuple*. And like the members of the counterculture, Truffaut preferred constructed, creative families—like those ephemeral families summoned up by the filmmaking process—to biologically inherited nuclear families.

Like Paris and Berlin, New York took on the status of an urban myth linked to modernist experimentalism. Andrea Barnet describes the atmosphere in Greenwich Village at the time of Roché's sojourn during World War I: "In Greenwich Village, cradle to the avant-garde, the dream of a cultural revolution was ubiquitous. Creative dissent, whether expressed as artistic innovation or as liberating lifestyle, was the revolutionary cri de coeur; sparkling talk and racy innuendo were the fashion. Sexual relations between men and women were lusty and unbinding. In bars and crowded basement restaurants, literary salons and former stables turned into ateliers, the talk was of Freud, free love, feminism, homosexuality, modern art, birth control, personal fulfillment, and radical politics."[2]

New York in the period of Roché's visit featured a cosmopolitan array of European and American modernists. The city became a temporary home to French-based figures like the composer Edgar Varèse, the originator of *la musique concrète*; to Francis and Gabrielle Picabia; and to poet/actor/boxer/womanizer Fabian Lloyd (a.k.a. Arthur Cravan, the putative nephew of Oscar Wilde), who had earlier been a part of the Parisian scene. On the American side New York was home to such figures as the poet William Carlos Williams, the photographer Alfred Stieglitz, and the modernist poet/painter/actress Mina Loy, whose erotically explicit poetry depicted life, as she herself put it, as "generally reducible to sex."[3] Linked to the European avant-garde through her affair with the futurist Marinetti, Loy, like Helen Grund in the same period, was wrestling with the challenge of simultaneously pursuing artistic and sexual experimentation in a generally phallocentric milieu.

Apart from its exploration of bohemia, however, this book hopefully offers other levels of interest. First, it gives us a glimpse into the fascinating story of the amorous triangle itself and the other satellite relationships. Here we enter an erotic and writerly territory reminiscent of that inhabited by other famous lover-artist couples given to multilateral erotic exchanges, such as Frida Kahlo and Diego Rivera, or Henry Miller and Anaïs Nin, or John Reed and Louise Bryant, or F. Scott and Zelda Fitzgerald. These artist/intellectuals lived their romantic and aesthetic lives as "bright, gemlike flames," but some of the participants and bystanders ended up "getting burned" by those flames. In a time of war and anti-Semitism the members of the ménage were German and French, Christian and Jew, and their story seems even more poignant when we reflect on its violent historical backdrop. Hessel, for example, belongs to a tragic period when many of Germany's best writers were forced into exile. Although these friends/lovers caused one another pain as well as pleasure, they tried to remain true to values of friendship, sincerity, and creativity. Even their stormy *folie à trois* seems in retrospect a form of sanity in comparison with the madness raging around them.

All of the principals, moreover, reflected on their lives in diaries and fiction, revealing themselves to be extraordinarily astute chroniclers of the tensions and aspirations at the center of modern love. As an experiment at once textual and sexual, the Helen-Franz-Roché ménage constituted a simultaneous exploration of eroticism and writing in ways that looked both backward to the more cynical tradition of eighteenth-century libertinage of *Les Liaisons dangereuses* and forward to the more naively utopian and sexually liberated counterculture of the 1960s. My hope is less to declare "what really happened" than to reflect on how the various participants narrated and interpreted what happened and how what happened was transmogrified into artistic form.

To tell that story, *François Truffaut and Friends* draws on biographical materials, but its genre is not, ultimately, biography. Rather, it is a work of contextualized film and literary analysis, a meditation on a series of novels, journals, films, and their intimate interconnections—one that constantly crosses the borders between art and life.[4] The goal is not to explore biography or history but rather the biographical overtones and historical reverberations of texts. Rather than pursue biography or history for their own sakes, I try to multiply perspectives, in a quasi-cubist manner, on the principal figures. Thus we look at Franz Hessel, for example, "through" Roché's novels and Truffaut's film but also through Helen Grund's memoirs, Walter Benjamin's essays, and the autobiographies of his son Stéphane and friend Charlotte Wolff. At the core of the book is a series of close readings of texts—novels, films, diaries—read against the backdrop of the broader history of bohemia, the arts, and sexuality. Nor is the approach strictly chronological; rather, it mingles various temporalities: the sheer consecution of biography, the uneven parallelisms between "real" and artistic history, the remembered time of diaries and novels, and the chronotopic duration of filmic representation (a time line is appended to clear up any confusion about basic history and biography).

As a second level of interest, the project delves closely into the actual writings of the three principals, in terms both of their shared themes and of the highly personal nuances and inflections that the writer-participants gave to them. This body of writing, I would suggest, has not received the critical attention it deserves. In the case of *Jules and Jim*, Truffaut's adaptation rendered an enormous service by popularizing the Roché novel. Yet at the same time the adaptation perhaps had the inadvertent effect of turning the spectatorial experience of the film into a substitute for actually reading and analyzing the source novel, with the result that the novel qua novel has received little in-depth analysis. Despite Truffaut's redemptive intentions, and despite his success in calling attention to the book, the adaptation both praised and, in a way, "buried" the novel, as if the adaptation had said all that need be said about the novel.

Third, the project explores one small instance of the gendered nature of modernism as it was lived differentially by men and by women, giving us insights into how gender and sexuality were experienced and reflected on at a specific point in history. Within the rather sexist and even misogynistic environment of the avant-garde, Helen Grund, the "Catherine" of the Truffaut film, represents an extraordinarily free and dazzlingly experimental figure who managed both to thrive and to suffer in a highly masculinist context. Her diaries offer an indispensable account of these issues as she lived them, filtered through her remarkably acute sensibility and intelligence. It is in this overall context that we will discuss the phenomenon of flânerie, so beloved to Walter Benjamin and Franz Hessel, and its relation to free-spirited flâneuses like Helen and her compatriot Charlotte Wolff. What did it mean to be a woman writer in a modernist milieu where the norms of literary authority were so often explicitly or implicitly masculinist and heterosexist?

Put differently, this book addresses the question of sexual modernism. We often speak of a military avant-garde—the root literal sense of the metaphor—and of the political and artistic avant-gardes, but can we speak as well of a sexual avant-garde? Laura Kipnis speaks of the "secret underground" of "conjugal saboteurs" who disrupt the "social machinery" of marriage as a disciplinary institution. Does love have its guerrillas and freedom fighters, or is the kind of sexual experimentation described here merely a form of patriarchal exploitation, dressed up in liberatory clothing? Do all the libidinous shenanigans merely end up reproducing in polyandry, as Flaubert wrote of Emma Bovary's adulteries, "all the platitude of marriage?" Kipnis speaks, with tongue firmly planted in cheek, of a kind of isomorphism between rule breaking in love (adultery, ménage) and rule breaking in art (the autographed *Urinal*, with which Roché was directly involved, or the mustache on the *Mona Lisa*). But while artistic rule breaking can trigger scandal and censorship, the consequences of rule breaking in love are more immediately demonstrable. Mona Lisa, to put it crudely, was not hurt by that mustache, but real women were hurt by Roché's infidelities. But that point should not let conventional marriage off the hook, since many people have also been hurt by the institution of marriage itself.[5] Moreover, we will discover a kind of uneven development; although sexually adventurous, our protagonists were also politically erratic and sometimes even conservative.

Fourth, the book forms part of a larger project that I began to explore, together with others, in a trilogy of books about the filmic adaptation of novels.[6] The goal of those books was to rethink the debates about adaptation by moving from a language of "fidelity" and "infidelity" to a language of "performativity" and "transtextuality." The notion of intertextual dialogism, seen as referring both to the play between individual texts and to the larger converse of all the utterances in which those individual texts are embedded, I argued, offers us a richer understanding of the "conversation" between various texts and media and art forms than do notions of "fidelity." Truffaut, for example, takes an activist stance toward his sources, intermingling them in new and often surprising combinations. I discuss his adaptations of Roché's novels not as a question of a simple dyadic relation between originary source and filmic adaptation, with the latter being judged in terms of the adequacy of the "copy," but as a series of dialogical turns, forming part of a veritable dance of relations between a wide spectrum of texts (novels, diaries, plays, paintings, sculptures, essays). Truffaut's adaptations of Roché's work, I argue, show how adaptations can be more than simply inferior "copies" of their "originals"; rather, they can become an immensely creative enterprise, a form of writing in itself. Adaptation studies, in this sense, can go beyond an evaluative measuring of "fidelity" by seeing artistic texts as part of the unending, recombinant work of transtextuality.

Fifth, the book gestures toward a study of friendship, indeed of many friendships: that of Franz Hessel and Walter Benjamin, for example, or of Franz Hessel and Henri-Pierre Roché, or of Marcel Duchamp and Roché, or of Helen Grund and Charlotte Wolff, or of Truffaut and Roché, and so forth. The many heterosexual liaisons in which these people were involved, in this sense, took place alongside complex forms of same-gender and cross-gender friendship. In a larger sense the book is about patterns of identification not only among individuals but also across cultures, across media, and across time periods. Reading and spectatorship, in this sense, constitute a form of friendship by proxy, a matter of fantasies and identifications shared across time and space. Along the way, as we stroll like flâneurs through various lives and texts, we will wander into the adjacent neighborhoods of such subjects as the aesthetics of flânerie, the politics of Jewishness and anti-Semitism, and the ethics of homoeroticism.

Sixth, the project will, I hope, shed new light on Truffaut's oeuvre, not only as reflected in the obvious impact of Roché's life and work on at least three Truffaut films—*Jules and Jim, Two English Girls (Deux Anglaises et le Continent)*, and *The Man Who Loved Women (L'Homme qui aimait les femmes)*—but also in the less obvious "diasporic" impact on such films as *Stolen Kisses (Baisers volés)* and *Shoot the Piano Player (Tirez sur le pianiste)*. What do these films reveal about Truffaut's approach to adaptation? More broadly, what do they reveal about the New Wave's attitude toward literary modernism and about their attitude toward the possibilities of adaptation in general?

Seventh, the book constitutes a meditation on the bookishness of sexuality and the erotics of bibliophilia. It is about the intimate entanglements of textuality and sexuality. Thus not only does sexuality generate an infinity of books and films, but books and films, in a feedback loop, inflect our common sexuality. *François Truffaut and Friends* explores, in sum, these mutual and hopefully pleasurable inflections.

With this ménage love becomes deeply enmeshed with literature, which partially shapes their conceptions and even their feelings about love. The ménage, in this sense, mingles not only individuals but also literary traditions, promoting an amorous exchange of literary fluids, as it were, between France and Germany, primarily, but also with Europe generally and with the United States. Literary love, in this sense, is palimpsestic. Embedded in Roché's work, for example, are traces of the long tradition of French literary representations of love, from the proto-romanticism and love-death of "l'amour courtois," to the sexual bawdiness of the "fabliaux" and Rabelais, on to the tragedies of unreciprocated love in Corneille and Racine, to the nuanced analyses of "les Precieuses," to Rousseau and *Julie; ou, La nouvelle Héloïse*, on to the sadism of the Marquis de Sade, to the Stendhal of *De l'amour*—whom Roché consciously imitated—to Flaubert and Proust and then the sexual-taboo breakers of the avant-garde (many of whom were Roché's friends), on, even, to *The Story of O*, the sadomasochistic novel published under a pseudonym in 1954, just a few years before Roché's *Two English Girls*.

On the German side the writerly sensibilities of Helen Grund (Hessel) and Franz Hessel were undoubtedly shaped by the German version of the *liebestod* tradition, with its conjunction of Eros and Thanatos, as well as by early German romanticism. It is noteworthy, in this sense, that the "Athenaeum" group, formed around the journal of the same name founded by the Schlegel brothers in 1797, constituted a

1. François Truffaut (left) and Jean Cocteau during the filming of
The Testament of Orpheus in 1950. Source: Photofest.

kind of proto-avant-garde, a close-knit group fascinated by revolutionary ideas in politics, art, and life, which anticipated the avant-gardes of the 1920s. Their dream was of an artistic-philosophical community where friendship would play a key role. As with Roché's project of "polyphonic writing" later, the Athenaeum group spoke of collective writing and the "fraternization of knowledge and talents" in the form of "sympoesie" (etymologically, poesy together) and "symphilosophy." At the same time, they spoke of innovative sexual arrangements such as "four-way marriage." Goethe too was an inevitable influence, especially the triangular love of *The Sorrows of Young Werther*, and it is hardly an accident that a copy of *The Elective Affinities* is briefly glimpsed in the film version of *Jules and Jim*.

Finally, the book can be seen as a meditation on translation, first of all in the most obvious sense of literal translations between French, German, and English. The prototypes were actively engaged in translation; Franz Hessel translated Proust's *A la recherche du temps perdu*, for example, and Helen Grund (Hessel) translated Nabokov's *Lolita*. But the book also concerns translation in a more figurative sense.

Pablo Picasso famously said of Roché that he was "very nice," but in the end "he was only a translation."[7] My discussion here treats translation not only between languages but also between cultural codes and traditions. It also treats the translation between the literary and the cinematic, with adaptation constituting a form of intersemiotic or intermedial "translation." As the same biographical and historical materials are filtered through various media—letters, journals, music, novels, films—each medium inevitably inflects the representation with its specific constraints and possibilities.

And on a personal note: If I am currently a professor of cinema studies, that fact has everything to do with my initially being overwhelmed by two films—Godard's *À bout de souffle* and Truffaut's *Jules and Jim*. I have spent decades, in a sense, explaining exactly why these two films gave me such a feeling of pleasure and freedom. This book continues that attempt at explanation.

To conclude, a few thank-yous. Thanks first to Leslie Mitchner for enthusiastically endorsing the project. Thanks to Richard Sieburth for an attentive last-minute reading and for suggestions concerning the German intellectual milieu. Thanks also to the film professors who helped me appreciate film and the New Wave—Michel Marie, Christian Metz, Roger Odin, Bertrand Augst, and many others. Thank you to the *Camera Obscura* group back in the time of its Berkeley incarnation. Thank you to Dudley Andrew for the pleasurable dialogue and for extremely useful materials concerning Franz Hessel. Thanks to mein Bruder Jim for his help with the Deutsch. Thanks to Joe Abbott for an impeccable job of editing. Thanks to the students in my "French New Wave" course, who have served as interlocutors and sounding boards during more than two decades of teaching Truffaut's films. Thanks to my brilliant research assistants Cecelia Sayad, Karen Wang, and June Monroy. Thanks also to Francine Goldenhar and NYU's Maison Française and to Frederic Viguier and Emmanuelle Saada at the French Institute at NYU for providing a steady stream of French celebrity intellectuals for our delectation and stimulation. And thanks, finally, to my perpetual and beloved interlocutor Ella.

FRANÇOIS TRUFFAUT AND FRIENDS

CHAPTER ONE

THE ORIGINS OF TRUFFAUT'S
JULES AND JIM

INITIALLY CONCEIVED IN the early 1920s during the first clutches of the Henri-Pierre Roché–Helen Hessel–Franz Hessel ménage, *Jules and Jim* was initially drafted as a novel in 1943 and finally published in 1953. After reading the novel, François Truffaut turned it into a film in 1961. According to Truffaut his reading of the novel in 1955 created such a strong impression that it cued his choice of profession: he felt that he simply *had* to film it. Truffaut corresponded with Roché between 1955 and 1958 about a possible adaptation and visited with him at his home in Meudon, where the pair developed a strong personal rapport. Truffaut writes of their encounter: "[Roché] was tall and slender, and had the same sweetness as his characters. He resembled Marcel Duchamp, of whom he spoke constantly. Painting was his great passion."[1] Truffaut's encounter with Roché and with *Jules and Jim* had seminal importance, then, for the history of the cinema in that it catalyzed the filmic vocation of a director who was to become a key figure both in auteur theory and in the French New Wave.

The Truffaut adaptation thus presents a number of salient and somewhat anomalous features in terms of film-novel relations: (1) the crucial impact of a novel on a filmmaker's career, (2) the close personal rapport between novelist and filmmaker, and (3) the redemptive role of the adaptation for the novelist's career. As will become clear over the course of this text, Truffaut's sympathetic rapport with the then octogenarian Roché was deeply rooted in Truffaut's biography. Like Roché, Truffaut had a complicated love/hate relationship with his mother, and, like Roché, he had never really known his biological father. Perhaps as a result Truffaut became attached to a number of substitute father figures, notably Roché himself, Jean Genet, and, especially, André Bazin, who all became paternal surrogates for Truffaut. Even before his encounter with Roché, Truffaut wrote to his friend Robert Lachenay that "Bazin and Genet did more for me in three weeks than my parents did in fifteen years."[2] As Dudley Andrew explains in his indispensable critical biography of Bazin, Truffaut's stepfather, after learning the whereabouts of his runaway stepson through an ad for the "Film Addict's Club," arranged for the stepson's arrest and imprisonment. At that point a furious Bazin began a campaign to convince the authorities to release the boy into his care. Later, when Truffaut was placed in military prison for desertion, the Bazins drove to the prison to see him, using the "strategic lie" that they were his parents.[3] In a kind of literalization of the Freudian "family romance," in which the resentful child conjures up ideal substitute parents, Truffaut was virtually adopted by Bazin and his wife, with whom he went to live during a very difficult period. Whereas Truffaut's stepfather mistreated him, and even had him sent to jail, Bazin protected him, snatching him from the pitiless jaws of the French justice system.

It is well known that Truffaut painted a hostile portrait of his parents in his first feature, *Les Quatre cents coups* (1959). And indeed, Truffaut's parents recognized their son's aggressivity, their pain aggravated by press reviews of the film that described the mother in the film in terms worthy of a narcissistic whore in love with nothing but her own body. In his response to an angry letter from his stepfather Truffaut acknowledged that he "knew [the film] would cause [them] pain" but that he did not care because "since Bazin's death, I no longer have any parents." Truffaut further explained to his stepfather that "although I silently hated mother, I liked you even while I despised you."[4] At the same time, Truffaut's perhaps disproportionate outrage partially displaces his intensely eroticized relationship with his mother. This feeling is captured in the many shots, in *The 400 Blows*, of the mother's legs and in the film's fetishistic preoccupation with her stockings and makeup. Truffaut's hostile feelings about his mother, at their height around the time of *The 400 Blows*, were still raw even at the moment of her death some years later, to the point that Truffaut hesitated even to go to her funeral.

2. Truffaut's beloved Bazin. Source: British Film Institute.

The Truffaut-Roché friendship offers a case of cross-generational identification, a strange confluence of adolescent rebellion and twilight-of-life nostalgia. Truffaut was intrigued by the notion of a first novel by an old man, one with whom he felt an uncanny bond. In his adaptation Truffaut claimed that he tried to make the film "as if he himself were very old, as if he were at the end of his life."[5] And Roché, conversely, was equally intrigued by Truffaut, seeing in him, perhaps, an artistic heir and adoptive son. Enthusiastic about Truffaut's short film *Les Mistons*, which he screened in 1957, Roché decided that Truffaut was the ideal director for *Jules and Jim*.[6] Roché was not completely unfamiliar with the world of cinema, having dabbled in the buying and selling of films and having worked briefly as a screenwriter for Abel Gance on the film *Napoléon*. Roché also approved, on the basis of photos, the casting of Jeanne Moreau as Catherine. Thus, the real-life lover of the fiercely independent Helen Hessel ironically came to exercise power, at a time when Helen was still alive, over her representation in the film. Truffaut even planned to ask Roché to write dialogue for the Catherine character, but the plan had to be given up when Roché died on April 9, 1959, just a few days after approving Truffaut's choice of lead actress.[7]

Truffaut had a highly fraught, almost Hamlet-like, relationship with his mother, whom he resented not only for what he saw as her maternal neglect but also for what he regarded as her "promiscuous" behavior. A moment in *The 400 Blows* captures this sexual jealousy. On a day that Antoine and his friend René have skipped school, the mother and son both catch each other in a "crime": the mother catches the son "playing hooky" from school, but at the very same moment the son catches the mother "playing hooker," at least in the son's fevered imagination, as he observes her engaging in a public, adulterous kiss. For Anne Gillain, Truffaut's tortured relationship with his mother is "the lost secret" that provides the key to his entire oeuvre. All of Truffaut's films constitute, for Gillain, an unconscious interrogation of "a distant, ambiguous, inaccessible, maternal figure" reminiscent of his own mother, Janine de Montferrand.[8] Although Truffaut's oeuvre provides very varied responses to this enigmatic figure, she nonetheless "remains always at the very source of his creative dynamic."[9]

At the same time, Truffaut never knew his biological father. Truffaut was an "illegitimate child," recognized and given a name by his stepfather Roland Truffaut. Truffaut's *Baisers volés* indirectly recounts the story of the young Truffaut's research (in 1968) into the identity of his real father, who turned out to be a German-Jewish dentist named Roland Levy.[10] Truffaut reacted ambivalently to the discovery, on the one hand declaring that he had always felt Jewish—a feeling that links him to the Jewish Franz Hessel—and on the other opting not to contact the man who had played such an important role in his life.[11] Truffaut often identified with literal and symbolic orphans. In *Le Plaisir des yeux* Truffaut expresses his admiration for "orphan" filmmakers like D. W. Griffith, Ernst Lubitsch, F. W. Murnau, Carl Theodor

Dreyer, Mizoguchi, Sergei Eisenstein, and Erich von Stroheim—all "orphans" in his view because their spiritual fathers were dead.[12] As Gillain suggests, Truffaut was doubtless intrigued by the fact that his mother alone possessed the key to the identity of his real father and thus the secret of his origins.[13] The obsession with mothers impacted Truffaut's tastes and sensibility and ultimately the films themselves. In his *Correspondence* Truffaut claimed to have a special shelf reserved for books "all about mothers." Invoking the names of Georges Simenon, Georges Bataille, Marcel Pagnol, and Roger Peyrefitte, Truffaut argued that the books about mothers were invariably the best books by the writers in question.[14]

An anxiety about paternity and origins, as Gillain suggests, feeds even the most apparently trivial details of Truffaut's films, for example the brief references to abortion and Cesarean section in *The 400 Blows*. In his films Truffaut took advantage of the psychic energies provoked by his secret, but he also took pains not to probe that secret too closely, carefully camouflaging the autobiographical dimension of his work, preferring to leave undisturbed the psychic springs of his creativity. Truffaut's films, for Gillain, thus allow for a double reading. The films simultaneously project two stories, one realist and obedient to cause-and-effect logic, the other phantasmatic, where the son tries to understand and dialogue, if only symbolically, with the absent and resented mother.

Like all creators, Truffaut makes films partially in order to move beyond childhood and become an adult. It is no accident, in this context, that Truffaut's films proliferate in references to writing, in ways that are often linked to sexual anxiety and aspiration. In a 1975 interview Truffaut acknowledged writing as an integral part of what might be called his creative DNA: "I can't get away from writing. In all my films there are people who send each other letters, a young girl who writes in her diary. . . . [That] simply is not done any more, but it's in my character."[15] In Truffaut's early short film *Les Mistons*, the titular rascals express their sexual frustration and aggressivity by sabotaging Bernadette's (Bernadette Lafont) love affair by writing on fences, tree trunks, and city walls, with the writing constantly increasing in size and intensity and public visibility, so that the object of the aggression will finally notice.

Truffaut saw filmmaking and writing as profoundly personal: "Tomorrow's film appears to me as even more personal than a novel, as individual and autobiographical as a confession or a diary. Young filmmakers will express themselves in the first person."[16] Truffaut's first full-length feature, *The 400 Blows*, in this same sense, proliferates in references both to writing and to paternal/parental authority in ways that lend credence to a psychoanalytic interpretation. The credit sequence—a series of tracking shots of Paris culminating in an image of the cinémathèque française—renders homage to the film "library" where Truffaut's "reading" of old films inspired and informed his subsequent "writing" of new films. The first postcredit shot shows a pupil writing, initiating a whole series of writerly references. Antoine gains vengeance against his teacher by chalking a poem on the wall and is punished by having to conjugate a sentence—in writing. Indeed, Antoine mimics his mother's penmanship in an excuse note. Learning French composition, his mother tells him, is invaluable, since "one always has to write letters." He subsequently steals a typewriter so that the principal will not recognize his handwriting, and as a runaway he falls asleep next to a printing press. Film too can be seen as a *machine à écrire*, a machine for writing.

In short, *The 400 Blows* rings the changes on the theme of *écriture* in a way that makes little sense except as a part of a structural metaphor subtending Truffaut's vision of filmmaking. And in this sense his work was in tune with the theoretical commonplaces of the period. In the postwar period in France, both film and literary discourse came to gravitate around such concepts as "authorship," "écriture," and "textuality." The New Wave directors' fondness for the scriptural metaphor was scarcely surprising, given that many of them began as film journalists who saw writing articles and making films as simply two variant forms of expression. A "graphological trope" thus informed a wide spectrum of coinages and formulations concerning film, from Astruc's *camera-stylo* to Resnais's *cine-roman* and Varda's *cinécriture*.

Antoine, as Truffaut's youthful surrogate, in this sense, "tries on" diverse writing styles in an attempt to become his own man. But writerly imitation gets him into trouble; his mother's writing is "hard to imitate," and Antoine's affectionate pastiche of Balzac elicits his teacher's accusations of plagiarism. (Mis)writing in *The 400 Blows* elicits the con-

3. French prosody in *The 400 Blows*. Source: Les Films du Carosse.

demnation of authority figures. The sentence dictated to Antoine by his teacher reads, "I deface the classroom walls and I mistreat French prosody." The phrasing suggests an analogy between classical literary prosody and the grammatically correct filmic heritage of the "tradition of quality," on the one hand, and between the calculated abuse of conventional filmic prosody and decorum by the French New Wave. The accusations of plagiarism anticipate the frequent charge against New Wave filmmakers that they borrowed their best ideas, that their films were merely collages of citations and cinematic in-jokes. The mistreatment of prosody thus corresponds to the New Wave's disrespect for the academic conventions of dominant filmmaking.

Antoine's writerly revolt has strong Oedipal overtones, a powerful "anxiety of influence." *The 400 Blows* combines a hostile portrait of Truffaut's stepfather, that is, his false father—the one who had him sent to prison—with an affectionate dedication to the beloved substitute father, Bazin, the man who had Truffaut released from prison. Within the family portrait called *The 400 Blows* Truffaut portrays himself as a revolted "batard"—to borrow Marthe Robert's terminology regarding the "novel of origins"—a parentless child in search of a true symbolic father who is in fact named in the film's dedication. Just as on a cinematic level Truffaut rejected the cinematic "father's generation" of the "tradition of quality" as "false fathers," preferring the grandfather's generation of Jean Cocteau and Jean Renoir, so Truffaut on a personal level preferred substitute real fathers like Roché, Bazin, and Cocteau to false fathers like his adoptive father, Roland Truffaut. *The 400 Blows* thus foregrounds the challenges of "writing" in the face of parental interdictions that define an emerging style as "incorrect" or "immature." In this sense the film is a thinly veiled plea on the part of an artistic adolescent for freedom from parental and stylistic constraints, a revolt against what the New Wave so symptomatically called the "cinéma de papa." Writerly adulthood entails forging one's own rules in defiance of "le nom/non"—the name and the "no"—of the scriptural father.[17]

CHAPTER TWO

THE NEW WAVE AND ADAPTATION

Ｇ IVEN OUR FOCUS on Truffaut's adaptations of Roché's novels and memoirs, it is pertinent to speak of the larger context of the New Wave's attitude toward literature in general and toward adaptations in particular. The *Cahiers du cinéma* critics who subsequently formed the nucleus of the French New Wave were profoundly ambivalent about literature, which they saw both as a model to be emulated and an enemy to be abjured. Haunted by the overweening prestige of literature in a country that had virtually deified its writers, the *Cahiers* critics forged the concept of the *cinéaste* as *auteur* as a way of transferring the millennial aura of literature to the relatively fledgling art of film. Novelist and filmmaker Alexandre Astruc prepared the way with his landmark 1948 essay "Birth of a New Avant-Garde: The Camera-Pen," in which he argued that the cinema was becoming a new means of expression analogous to painting or the novel.[1] Within this view film was no longer the rendering of a preexisting written text; rather, the shooting process itself became a form of writing performed through mise-en-scène, a kind of "filmécriture automatique."

Truffaut and the New Wave made a number of innovations in terms of adaptation, especially in comparison with earlier French cinema. First of all, they adapted new *kinds* of novels. Whereas the antecedent French "tradition of quality" preferred to adapt prestigious classical novels from the French realist tradition (Stendhal, Balzac, Zola), the New Wave directors favored less canonical (often foreign) and more contemporary writers such as David Goodis, Ray Bradbury, and Roché himself. Second, some of the directors reconceptualized the very idea of adaptation. The "ciné-roman" films by "Left-Bank" directors like Alain Resnais and Marguerite Duras, for example, were less interested in "fidelity" to an original text than in a synergistic collaboration between two artists, a process productive of quasi-experimental films that were at the same time more reflexively cinematic, and more reflexively and self-consciously literary, than conventional films. And Eric Rohmer, who began as a novelist, not only adapted his own novels but also made many films that, although not adaptations per se, had everything to do, as Maria Tortajada points out, with the novelistic tradition of "libertinage."[2]

The New Wave began to formulate its aesthetic principles, symptomatically, precisely around what came to be called the "querelle de l'adaptation." In a series of articles Truffaut's mentor, Bazin, argued that filmic adaptation was not a shameful and parasitical practice but rather a creative and productive one, a catalyst of progress for the cinema. In his essay "In Defense of Mixed Cinema" Bazin mocked those who expressed outrage over the crimes against literature supposedly committed by film adaptations, arguing that culture in general and literature in particular have nothing to lose from the practice of adaptation. Filmic adaptations, for Bazin, help democratize literature and make it popular: "there is no competition or substitution, rather the adding of a new dimension that the arts had gradually lost . . . namely a public."[3] In another essay, "Adaptation, or the Cinema as Digest," Bazin suggested that the adaptation, far from being illegitimate, has been a perennial practice in all the arts. While admitting that most films based on novels merely usurp their title, Bazin also argues that a film like *Day in the Country* (1936) shows that an adaptation can be "faithful to the spirit of Maupassant's story while at the same time benefiting from . . . Renoir's genius. With Renoir, adaptation becomes "the refraction of one work in another creator's consciousness."[4] For Bazin, Renoir's version of *Madame Bovary* (1934) reconciles a certain "fidelity" with artistic independence; here, author and "auteur" meet as equals.

In his manifesto essay "A Certain Tendency in French Cinema" (first published in *Cahiers* in 1954), Truffaut himself also turned to the issue of adaptation. Distancing himself from his mentor's cautious approval of adaptation in general, Truffaut excoriated a specific genre of adaptation, that of the "tradition of quality," which turned French literary classics into predictably well-furnished, well-spoken, and stylistically formulaic films. The prestige of the "tradition of quality" partially derived from the borrowed luster of the literary sources it adapted, so Truffaut was striking at the very source of a prestige that he saw as illegitimate. Truffaut especially lambasted adaptation as practiced by two "quality" screenwriters—Jean Aurenche and Pierre Bost. In his 1948 "Adaptation, or the Cinema as Digest" essay, Bazin had suggested that Aurenche and Bost simultaneously "transformed"—in the manner of an electric transformer—and "dissipated" the energy of their source novels.[5] Truffaut, in contrast, was infinitely more harsh and unforgiving. Truffaut accused the two screenwriters of being disrespectful to both literature and film. He mocked the two screenwriters' claim to have revolutionized adaptation through a "creative infidelity" that produced "equivalencies" between literary and cinematic procedures. What this amounts to in practice, Truffaut argued, was a cynical triage that discarded everything that was arbitrarily decreed to be "unfilmable." Every novel became for these screenwriters an excuse to smuggle into the adaptation the same old anticlerical and (innocuously) anarchistic themes. Since one cannot possibly be "faithful" to the style and spirit of writers as diverse as André Gide, Raymond Radiguet, Colette, and Georges Bernanos, according to Truffaut, the screenwriters chose to be faithful instead to their own myopic vision. Basing his critique on adaptations of Bernanos's *Journal d'un cure de campagne* (Diary of a Country Priest, 1951) and Radiguet's *Le Diable au corps* (1946), Truffaut argues that the "quality" screenwriters simply exploit their source texts to introduce a limited set of secularist, antimilitarist, and left-wing ideas. The result is a flattening out of the heterogeneity of literary sources. But, even more gravely, the search for "equivalencies" for the putatively "unfilmable" passages from the novel masks a profound scorn for the cinema, seen as fundamentally incapable of ever achieving the grandeur of literature. For Truffaut, not only traveling shots but also adaptations were a "question de morale." In retrospect, Truffaut clearly mingled valid insights with a passionate, perhaps Oedipal, hostility to the cinema of those he saw as (false) fathers.

Bazin gently rebuked the violence of Truffaut's language in his own response to Truffaut's polemical tract.[6] Truffaut denounced "quality" adaptations in the name of "fidelity," but it seems that since the time of the New Wave, adaptation studies have oscillated between a "fidelity" discourse and a more theoretically sophisticated "intertextuality" discourse. It was the supposedly conservative and "realist" Bazin, ironically, who anticipated some of these currents in his 1948 "Adaptation, or the Cinema as Digest" essay. There he argued for a more open conception of adaptation, one with a place for what we would now call "intertextuality" and "transécriture." Bazin's words about adaptation in 1948 ironically anticipate both "auteurism" and its critique. The "ferocious defense of literary works vis-à-vis their adaptations," Bazin suggested, rests on a "rather recent, individualist conception that was far from being ethically rigorous in the 17th century and that started to become legally defined only at the end of the eighteenth."[7] Here Bazin anticipated Foucault's devalorization of the individual author in favor of a "pervasive anonymity of discourse." Bazin also anticipated Roland Barthes's prophecy of "the death of the author" by forecasting that "we are moving toward a reign of the adaptation in which the notion of the unity of the work of art, if not the very notion of the author itself, will be destroyed."[8] Thus Bazin, whose "humanism" later made him the whipping boy for film structuralists and semioticians, ironically foreshadowed some of the later structuralist and poststructuralist currents that would indirectly undermine a fidelity discourse in relation to adaptation. All of these various positions on adaptation, we will see, resonate with the Truffaut adaptations of the Henri-Pierre Roché source texts.

A number of the essays in the Truffaut collection *Le Plaisir des yeux* are gathered under the rubric "Literature and Cinema."[9] There Truffaut speaks of his relationship not only to the work of Henri-Pierre Roché but also to other writers such as Jean Giraudoux, William Irish, André Gide, and François Mauriac. In his essay "Literary Adaptation in the Cinema" Truffaut acknowledges that one cannot apply general rules and that each case is special and unique. Nevertheless, Truffaut posits three legitimate forms of successful adaptation: those that do the "same thing" as the novel, those that do the "same thing, but better," and those that do "something different, but interesting." Although Truffaut does not give examples of the three types, I would suggest that directors like David Lean (for example in *Passage to India*) do the "same thing" as the novel, that a director like Orson

Welles (for example in *The Trial*) does "something different, but interesting," and that a director like Truffaut himself, in *Jules and Jim*, does "the same thing, but better." Truffaut concludes on an auteurist note: "In sum, the problem of adaptation is a false problem. No recipe, no magical formula. All that counts is the success of the particular film, which is linked exclusively to the personality of the director."[10]

Truffaut and the New Wave are very much linked to modernism and to the avant-garde. The question of adaptation, for the New Wave, stood at the point of convergence of a number of crucial issues—cinematic specificity, modernist reflexivity, and interart relations. But these questions were all inextricably interrelated; the foregrounding of specificity was often linked to a modernist stance or aesthetic, and filmic modernism necessarily passed through comparison to other, more markedly modernist-dominated, arts like painting, music, and theater. It is hardly surprising, in this light, that the *Cahiers* writer/filmmakers constantly draw comparisons between film and other arts, usually in terms of their relative coefficient of realism or modernism. The 1959 *Cahiers* roundtable devoted to *Hiroshima mon amour*, for example, elicits a number of interart comparisons. Rohmer describes Resnais as a "cubist" and the first "modern" filmmaker of the sound film. And for Godard *Hiroshima* can only be appreciated in relation to other arts, as "Faulkner plus Stravinsky" but not as a combination of any two film directors.[11] And Truffaut said that one had to speak of cinema "before and after" Godard's *Breathless*, much as one had to speak of painting "before and after" Picasso.

While the New Wave drew on the early avant-gardes, contemporaneous with the bohemian period of Roché, Franz Hessel, and Helen Grund—that is, the avant-garde of filmmakers like Buñuel and Vigo—the emergence of the New Wave movement in the late 1950s also coincided with and was inflected by the emergence of various experimental movements—Barthes and "nouvelle critique" in literary theory, Beckett and absurdism in the theater, Boulez in music, and the "new novel" in literature. It was hardly an accident that the title of Astruc's landmark 1948 "Camera-Stylo" essay was "Birth of a New Avant-Garde." What would differentiate the "new avant-garde" from the "historical avant-gardes" of the 1920s was its hybrid character as a compromise formation negotiating between entertainment and vanguardism. Whereas the avant-gardists of the 1920s had called for "pure cinema," New Wave directors like Truffaut preferred a "mixed cinema" that mingled formal audacity (reflexivity, sound/image disjunction) with the familiar pleasures of mainstream cinema (narrative, genre, desire, spectacle).

CHAPTER THREE

THE PROTOTYPE FOR JIM
HENRI-PIERRE ROCHÉ

*J*ULES AND JIM, as I noted earlier, was based on real-life prototypes, all of them artists and bohemians. The prototype for the
character "Jim" was Roché himself, played in the film by Henri Serre
(who was chosen partially because he physically resembled the young
Roché). Born in Paris on May 28, 1879, Roché was a writer/artist/bohe-
mian whose circle of friends and acquaintances included Pablo Picasso,
Marcel Duchamp, Erik Satie, Darius Milhaud, Le Douanier Rousseau, Le
Corbusier, Paul Klee, Diego Rivera, Isadora Duncan, Abel Gance, Blaise
Cendrars, Ezra Pound, Ford Madox Ford, James Joyce, Gertrude Stein,
Heinrich Mann, Thomas Mann, Edgar Varèse, Man Ray, Modigliani,
Marie Laurencin, Sergei Diaghilev, Francis Picabia, Vaslav Nijinsky—in
short, a veritable "who's who" of artistic modernism. It was Roché who
boxed in the ring with the painter Georges Bracque. It was Roché who
first presented Stein to Picasso. In *The Autobiography of Alice B. Toklas*
Stein describes Roché as a "very earnest, very noble, devoted, very faithful and very enthusiastic man who was a general introducer. He knew
everybody, he really knew them and could introduce anybody to anybody."[1] For Stein, Roché was a "born liaison officer, who knew everybody and wanted everybody to know everybody else."[2] A shrewd and
cosmopolitan observer of the art scene, Roché moved easily and grace-
fully among very diverse milieux and communities. Gertrude's brother,
Leo Stein, described Roché as a "tall man with an inquiring eye under
an inquisitive forehead" but a man who was "more ear than anything
else."[3] Roché was thus a kind of medium, a vehicle of communication
between persons and arts and movements.

4. Five-way portrait of Henri-Pierre Roché, the prototype for "Jim" of *Jules and Jim*. Photo courtesy Carlton Lake Collection, Harry Ransom Humanities Research Center, University of Texas at Austin.

Roché also became an inveterate, obsessive collector of objets d'art, perhaps in compensation for the untimely loss of his father, or in function of his regrets about his complicated relationship to his mother and his inability to sustain stable relationships with women.[4] Susan Stewart has suggested that whereas women collect souvenirs and memorabilia, men are more likely to be serial "completists," more invested in the completeness of their collections than in the emotional resonances of the objects collected. It might even be suggested, in a somewhat vulgar Freudian manner, that in seeking plenitude the collector is essentially warding off a fear of castration. For his biographers Roché's collecting was "a way of protecting himself from loss, absence, and the means of communicating symbolically with loved ones. Like collectors of religious relics or the man of archaic civilizations who believes in fetishes, Roché attributes supernatural qualities to the pieces in his collection, endowing them with power and virtues of an almost curative nature. Quite logically, he refuses to speak of works of art, words which 'leave me cold. Rather, the works are secretions or the fantasist/natural fruits of [his] friends and the toys of their agile hands.'"[5]

It is not an accident, Roché's biographers point out, that Roché placed near his bed such erotically charged paintings as Brancusi's *La Princesse X* or Duchamp's *Neuf Moules* or *Machine Optique*. Roché indulged a parallel passion for collecting women and paintings, but whereas his "collection" and "ownership" of living beings like wives and mistresses was necessarily always precarious and tentative, inexorably doomed to incompletion or loss, the collection of dead objects such as statues or *natures mortes*, as they were so suggestively called, seemed a way of cheating death by possessing objects that would not change or betray or die. And while Roché's "collecting" of women left a lot of human wreckage in its wake, his collecting of art objects was much less destructive, leaving a legacy of beauty.

As a young man Roché, in a kind of "advertisement for himself," described himself as follows:

> H. P. Roché (born 1879), graduate in law, former student at the École de Sciences Politiques, member of various international and humanist organizations, belongs to the "modern movement" in France in literature and art (as well as philosophy, feminism, socialism), works currently in this movement in England, will be studying in Germany and in the United States on a project concerned with "modern psychology"; he wishes to begin communication with persons concerned with the same subject and to give lessons or papers in London, Paris, Berlin and Vienna. Languages: English, German, Latin, Esperanto.[6]

Carlton Lake characterized Roché as spending his life in three principal ways: "1) making friends, 2) being a kind of private art dealer . . . and 3) keeping a journal. Transcribed single-spaced on 8"-by-11" sheets, his journal runs to about seven thousand pages. Among other things it established two facts: 1) Roché was, without any doubt, one of the greatest lovers in the history of literature, and 2) he documented that aspect of his life in such a thoroughgoing and convincing manner as to make him . . . one of the greatest diarists in the history of love."[7] Roché saw himself, meanwhile, as a contemporary Stendhal, a chronicler of love writing for a future time when writers could "show sex in the light of day, when one will speak of the touch of sex organs as one speaks of the knees, with all possible nuances, since each situation is emotionally and sexually unique."[8]

Roché's own sexual life was an endless marathon of obsessive sexual conquests. Roché first ejaculated at the age of twelve after glimpsing the breasts of his mother's maid in the next room.[9] Already as an adolescent, Roché established a pattern of pursuing women, but he usually engaged in that pursuit in the company of other men. He also developed the habit of using writing as an invaluable instrument of seduction. With his lycée friend Jo Jouanin, Roché developed a way of meeting women through paid newspaper advertisements that invited women to meet them for "discussions." In Ian MacKillop's account, this scheme "worked spectacularly: in one day alone Jo and Pierre received a hundred replies, so they rented a back room at a café to spread out the letters into categories and discuss tactics. Sometimes immediate meetings were arranged, [and] sometimes no meeting materialized."[10]

Roché kept careful records of his exploits. Public writing served to initiate conquests, while private diary writing allowed him to register his private impressions of conquests already achieved. In this period of his life writing, eroticism, and male friendship became mutually cathected, initiating Roché's career as a relentless self-chronicler. An ascetic orgiast, Roché enjoyed both the stormy erotic encounters themselves and the remembering of them, through writing, in the cloistered calm of solitude.

A later Roché novel—*Two English Girls*—was based on Roché's real-life relationship with two English sisters: Margaret (Muriel in the novel) and Violet (Anne in the novel) Hart. At the time of their meeting, Roché was a Tolstoyan idealist and a student in political science, and Violet was a student of sculpture. The real sequence of events, refracted in the novel, is delineated in loving detail in Ian MacKillop's *Free Spirits: Henri Pierre Roché, François Truffaut, and the Two English Girls*. The events of this story went more or less as follows. Roché (Claude in both novel and film) met Violet when his mother, Clara ("Claire" in the novel), proposed that she teach English to Henri-Pierre. During a trip to Wales, Henri-Pierre met the other sister, Margaret. After maintaining a Platonic camaraderie in which the three called each other "brother and sister," Henri-Pierre became enamored of Margaret. Ultimately, Claude/Roché proposed to Margaret, but she hesitated, and in any case Roché's mother, Clara, was opposed to the marriage. Margaret slowly began to relent, but Claire demanded a year of separation for the couple, which effectively foreclosed marriage as a possibility. In 1902 Roché read Nietzsche and began to see himself as a partisan of erotic freedom, flying high above the earthbound social constraints of conventional monogamy and reality.

From 1903 to 1906 Roché became the lover of the other sister, Violet. In 1907 Margaret visited Roché in Paris, but she was shocked to learn of Roché's affair with her sister. In 1908 Violet married someone else, thus freeing Margaret to marry Roché. But by this time it was too late, since Henri-Pierre found Margaret "terrifyingly virtuous," and he was already beginning to enjoy his new life as an adept of *amour libre*. During this time, the sisters had generally been romantically monogamous, or in Anne's case at least serially monogamous, while Claude had been enthusiastically, even religiously, polygamous. For Margaret, Henri-Pierre was the only one, but for him, she was but one of many. In 1913 Margaret married as well. Margaret died in 1926, leaving a husband and daughter. In 1939 Roché had the perhaps hallucinatory impression of glimpsing Margaret's daughter in the Paris metro.

CHAPTER FOUR

NEW YORK INTERLUDE

ROCHÉ'S LIFE ALSO intersected with another urban center of the bohemian avant-garde—New York—as part of what has been called the "Modernists' TransAtlantic Shuttle."[1] Like other emissaries of the modernist French art world in New York during the war, Roché was partially pushed by the stick of the First World War and pulled by the carrot of artistic effervescence. He ultimately spent three years (1916 to 1919) in the city. Yet the choice of New York was hardly fortuitous; a strong Paris–New York artistic connection had been building for decades. More and more New York artists were studying in Paris, while French impressionist paintings "became coveted trophies in the rivalry among wealthy American collectors."[2] On February 17, 1913, the International Exhibition of Modern Art, usually known as the "Armory Show," exhibited some fifteen hundred works by European artists such as Paul Cézanne, George Bracque, Paul Gauguin, Pablo Picasso, Marcel Duchamp, Wassily Kandinsky, and Francis Picabia. The Armory Show was an important event for Roché as a collector, for it was there that European artists met American collectors like Walter Arensberg and John Quinn, both of whom Roché met and befriended. (Quinn served as defense counsel in the famous 1921 censorship trial concerning Joyce's *Ulysses* and was the major funder of the Paris-based *TransAtlantic Review*, where writers like Joyce and Ezra Pound were published.) The moment was especially opportune because the Paris art world had been virtually closed down because of the war; as a result, European artists were ready to take a chance on *TransAtlantic* collectors. Together, Quinn and Roché acquired some of the most famous modernist paintings.[3]

Fleeing Paris for New York, some members of the Parisian avant-garde encountered a city very much in the vanguard of sexual and artistic liberationism. New York was the home of that Village bohemian par excellence, poet /reporter Djuna Barnes, with her innumerable lovers and polymorphous artistic practices. It was a time in the Village when socialist radical Emma Goldman was calling for a danceable revolution. The Village was home as well to Gertrude Stein's friend Mabel Dodge. It was in Dodge's weekly salon that the usually segregated bohemias of Harlem and Greenwich Village came into contact. Dodge was herself a friend of Margaret Sanger, an advocate of birth control and an adept of the sexual theories of Havelock Ellis. Dodge described Sanger as an "ardent propagandist for the joys of the flesh [who] made love into a serious undertaking."[4] In 1915 Sanger founded the magazine *The Woman Rebel*, which called for the questioning of Victorian sexual mores. The duty of modern women, she wrote, was to "look the whole world in the face with a go-to-hell look in the eyes, to have an ideal, to speak and act in defiance of convention."[5] In her pamphlet "Family Limitation"—Sanger later founded "Planned Parenthood"—Sanger argued that women who did not have orgasms would suffer "disease of her generative organs."[6]

Restless intellectual women in the Village created a space for experimentation that mingled art, politics, and eroticism. A movement, led by women but joined in by men, experimented with sexual revolution and open marriage. Many put their "advanced ideas" about "free love" into practice through multiple love affairs. But what is most interesting for our purposes is the extent to which these currents were expressed *verbally*, whether in salon discussions or in letters, novels, and plays. Emma Goldman, for example, left vivid accounts of her sexual life with Ben Reitman. In a "progressive" literary version of *Les Liaisons dangereuses*–style libertinage, Hutchins Hapgood and Neith Boyce Hapgood, similarly, wrote up their relationship and affairs in letters, diaries, and books, and letters were exchanged not only between the partners but also with friends. "Talking publicly about sexual matters—erotic exchanges, configurations of partners, and the attendant emotions of passion, jealousy, humiliation, rapture—became seen as political in itself."[7] The later Franz-Helen-Roché ménage, and Henri-Pierre Roché's project of "polyphonic writing," in this sense, must be seen as part of a much broader transnational current—the literarization of experimental sexuality—flowing through many of the capitals of artistic modernity.

The left intelligentsia of New York, perhaps more than Paris or Berlin, was deeply marked by the feminist movement. "The emancipated woman," as Christine Stansell puts it, "stood at the symbolic center of a program for cultural regeneration." Men like John Reed and Randolphe Bourne, meanwhile, "saw themselves as coconspirators of the heroines of the day."[8] Feminism, it was thought, would enable even men to be more free. The egalitarian thrust of feminism was registered in concrete programs such as the legalization of birth control in 1916 and the achievement of women's suffrage in 1920. And while modernism is often seen as a male-dominated movement, the New York scene was animated by many women artists and cultural activists. Women like Nancy Cunard, Caresse Crosby, Adrienne Monnier, Janet Flanner, and Silvia Beach played a crucial role in disseminating the modernist movement through their journalism and publishing efforts. Shari Benstock compares these women to "midwives to the birth of Modernism," the facilitators of a "literary accouchement."[9] The empowerment of women was also reflected in the fact that a quarter of American artists in Paris were women who discovered that Paris, no matter how progressive in artistic terms, was less so in gender terms. Unlike the United States, where women were admitted into art classes, in Paris in the same period they were denied access to the École des Beaux-Arts.[10]

In New York, as a representative of the French diplomatic delegation, Roché lived in a basement apartment near Washington Square with his friend Marcel Duchamp. Through Duchamp, who Roché himself called "the most famous Frenchman in America," Roché gained access to the inner sanctum of the New York modern art scene. Together with Picabia, they frequented Mabel Dodge's leftist salon in Greenwich Village, where they probably met people like John Reed, Louise Bryant, and Emma Goldman. They also frequented Alfred Stieglitz's "Little Gallery" on Fifth Avenue. Roché, Duchamp, and Picabia all adored New York for what they saw as its "rapidity, efficacity, mobility, and generosity."[11] For them New York was itself an artistic achievement in that it "created, in architectural panels, the equivalents of Cubist dreams, long before European painters," and New York's bridges were as beautiful as European cathedrals.[12]

Henri-Pierre Roché and Marcel Duchamp resembled each other in their beauty, captured in the famous multiple-view photographs

5. Five-way portrait of Marcel Duchamp. Photo courtesy Carlton Lake Collection, Harry Ransom Humanities Research Center, University of Texas at Austin.

made separately of them in 1917. Duchamp and Picabia, and subordinately Roché, invented what has been called "New York Dada." Duchamp and Roché indulged in Dada-like pranks, the most famous being their joint submission to an exhibition of the readymade "Fountain," an upside-down porcelain urinal, signed "R. Mutt 1917." Shortly thereafter the two friends, together with Beatrice Wood, founded a magazine called *The Blind Man*, founded to defend the legitimacy of Mutt's contribution, developing concepts that foreshadow pop and minimalist art: "Whether Mr. Mutt with his own hands made the fountain or not has no importance. He CHOSE it. He took an ordinary article of life, placed it so that its useful significance disappeared under the new title and point of view, creating a new thought for that object."[13]

We know that Duchamp and Roché frequented the home of Walter and Louise Arensberg, which became the social epicenter of New York modernism. (A photo of Roché with Louise Arensberg and Francis Picabia graces Andrea Barnet's book *All-Night Party*.)[14] Gabrielle Buffet-Picabia recalled the parties at the Arensbergs' as engaging a "motley international band," which managed to turn "night into day" and featured "conscientious objectors of all nationalities . . . living in an inconceivable orgy of sexuality, jazz, and alcohol."[15] The soirées at the Arensbergs' often included group flirtations and sexual play. The poet William Carlos Williams recalled seeing a young Frenchwoman surrounded by young men, each kissing different parts of her body.[16] As occurred later with Roché and Franz Hessel, Roché and Duchamp participated in several sexual ménages linked to these circles. Also present at the Arensberg parties was Baroness Elsa van Freytag-Loringhoven, a protégé of Duchamp known as the "Mama of Dada," who had been arrested for public nudity and who liked to brandish a "life-size plaster-cast penis . . . to shock old maids."[17]

Roché made Duchamp the subject of his unfinished but posthumously published novel *Victor*. The novel was a roman à clef in which the eponymous protagonist, based on Duchamp, faces the same choice that confronted Roché himself: the choice between a risky freedom, on the one hand, and a cozy familial responsibility, on the other, but where the character always opts, in the end, for freedom. In the novel Roché describes Victor/Duchamp as attractive because of his combination of celebrity, physical beauty, and sheer elusiveness. Because of his charisma, Duchamp was constantly surrounded by women, "like a great flower of fragrant dresses that constantly renewed itelf."[18] In terms that might characterize Roché himself (and Helen Grund during certain periods), Roché has the novel's heroine Patricia say of the protagonist, "Everybody loves him. He's everyone's and no-one's. Wherever he goes he becomes the center, the leader." The Patricia character was based on Beatrice Wood, who became the lover of both Duchamp and Roché. In her memoir Wood described their relationship in terms reminiscent of the Helen-Franz-Roché ménage later: "The three of us were something like an amour à trois. It was a divine experience of friendship."[19] This fashion of polyandrous caresses was apparently quite common in the Arensberg circles. In *Victor*, Roché has the Beatrice Wood character suggest to Pierre (based on Roché) that they sit down on the bed with the words "Foutons-nous sur votre lit" (Let's relax/fuck on your bed). This kind of languorous encounter, as we will see, became a regular experience in Roché's life.

CHAPTER FIVE

THE DON JUAN BOOKS

WHILE MOST BIOGRAPHICAL AUTHORS of romans à clef tend to exaggerate their exploits, in the case of Roché the real-life events themselves were even more dramatic than those related in his books. A twentieth-century Don Juan, Roché not only wrote about Don Juan in two books—*Fragments sur Don Juan* (1916) and *Don Juan et . . .* (1921)—but also emulated Don Juan in life, remaining an inveterate womanizer until his very last days. In 1919 he wrote, "My desire [is] to write the story of my life, like Casanova, but in a different spirit."[1] In 1898 Havelock Ellis had emphasized that seducers like Casanova succeeded owing to their close attention to the psychical and bodily states of their erotic "interlocutors," and Roché certainly exemplified this capacity. In what Shoshana Felman calls a "specular illusion," the male seducer holds out to women the narcissistic mirror of their own desire for themselves. The rhetoric of seduction, for Felman, consists largely in the "deployment of speech acts," and specifically in variations on the "performative utterance par excellence: 'I promise.'"[2]

In his *Don Juan et . . .*, written under the pseudonym "Jean Roc" to spare the delicate sensibility of his mother, Roché portrays a knight-errant of Eros, the mounted one who also "mounts" women. The prefatory prose poem describes, to take up a Truffaut film title, an "amour en fuite" (love on the run):

> *And I made an effort with this one*
> *and with that one*
> *and with still others as well.*
> *And this one said: "I need your eyes"*
> *And that one said: "I need your arm."*

And the others said still other things.
And as for myself I know what that means:
My effort, my pleasure,
When they explode
They are astonished and want more.
And these women weigh one down like a debt,
And I don't like to repeat.
Tonight the road will be my bed
The reins of my horse will move beneath me
and an unknown city will welcome us tomorrow.[3]

In his study (first published in German) of the prototypes of the characters in *Jules and Jim—Gesprungene Liebe: Die wahre Geschichte zu "Jules und Jim"*—Manfred Flügge describes Roché as an "improbable Casanova" who had a fetishistic fixation on specific body parts—ears, wrists—which served to help him forget and transcend previous lovers. In Flügge's view diary writing and serial seduction were for Roché linked and cognate activities.[4]

What is striking in *Don Juan et . . .* is the frequent conjunction of religion and eros, in a manner reminiscent of another artist whose life spans the same period as Roché's—Luis Buñuel. Much as Buñuel paradoxically proclaimed, "I'm an atheist, thank God," Roché expressed his ambivalent feelings about religion, and his phallocratic attitudes toward women, in the following way: "I can conceive only of a God, who, in his own way, does with the world what we do with the women he has given us."[5] It is not clear whether Roché is implying that God loves human beings, or screws them, or both. Like Buñuel, Roché worshipped at the shrine of an unholy Trinity that linked religion, death, and sexual desire. Don Juan and Roché choose seduction as a sacred vocation. "Don Juan," he writes, "makes love the way a priest does" (8). Some of the chapter titles—"Don Juan and His Prayer," "Don Juan and the Cathedral"— evoke this fiery concatenation of love and religiosity. Roché suffuses sex with religiosity and sacrilege, exploiting religious prohibition in order to intensify what the prohibitions are designed to prevent—desire. As with Buñuel, religion becomes an aphrodisiac, a trampoline for passion. Religion (the Law) anoints sex with a halo of tantalizing interdiction, resulting in a "positively voluptuous" feeling of sin.[6] Buñuel once cited

6. Roché at the time of *Don Juan*. Photo courtesy Carlton Lake Collection, Harry Ransom Humanities Research Center, University of Texas at Austin.

with approval Saint Thomas's idea that sex even in marriage is a venal sin. "Sin multiplies the possibilities of desire." Lacan could hardly have said it better: the Law catalyzes desire. It is as if, as Buñuel once put it, "religion makes sex sexier." In the same spirit, Roché's Don Juan transforms the House of God into a *maison close*, at one point asking himself: "Will I go to Church to lie in wait for the flesh that prays?" (11). Don Juan's experience of desire in a cathedral reminds us of the opening of Buñuel's *El*—one of the films favored by Jacques Lacan, who screened it as part of his lectures on sadomasochism and paranoia—where the protagonist, Francisco, becomes transfixed at the sight of the heroine's feet during mass. Elsewhere in the book, Roché's Don Juan conjures up ecumenical orgies featuring not only Christian saints but also classical Greek gods and satyrs.

Like Roché, Truffaut was something of a Don Juan, although hardly on the same scale or at the same level of calculated egotism. Both Roché and Truffaut were shy men who attracted women through their soft-spoken but passionate intensity. Both were, in their way, perhaps unconsciously, cruel. Throughout his life Truffaut practiced the art of what might be called the erotic combinatoire. Already at age eighteen, according to his biographers, Truffaut had acquired a taste "for parallel relations, at once happy and sad, as if each woman, separately but simultaneously, seemed even more loveable, indispensable in her difference."[7] Even after marrying Madeleine Morgenstern, Truffaut continued his old liaisons and initiated new ones, even while continuing to visit prostitutes.

Roché and Truffaut also shared an eroticized gaze on art. For both, art-related activities became the locus for sexual encounters. Just as Roché met women through art connoisseurship, Truffaut met women through the cinéclubs and at the cinémathèque. Roché's love of art was inextricably linked with his pursuit of women. His passions came wrapped in the aura of art, as he sought out women in art schools and academies, ateliers and salons. While Roché eroticized the arts of sculpture and painting, Truffaut eroticized the seventh art—the cinema. If Roché's sexual attitudes were shaped by the Catholic Church, Truffaut's were shaped not only by Catholicism—especially in terms of the Madonna/whore dichotomy—but also by the contemporary, secular substitute for the religious shrine—the movie theater.

Many film theorists have called attention to the voyeuristic aspects of the cinematic medium as the privileged medium of the eye. The most appropriate format for the cinema, some have suggested, would have been that of a keyhole. An ineluctable logic leads from Vitascope's *The Kiss* in 1896, made just before Roché began courting the Hart sisters, to the latest pornographic productions. Founded upon the pleasure of looking, the cinema, as feminist theorists have pointed out, has endlessly exploited the spectacle of the female body. But in Truffaut's case cinematic voyeurism was deeply rooted in both biography and history. As an adolescent growing up in the Vichy period, Truffaut associated

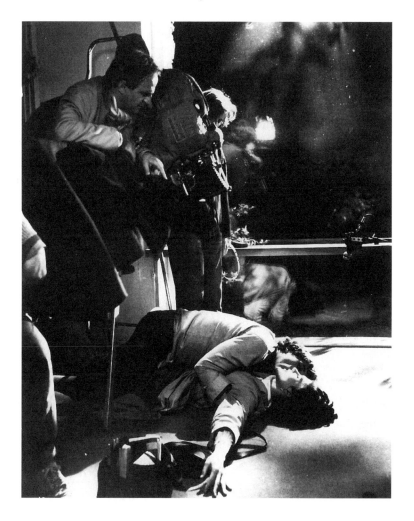

7. Truffaut filming *The Woman Next Door*. Source: Photofest.

the cinema with sexuality and sin, with naughty and forbidden pleasures. To hide his vice of moviegoing, he would often lie to his parents about his activities outside the home. Truffaut paid for the guilty pleasures of cinephilia, by his own account, in the coin of "stomach aches, nausea, fear and a feeling of culpability which inevitably became mixed with the feelings provoked by the spectacle."[8]

But in Truffaut's case cinephilia became linked to sexuality in an even more palpable way. Truffaut adored female stars, first as a fan and at a distance. This form of distant adoration is evoked in *The 400 Blows* by Antoine's stealing a movie theater poster of the young female star of Ingmar Bergman's *Monika*. Yet it was eventually through the process of filmmaking itself that Truffaut managed to meet, engage, and even bed such stars as Catherine Deneuve, Françoise Dorléac, Kika Markham, and Fanny Ardent. In terms of behavior, however, Truffaut was timid like his character Jules, not audacious like Jim. If Roché was a major-league and somewhat cynical Don Juan, Truffaut was a sincere, at times even masochistic, minor-league Don Juan, weighed down by guilt and cursed by a late-romantic tragic sensibility.

When Henri-Pierre Roché was only one year old, his father suddenly died, in a bizarre fashion evoked verbally in the film version of *Two English Girls*. Just as Roché's père was inviting his wife, Clara (Henri-Pierre's mother), for a walk in the Luxembourg Gardens, the father fell off a balcony and died. In the wake of her husband's death Clara maintained an extremely close, almost incestuous, relationship with her son, who actually lived with his mother until her death in 1929. In his *Carnets* Roché quotes Helen Grund Hessel to the effect that in the end he loved only his mother: "she is the woman that you love the most."[9] Roché's mother was also a writer, who published, in 1926, a treatise on the education of children. The novel *Jules and Jim* alludes to Roché's mother when it says of Jim that he "had a high opinion of his mother. When he was a child she had taught him never to talk back; her yes meant yes and her no meant no."[10] Jim also speaks of the strangeness of having Kate visit the home "sanctuary" that he shared with his mother: "the atmosphere was so full of his mother's presence, and she was so much against the life he led with Kate" (195).

Roché delineates the relationship with his mother in fraught detail in *Two English Girls*, where the mother plays a paradoxically central role as at once cheerful mistress of the courtship revels and symbolic castrator of the reveling son. In transparently Oedipal terms Roché ("Claude" in the novel) refers to his mother as someone he "wanted to marry" and as "the fiancée of my childhood."[11] At age fifteen Roché had a strange dream, one mingling echoes of the Marquis de Sade with overtones of Marcel Proust, a dream that haunted him throughout his life. He recounts the dream in *Two English Girls*:

Claire, the fiancée of my early childhood, entered my room, looking very serious, half naked, wearing archaic jewels. With the gestures of a priestess, she stretches over me. Thanks to I don't know what kind of needle, she penetrates my penis, and enlarges the narrow opening the way one stretches the finger of a glove. It hurts badly. Sweat flows down my flanks. Claire disappears.

A short time later, she comes back with even more colorful ritual ornaments. She takes me again with her needle, which now enters more easily, enters even farther, in a way that is extremely painful, and she pierces something deep within me, for a splitting pain and a jet of blood awaken me.[12]

On April 18, 1927, Roché, who like many modernists had always been fascinated by the work of Sigmund Freud, and who had often played "Freudian games" with his friend Franz Hessel, used the pretext of sending Freud his book on Don Juan to ask the Viennese psychoanalyst to decipher his dream. (Freud thanked him for the gift but ignored the request, although in a later correspondence Freud remarked of Roché's book that it showed "correspondences with our own insights.") In uncanny complementarity to the mother's taboo on his having any long-standing relationship or marriage with a woman, Roché expressed in *Don Juan et . . .* a corresponding desire that his mother never abandon herself to the transports of love: "[Don Juan] began to think about his own mother, and suddenly he began biting his fingers. He does not want, does not want his mother ever to have rolled her head and cried out like Annette [in the transports of love] just did! But still, it was beautiful with Annette, and nevertheless his mother . . . that would have been beautiful, too. But it's impossible! He doesn't want it!" (114).

The son's thoughts about his mother's sexuality remind us of Hamlet's anguished imaginings of his mother as a sexual being. It is possible to speak, in Roché's case, of a kind of transformational grammar of eroticism, a predictable and interlocking series of elements constantly reconfigured in surface appearance but always prolonging the same substratal matrix. This matrix includes the various elements that Roché conceives as necessary to his narcissistic sense of well-being: close male friendship (successively with Jouanin, Marcel Duchamp,

Franz Hessel); the reliable companionship of patient, long-suffering, wifelike figures (Germaine Bonnard, Denise Renard); strong, passionate mistress figures (Helen Grund, Marie Laurencin); an endless series of more or less meaningless love affairs, all conducted under the surveillance of the mother, as the panoptical "warden" scrutinizing her son in the cramped cells of his lovemaking.

In 1899 Roché's mother placed Henri-Pierre (Claude in the novel) in contact with the young Englishwoman, Violet Hart, who was to teach him English and whom he visited in Wales. While there, Roché formed a "Platonic" trio with Violet and her sister Margaret. Roché eventually fell in love with Margaret and asked her to marry him. But Margaret was all too aware of the danger of antagonizing Mrs. Roché: "Think of the horror," she warned Roché, "of living with Mme. Roché's hatred and misery forever hanging over you."[13] If Henri-Pierre married Margaret, Violet worried, Mme Roché would "never see them again, or their children if they had them."[14] And, indeed, Roché's mother strongly opposed the marriage, insisting on a year of separation, which effectively destroyed its possibility. Shortly thereafter, Roché decided to dedicate himself to amorous conquests. Later in life, after his mother's death, Roché referred explicitly to the link between his mother's controlling attitudes and his Don Juanism. In his *Carnets* (February 10, 1952) he says of his wife, Denise, that "she is always, silently or not, reproachful of the past . . . says I have done much harm . . . through my polygamy, helped, created, by my mother."[15] (We will return to Roché's complex relationship with his mother when we discuss Roché's novel *Two English Girls* and Truffaut's adaptation of it.)

A mixture of dandy and rake, Roché was never a vulgar, ordinary Don Juan. Although his behavior was ultimately misogynistic, it was wrapped in the allure of what would later be called the "sensitive, New Age Man." In his "self-advertisement," we recall, Roché had listed "feminism" as one of his interests. When Lucie, in *Jules and Jim*, expresses surprise that Jules calls Jim "chaste," Jim replies: "But of course he is. . . . All passionate men are. He's chaster than I am, and than most other men. I've known him to go without a woman for months, without even looking for one. He's not the sort that runs after someone passing in the street. What he's mad about, what he worships, is character, and he doesn't go for sensuality in itself" (*Jules and Jim*, 67).

8. Kika Markham (left) and Stacey Tendeter in Truffaut's
Two English Girls. Source: Photofest.

Although in many ways a macho-style man in his behavior, Roché
was also somewhat ambidextrous in his gender identifications. In
this sense his attitude and behavior conform to Freud's claim that the
human libido is essentially bisexual but that social constraints usually
serve to conjure away the temptation of same-sex attraction. In some
ways Roché conforms to the archetype of what Robert Greene calls
the "feminine dandy," the man who lures women through a familiar
and graceful presence, where the sexuality is clearly heterosexual but
where its modalities oscillate between the feminine and masculine
poles: "Mirroring feminine psychology, [the feminine dandy] displays
attention to his appearance, sensitivity to detail, a slight coquettishness, but also a hint of male cruelty.[16] Since seduction is a classical
form of female power against overwhelming odds, premised on the
absence of real power in the public sphere, the feminine dandy in a
sense uses "feminine" weapons against women themselves.

Fascinated by Otto Weininger's misogynistic and self-hating anti-
Semitic tract *Sex and Character* (1906), Roché identified with Weininger's

portrait of women as totally sexual and saw himself as "feminine" and in some ways "hysterical." Weininger had written, "It is always relatively feminine men who continually run after women and who are interested only in romantic affairs and sexual relations."[17] Roché was a strangely passive seducer who waited for women to respond to him. Even in his erotic dream about his mother, it is she who is the aggressor who symbolically "deflowers" him. Furthermore, Roché did not look for blind obedience from women; rather, he was fascinated by strong, outspoken women who were emotionally independent and sexually free. At the same time, he also liked to have available, as a kind of amorous insurance, a perennially patient and long-suffering woman, who could function as "default setting" for his affective needs.

Rakes like Roché are appealing to the kind of women who hope to domesticate them; the rake's disloyalty and opportunism, for these women, only adds to his appeal, at least momentarily. Yet Roché's undeniable sexism was mitigated, up to a point, by his respect for women as artists and as intelligent human beings. In 1903 he contemplated writing a short story on the theme of the superiority of women to men, especially the superiority of modern, intelligent women. In his work as art critic and collector Roché often served as a midwife—Pygmalion?—for feminine talent. He encouraged Marie Laurencin to paint, for example, and prodded Helen Hessel to write. Rather surprisingly in an axiomatically masculinist age—including even (and perhaps especially) in the avant-garde milieu—Roché developed an art collection uniquely devoted to women painters, and in 1904 he wrote a short critical essay titled "Several Works by Women." After his stay in New York, at a time when a standard motif of French anti-Americanism was that the United States was a gynocratic country populated by castrating harpies and "hen-pecked" husbands, Roché praised American women to a *New York Tribune* reporter: "American women are the most intelligent in the world . . . the only ones who know what they want and who, therefore, always get it."[18] Roché's admiration for strong, smart women certainly reverberates with his respect, expressed in his diaries, for his own mother and for the supremely intelligent Helen Grund Hessel.

CHAPTER SIX

THE PROTOTYPE FOR JULES
FRANZ HESSEL AND FLÂNERIE

T HE CHARACTER JULES was based on the German-Jewish writer Franz Hessel (played by Oscar Werner in the Truffaut film). Born in Stettin on November 21, 1880, to a Polish Jewish family that became wealthy through the grain trade, Hessel moved to Berlin with his family in 1888, which by this time had converted to Protestantism. At that time Franz's father, Heinrich, had his children baptized and catechized. Like both Roché and Truffaut, Hessel did not know his father very well, since his father had died when Franz was very young. According to the Hessel's son Stéphane's autobiographical account, there were three children in his father's family. One, Anna, died of tuberculosis when Franz was ten, leaving him traumatized, which perhaps explains the air of melancholy that seems to have surrounded Franz throughout his life. Stéphane describes his father as having "a subtle mind in an awkward body," with a "sweet face and sweet gestures." Apparently he was not the most devoted of fathers, but he did take a strong interest in the children's education, especially in terms of learning about Greek mythology.[1] As Stéphane Hessel puts it in his autobiography: "Franz inculcated in me a taste for polytheism, which did not reduce the divine to the unique and rather anxiety-provoking figure of the Eternal Father, but which delivers us instead to the moving arbitrariness of Athena, Aphrodite, Apollo and Hermes."[2] Instead of a Jewish or Christian-style monotheism, then, Franz displayed a preferential option for the plural, whether in relation to lovers or to divinities.

In Germany Franz Hessel came to form part of Munich's bohemian circle, dominated by the poet Stefan George. In Munich, and especially in the artsy neighborhood of Schwabing, Hessel took part in the carnivals and masked balls typical of that intellectual milieu. Hessel became a friend and kind of disciple of a dominant figure in the artistic milieu, Karl Wolfskehl, an assimilated Jew with pan-Germanic enthusiasms, who also advanced Johann Jakob Bachofen's valorization of primitive matriarchy in the Mediterranean. Michael Hollington points out that Wolfskehl's closeness to Franz Hessel can be measured in the fact that it was Wolfskehl who saw off Hessel at the Munich train station when he left for Paris.[3] At that time many audacious ideas about sexuality were circulating—contradictory ideas about phallus worship and primitive matriarchy, pagan amorality and mother-earth goddesses, eugenics and the feminization/Judaization of modernity.

Hessel also admired another figure from Munich bohemia, the countess Franziska zu Reventlow, whom Hollington describes as "the first person to actually attempt to live out, or to have thrust on her, the role of the primal earth goddess mother figure."[4] (One is reminded of Jules's description of Catherine, in *Jules and Jim*, as a "queen" and a "force of nature.") Known as the "heathen Madonna," the countess had many prestigious lovers. Franz Hessel shared a ménage à trois in Schwabing with the countess and the Polish painter Suchocki, a kind of dry run for the later ménage with Roché and Helen. (Roché also became the countess's lover for a brief period.) Jean-Michel Palmier sees the ménage as prefiguring Hessel's relations with women in general: "He becomes their confidant, he loves them and admires them at a distance, preferring the role of friend to that of lover, consoler rather than conqueror."[5] The novel picks up on these ideas by describing Jules as a "delicious friend" but an "inconsistent husband and lover" (p. 18 in the French version) who loves women "too much and not enough" (20).

Hessel first met Henri-Pierre Roché in Paris in 1906 when Roché took him to the "Bal des Quat-z' Arts," in an episode picked up both in the novel and in the film versions of *Jules and Jim*. "It was while Jules was looking through the materials and choosing a simple slave costume that Jim's love for Jules was born" (9). That Jules chooses a "slave costume" hints at an element of masochism in his relation not only with women but also with Jules/Henri-Pierre. In his diaries Roché described Franz Hessel as "Jewish, German, small, round, endowed with great understanding and a charming sensibility" (*Car-

nets, November 10, 1906). Like Roché, Franz Hessel lived at various epicenters of European modernism—Munich, Berlin, and Paris. Ultimately, Franz became a friend of prestigious artists and intellectuals such as Hermann Hesse, Siegfried Kracauer, Heinrich Mann, Aldous Huxley, Stefan George, Robert Musil, Kurt Weill, Marlene Dietrich, and Ernst Bloch.

Hessel was also especially close, in both Paris and Berlin, to Walter Benjamin. Hessel became Benjamin's Berlin editor, and together they articulated the first phase of the "Passagen" project, a meditation on the phenomenon of the commercial "arcades."[6] Benjamin wrote his essay "The Return of the Flâneur" on the occasion of Hessel's *Spazieren in Berlin*. In that book Hessel spoke of the powerful feelings, the "damp chill," the "absent center," and the "ghostly, hidden crowds of people from days gone by" that were triggered by a stroll through Berlin's Kaisergalerie, a shopping gallery modeled on the Paris arcades.[7] Hessel evokes Berlin, in a kind of verbal equivalent to the city-symphony films (such as Walther Ruttman's *Berlin, Symphony of a City*) then being screened in Europe, as places where rich and poor rub elbows, as places of both beauty and ugliness. Unlike Benjamin, Hessel pays attention to the random and the gratuitous, to the lived surfaces of urban life; he is less interested in allegory. The physical experience of the confrontation of past and present in these passages, as Susan Buck-Morss points out, "paralleled the internal, mental experience of 'involuntary memory'" described in Proust's *Remembrance of Things Past*, which together Hessel and Benjamin translated.[8]

Roché met Helen Grund, Hessel's wife-to-be, in 1912, when she arrived together with "a new shipment of girls from Germany," a moment registered in a memorable early sequence in the Truffaut film. Benjamin spoke of Hessel's uncanny magnetism and told Helen that Hessel was a "magician": "We come to life in his company, are ourselves once again, this self that fills us with the joys of discovery and with as much interest and pleasure as he finds in us. And then we simply sit there, caught up in his spell."[9]

In 1926 Helen Hessel invited Benjamin to move in with her and her husband, but Benjamin hesitated, partially because, as he told Julia Radt in an April 8, 1926, letter, "Helen sometimes has a strange desire to flirt with me, and I do my best . . . not to flirt back."[10] Yet in 1929 Benjamin

9. Walter Benjamin. Source: Walter Benjamin Archiv der Akademie der Künste, Berlin. Photographer: Studio Joël-Heinzelmann.

ultimately did move in with the couple, in their apartment in an old neighborhood in west Berlin.[11]

As a well-published author and as the editor of a major German publishing house, and as a habitué of artistic cafés, Hessel, like Roché, was close to both the German and the French branches of artistic modernism. Hessel translated and edited French writers like Stendhal and Balzac, and in 1927 Benjamin and Hessel together worked on translating into German Proust's *A la recherche du temps perdu*, specifically *À l'Ombre des jeunes filles en fleurs*. Hessel's own writing, steeped in nostalgia for the lost world of bohemian Paris, is reminiscent in some ways of Proust, as is his view of his childhood as a lost paradise of pampered security. The Proust translation was praised by critics for not merely creating the atmosphere of the novel but also for transposing Proust's "spiritual zone to another landscape."[12] In a letter to the *Literarische Welt* Friedrich Burschell stressed the symbiotic hybridity of the translation, in words redolent of the real-life friendship of Benjamin and Hessel:

> What makes this new translation so special is the happy fact that it is the successful collaboration of two authors, each of whom is more suited than any other to translating Proust—the most cultivated and demanding of all modern authors—as a result of their linguistic knowledge, education, and taste. Yet they have exchanged their ideas, merged together and amalgamated to produce—even where their individual contributions can be clearly distinguished from one another—an astonishing approximation . . . of not only the original, but also of that which the author had intended to underlie his words. The elements which they each contribute from their individual personalities and scholarly backgrounds seem to have been predestined to blend within the great medium of Proust's ingenuity.[13]

Burschell goes on to delineate the complementarities and contrasts between the two translating personalities:

> Essentially Franz Hessel represents the engaging, affectionate, intuitively acquisitive side of Proust the charmeur, the well-versed, ironic, creatively superior connoisseur; the genius with a mastery of enchanting, beguiling details, of tact and delicate exposition. Walter Benjamin represents the subtle, exact, unremittingly probing, critically transcending side which is never satisfied with a single solution, and that corresponds to the other aspect of Proust's talent: the passionate compulsion not to leave anything untouched and to retain in the depths of memory and knowledge all that has been experienced. . . . Hessel is sufficiently thoughtful, while Benjamin has shown . . . just what strong emotions and powers of expression he can summon to convey poetic virtues and resonances. Consequently, this new translation is built on the best of possible foundations. It

would have been difficult to entrust this work to more solid, skillfully interlocked hands. The German version of Proust that matches up to the original is at last emerging.[14]

The collaboration of Hessel and Benjamin on the Proust translation thus recalls and anticipates other cross-cultural friendships and collaborations involving Roché and Franz and Helen, the same kinds of international collaborations also evoked in *Jules and Jim*. The Proust connection also anticipates certain "Proustian" aspects of Truffaut's own oeuvre, where "involuntary memory" can sometimes be glimpsed as an organizing principle behind some of the motifs in the film.[15] (We note this Proustian motif, for example, in the memory sequences of *The Man Who Loved Women*.)

Walter Benjamin revived the term *flâneur* to describe Hessel in his review of Hessel's 1928 book *Spazieren in Berlin*. The flâneur was originally linked to nineteenth-century Paris as conjured up by Benjamin in his analysis of the life and work of Charles Baudelaire. The flâneur wandered through the city, seen as a kind of "forest of symbols." For Benjamin the flâneur in the Baudelairean mode was linked both to bohemian life and to the commercial marketing typical of those proto–shopping malls called arcades.[16] Indeed, Benjamin's arcades project was first elaborated in conjunction with Hessel during a visit to Paris. Inveterate walker in the city, and author of the essay "On the Difficult Art of Walking" [Von der schwierigen spazieren zu gehen], Hessel roamed the streets of various European capitals, reading them, as Benjamin would have put it, "like a book." As passive spectator of the life of the streets, Hessel became the unhurried ambulatory reader/writer, without concrete goal or destiny, the man who privileges the ephemeral and the apparently superficial.[17] For Manuela Ribeiro Sanches, reading Hessel is like "paging through an album of photographs where . . . absorbed and attentive, we fix moments, little gestures, little nothings of a quotidian where everything is only insinuated."[18] For Hessel flânerie was characterized by a delicious aimlessness, a suspension of pragmatic goals. "If you want to observe something along your route," Hessel warns prospective flâneurs, "do not greedily rush into it. In that case, it will escape you."[19] "The incomparable enchantment of the stroll," for Hessel, was that it detaches the stroller from the private and practical life, offering the freedom of anonymity and an oceanic mingling of self and city.

In her indispensable *The Art of Taking a Walk: Flânerie, Literature, and Film in Weimar Culture*, Anke Gleber sees Franz Hessel as one of the last avatars of the bohemian intellectual typical of early modernist European culture. She describes the flâneur as "at once a dreamer, a historian, and a modern artist, someone who transforms his observations into texts and images."[20] In his writing Hessel defines *flânerie* as a way of "reading the street, in which people's faces, displays, shop windows, café terraces, cars, tracks, trees turn into an entire series of equivalent letters, which together form words, sentences, and pages of a book that is always new."[21] Intoxicated with the search for hidden resemblances, Weimar flâneurs were semioticians avant la lettre who decoded the phantasmagoria, the consumer products and street signs, of the modern metropolis. According to Benjamin the flâneur is an "artist of modern life" who registers his highly visual impressions in literary form, thus becoming the "chronicler" and the "philosopher" of his age.[22]

On one level the flâneur is an aesthete who enjoys the intensification of perception triggered by the city's variegated stimuli. In this sense flânerie is an exercise in cubist multiperspectivalism, a form of mental montage, a way of superimposing one set of experiences and associations on another set of experiences. Yet on another level the flâneur is also a critical observer, whose perambulations constitute an exercise in what the Russian Formalists would have called (social) *ostrenanie* ("making strange") or what Bertolt Brecht later called "verfremdung-seffekt." Formulated in another critical idiom, the flâneur performs, in ambulatory form, what the Frankfurt School Marxists might have called *Ideologiekritick* (critique of ideology). Or, to borrow from the language of the 1960s counterculture, the flâneur moves in a free-floating "liberated territory," a zone of experimental identifications, free from bourgeois constraints. Flânerie is slackerism avant la lettre, a form of redemptive laziness, a European equivalent of what the Brazilian modernists, tropical flâneurs in their own fashion, called *sacerdocio* (sacred leisure).[23] Flânerie is above all a question of what André Gide later called "disponibilité" (availability) to the moment. Gleber sees in Hessel's flânerie a nostalgia, as well, for a protected childhood, a "way of looking at the world [that] preserves a childlike affinity with things" through what Hessel calls the child's "fairy tale gaze."[24] Both the novel and the film *Jules and Jim*, I would argue, convey this sense of childlike wonder and (perhaps illusory) innocence. But flânerie also had its dark underside. For Rob Shields flânerie constitutes "a sociability of Ones . . . an atomized form of sociation where individuals congregate in an anonymous crowd of randomly strolling people [keeping] their social distance from each other."[25]

Flânerie also had a clearly gendered and erotic dimension, shaped by the male-dominant environment, where the urban scene/seen formed the site/sight of a masculinist gaze. For men it sometimes constituted a flight from a lifeless marriage into the wifeless streets. For women, hemmed in by all sorts of restrictions, it was usually a taboo activity. In erotic terms flânerie implied a libidinal openness to what the city had to offer in sexual, or at least scopophilic, terms. To a somewhat passive, voyeuristic, and not conventionally attractive figure like Hessel, flânerie offered a lottery in flirtation, a desperate, anxious hope for the "prize" of a reciprocated glance from those women who "walk by and do not look at me."[26] Anke Gleber contrasts the misogyny of some flâneurs from the same period with what she sees as Hessel's "polymorphous" curiosity about all the appearances of urban modernity. In words that evoke the portrayal of the character Jules in both novel and film, she writes that in Hessel's texts "women receive an incomparable degree of visual autonomy and attentive regard."[27]

It is also appropriate and suggestive, I think, to flash-forward and see New Wave directors like Truffaut, and the characters in their films, as latter-day flâneurs. Quite apart from the indissoluble link that joins flânerie to narrow and well-worn Parisian streets, the New Wave cinéastes themselves displayed flâneurlike qualities as they carried their jiggling handheld cameras—in movements that inscribe the traces of the moving gaze of their errant sensibilities—around the streets of Paris, seeing it like a painting and reading it like a book. Picking up on Sartre's Roquentin in *La Nausée*, these filmic flâneurs searched for meaning and pleasure on the sidewalks and in the signs of the metropolis. Recalling their movement from movie theater to movie theater, and from bookstore to bookstore, we are reminded of the innumerable urban walking sequences in New Wave films, for example Antoine and René's "playing hooky" gambols/gambles around Paris in *The 400 Blows*; or Patricia and Michel's long stroll down the Champs-Elysées as Patricia hawks the *New York Herald Tribune* in Godard's *Breathless*; or Riva walking and being flirted with by Japanese men in Duras/Resnais's *Hiroshima mon amour*; or the metal worker Angelo's long walk home in Jean Rouch's *Chronicle of a Summer*; or the two girlfriends' jump-cut promenade in *Adieu Phillipine*; or Cléo's walk from the Café Dome through Left Bank streets in Agnès Varda's *Cléo from 5 to 7*; or Frédéric's eroticized strolling (and reading) in Eric Rohmer's *Chloé in the Afternoon*, to cite just a few of innumerable examples.

Although their artistic practice was resolutely modernist, their auteurist theory was drenched in romanticism, an expressive aesthetic that idealized the artist as visionary, seer, and magus. In *Le Poétique du mâle* Michelle Coquillat argues that romanticism entailed a claim of "self-engendering" that associated creativity and masculinity, relegating women to the realm of nature, reproduction, and contingency. The New Wave wrote cinema, as Genevieve Sellier puts it, "in the first-person of the masculine singular."[28] For Sellier the "ontologically misogynistic" side of romanticism, which was nevertheless capable of creating very moving female characters, established a zero-sum game in relation to masculine identity and any deep connection to women, a feature that characterized many New Wave films.[29] Few women, symptomatically, formed part of the New Wave movement, especially in the core *Cahiers* group. (Agnès Varda and Marguerite Duras were both associated more with the "Left Bank" subgroup of the movement.)

It is revealing to examine, in this regard, the crucial role of public-space flirtation—what is known in French as "la drague"—in the films of the New Wave, beginning already in the 1950s with shorts like Godard's *Tous les garçons s'appellent Patrick* (All the Boys Are Named Patrick), where the Jean-Claude Brialy character flirts with two women simultaneously, unaware that they are roommates. In Truffaut's *The 400 Blows* Jean-Claude Brialy accosts Jeanne Moreau as she walks her dog. In *Chloé in the Afternoon* Rohmer's character Frédéric fantasizes about an amulet that inspires women pedestrians to fall magically into his arms. In real life, women like Françoise Sagan, Simone de Beauvoir, and Juliette Gréco were entering public space. But as Ginette Vincendeau points out, the New Wave *flâneuses*, unlike their male counterparts, are often "trapped by brutal sexual encounters (*Les bonnes femmes*), prostitution (*Vivre sa vie*), and [are] relentlessly brought back to [their] sexuality."[30] Yet on rare occasions New Wave films do offer glimpses of the resentment engendered in the women who have to put up with the relentless stalking of *les draguers*. In a 1969 essay in *Esquire* Truffaut speaks of his "solidarity" with the women who confront the outrages of the draguers, scenes he witnessed so often in Paris, and imagines a reversal of roles whereby "the humiliation switches sides."[31] In fact, Truffaut is describing a scene that he already filmed, in *La Peau douce* (1964). There, the Francia character, at a moment when she is already outraged by evidence of her husband's infidelity, tells an obnoxious draguer (played by Jean-Louis Richard, the coscreenwriter of the film): "Who do you think you are? Did you imagine that I was going to go to bed with an idiot like you? Have you ever looked at yourself in the mirror?!" Taken aback by her anger and sarcasm, the man beats a hasty and embarrassed retreat. (We will return to flânerie when we get to Helen Hessel.)

CHAPTER SEVEN

HESSEL AS NOVELIST

Although both Roché and Truffaut downplay Hessel's Jewishness, it is hardly an incidental feature of his identity, especially in an age of rising anti-Semitism. The Jules of the Roché novel reports anti-Semitic incidents. At the age of ten, he recalls, he was struck by his "friend" Hermann, who called him "a dirty Jew" (28). With the rise of Hitler to the rank of chancellor of the Reich, things got worse for Jews. The Hessels' son Stéphane describes the family's reaction as follows: "Our refusal was total and immediate. For us, this clownish megalomaniac who brayed in an atrociously vulgar language could not possibly last very long. The Germans could never be so stupid."[1] But in fact things were more complicated. The narrator of *Jules and Jim* describes Hessel as an assimilated Jew, "one of those who, apart from a few close friends, avoid other Jews" (160). But Hessel's family's conversion to Christianity and his marriage to Helen did not protect him from discrimination. His own patron, Ernst Rowohlt, told Hessel that, as a Jew, he could no longer write under his own name. In 1933 Hessel was forbidden to publish in Germany and was even "excommunicated" by the Germans' Writers Chamber in 1935.[2] Helen divorced Franz in this period because she could not continue to publish her articles while she was married to a Jew, even to an assimilated Jew like Franz.

Hessel touched briefly on these issues in his novel *The Bazaar of Happiness*, where his character Gustave, largely modeled on himself, knows little about Judaism. When a schoolmate taunts him as a Jew, Gustav asks, "What's a Jew?" Later he attends a Zionist Congress in Basel, where he hears Orthodox Jews talk about anti-Semitic pogroms in Russia, yet he feels ill at ease with the Orthodox milieu. Always passive, Hessel let himself be seduced by the men and women and objects around him. In the end he remained always the outside observer. His power, such as it was, was that of the serene, disinterested voyeur. As Manuela Ribeiro Sanches puts it, Hessel was equally alienated from a wide variety of contemporaneous lifestyles and ideological currents, equally distant "from the progressive enlightened ideas of his Jewish father; from the Christianity that, for sentimental reasons, he tried to adopt; from the Zionism in which he could not see himself; and from the bohemian life which seduced but did not convince him."[3]

In actuality Hessel also suffered from the anti-Semitism of Helen Grund's family—who were reluctant to see her marry a Jew. At the wedding reception, according to Stéphane Hessel, Helen's brothers thought too many Jews had been invited, while Franz's relatives wondered if Helen hadn't married him for his fortune. Few seemed to understand the deep, uncanny connection between them. But even Helen at times suffered mild forms of the anti-Semitic infection. When Helen has a difficult delivery with their son Ulrich, she wonders if God isn't punishing her for having married a Jew. Indeed, it is difficult not to conclude that Hessel was in some ways a self-hating Jew like Otto Weininger, one of those highly assimilated Jews who played a hiding game with their Jewishness. In Hessel's short book *Seven Dialogues* (1924) a character describes Jews as those who invert Christ's command to "love those who hate you" in favor of "hating those who love you." Like so many Jews in this period, Hessel was caught between contradictory demands—to assimilate on the one hand, and to honor his Jewishness on the other—with the result that he was obliged to constantly "code-switch." Hessel sometimes describes Jews as those who undergo metamorphoses, a description reminiscent of Woody Allen's chameleon man in *Zelig*, a fictional Jewish character who lived in exactly the same period as Hessel and who conformed his appearances according to the reigning stereotypes, to the point even of joining the Nazi movement.[4]

Despite the rise of the Nazis to power, Hessel refused to leave Berlin, arguing on antielitist grounds that he should not be "spared the fate accorded other Jews." Hessel's refusal betokens the inappropriately serene passivity—in this case a kind of social masochism—that characterized his temperament. At the same time, Hessel's blinkered response to Nazism reveals the limits of his aestheticism, pointing to the art-for-art's-sake blinders that allowed him to idealize the early Nazi rallies as a "kind of gigantic cheerfulness."[5] But Hitler's storm troopers were gradually sanitizing Berlin's streets not only of prostitutes and vagrants but also of "cosmopolitans" and "flâneurs" and "wandering Jews" like himself. According to Stéphane Hessel it was only in 1938, a few weeks before Krystallnacht (November 9) that Helen went to look for Hessel in Berlin to put him on a train for Paris. Helen stayed in Berlin, where she witnessed Krystallnacht, and wrote about it in an article for the *New Yorker*. When war broke out, Franz was arrested and placed in the Colombes Stadium, along with all the Germans living in Paris, whether Nazi sympathizers or not. Freed, he rejoined Helen in Sanary, where many exiled German intellectuals and artists—such as Heinrich and Thomas Mann, Ernst Bloch, Bertolt Brecht, and Arthur Koestler—were awaiting some outcome that would allow them to return to Germany. With Vichy, both Franz and the Hessels' son Ulrich were conducted to a prison for "ennemis citoyens" in Aix-en-Provence. Hessel there found himself imprisoned along with three thousand others, among them the German dramatist Walter Hasenclever. Lion Feuchtwanger evokes his memory of Franz as "this sweet little man who lived at Milles [the prison] as if [he] were in the middle of cosmopolitan Berlin."[6] They were ultimately freed, but the harassment had taken its toll. At the time, Hessel continued working on his novel *Alter Mann*, which remained unfinished at the time of his death and was completed only with the help of Helen. Hessel died in 1941 at the age of sixty, in France, his health and spirit broken, an early victim of French anti-Semitism. (We do not know if he was aware of his friend Walter Benjamin's death earlier.)

Helen evoked the funeral in Sanary in a text written for the tenth anniversary of Franz's death, in words that only partially correspond to the accounts of the funeral in both novel and film:

> Yes, many people came, a cortege of very diverse people who came to say Goodbye to him. No one, not even we ourselves, suspected that he was so close to death. He approached death so sweetly that we became aware of it only when it was too late.
>
> Only the old bum, who lived in a cabin near the garden gate, with his eternal bottle of wine . . . was not surprised. Franz had

often chatted with him, and when I expressed astonishment, Franz said: "Drunks are lucky; when they stagger, they feel through their feet the happy rotation of the earth." The old vagabond came to the funeral . . . and said: "He was a good man," which in the language of simple people is the expression of the highest respect. And then the bum asked for Franz's shoes, which Franz had promised to him once he no longer needed them. . . . Other people, some poor and some poorer, came, and what little material goods remained to Franz were distributed right there before he was placed in the coffin.[7]

"He died," Helen writes, "as he had lived, possessing nothing, softly, without complaining and without struggling."[8]

Evoking their relationship, Helen writes: "When I reflect today on my marriage with this very singular man, it seems to be, despite the certificates concerning our married status, that I was never his wife. Something very different bound us together, something voluntary and therefore even more binding."[9]

The eternal outsider, Franz was regarded in Germany as a Jew and in France as a German. Roché, for his part, had a number of Jewish friends like Hessel, but he was not especially sensitive to the evils of anti-Semitism. When his good friend the anti-Semitic American art dealer John Quinn rails against Jews and their conspiracies, Roché says nothing. When Quinn railed against Jews in letters, Roché would merely note that he didn't know the person in question was Jewish, without questioning the assumptions behind the remarks. A misconstrued Nietzscheanism, at the same time, attracts Roché to strong personalities. Roché reportedly drafted a new version of "La Marseillaise" for the head of the Vichy government, Marechal Petain. Roché's reaction to Hitler's *Mein Kampf* was even more disconcerting. On July 17, 1941, Roché writes of Hitler's diatribe: "Very powerful. A book of action. I understand its success."[10] None of this prevented Roché from being very much shaken when he learned of Franz's death: "How we counted on having the leisure to continue one day our eternal conversations. We didn't write to each other, see each other, out of fear of and pity of Helen. . . . This death for me is such a deep sorrow, and not to have been able to help him."[11]

Hessel's death also triggered one of Roché's first contacts with the world of cinema. Roché considered scripting a film about Franz, hopefully to be made by Jean Renoir, to be entitled *L'Homme unique*. Roché even got so far as fashioning a rough outline, but memories of Helen's warnings and ultimatums forbidding any contact with Hessel intimidated him.[12]

CHAPTER EIGHT

HESSEL'S *PARISIAN ROMANCE*

FRANZ HESSEL WROTE about his relationship with both Helen Grund and Roché in his 1920 novel *Pariser Romanze* (translated into French as *Romance Parisienne* in 1990).[1] Supposedly written in the trenches of World War I, these "notebooks" are presented as a series of four letters composed by a "missing man" to his Parisian friend "Claude" (Roché), dedicated to reviving their common memory of prewar bohemian Paris. As if in uncanny premonition of his own untimely death, Hessel subtitled the novel (in German at least) *Papers of Someone Lost without a Trace.* The account of male friendship mingles the shared experience of flânerie with reflections on that experience. Here, in words that clearly evoke the camaraderie shared by Hessel and Roché, is Hessel's account of the friendship between Claude and the narrator: "The silences of our conversations were full of neighboring thoughts. Whether we would read together in books or read the people who we would encounter in the street, whether we lived an event together or told each other about what we had experienced, everything transpired under the same sign of meditation and silence."[2]

Much of *Romance Parisienne* is taken up with affectionate memories of Paris, where Roché spent six years, a city that was then a veritable melting pot of international artists—Pablo Picasso from Spain; Constantin Brancusi from Romania; Franz Hessel from Germany; Gertrude Stein from the United States—who created their own cosmopolitan, ad hoc version of the French language. The narrator recalls a cosmopolitan, bohemian Paris that transcended narrow national chauvinisms: "We are all exiles. Only Paris was our country. It's strange and difficult to explain. Paris had become a destiny, a necessity. . . . I knew several painters and the friends of painters, mostly foreigners like myself. As a foreigner, I lived on the margins of life and I loved this city" (262).

Or again, referring to the way Roché (here "Claude")—welcomed Hessel to Paris: "As a foreigner, I lived on the margins of life and I loved that city. And perhaps in recompense for my love, which coveted nothing and strove for nothing, Paris gave me the gift of the friendship of one of its authentic children. It gave me your friendship, Claude" (263).

At one point Hessel strikes a nostalgic note about one of the foremost modernist Parisian eateries—the Closerie des Lilas in Montparnasse—precisely the place where Hessel and Roché first met: "Claude, what has become of our world? Do you remember the belle époque where all the nations of Montparnasse came together at the Closerie des Lilas?" (258).

Hessel was writing in Germany, we must remember, at a time when official German propaganda was more and more demonizing France and the French. In this sense Hessel had already become a psychic émigré, a man whose heart and mind had partially abandoned his country of birth, even while remaining on its soil. At times these reflections take on clear pacifist overtones. While "some rejoice over reports of military victories," Hessel's narrator "feels no joy" (258). What he calls the "monstrous system" of military life deprives "human beings of the right to think" (271). At times, the narrator excoriates militarism in terms that encode Judaic and Protestant iconoclastic hostility to "idolatry" and the taboos on the "graven image." Describing a moment where "horror embraces the world," the narrator asks: "How can I live and tolerate the fact that my peers shed their blood for idols which no longer carry the names of gods but rather of scientific abstractions? That kind of death is a sin, that shedding of blood is an outrage. It is no longer a question of idols made of stone, wood, or gold, but rather of machines made of steel, equipped with perfectly precise moving parts" (269).

Claude and the narrator are determined not to let the war open up any fissures in their friendship. Speaking of a French poet-friend (Paul Fort) who has begun to compose "hymns of hatred" against the Germans, the narrator asks Claude: "Is this conceivable? What do you think, Claude? Do you hate us too, you the fair and just one, who knowingly weighed the virtues and vices of nations? We who had the hope that the era of money, of exchange, of industry, with its renewed outbreaks of chauvinism, would reach the point of the absurd, until humanity would wake up from the horrible dream. Might that be the final meaning of this war? Will not much blood have been shed in vain?" (21).

Elsewhere the pacifist plea takes on tones of a very personal vulnerability. For Hessel collectivities and ideologies do not exist, only individuals. Doubting that "goodness can save us," the narrator wonders if he will ever "see spring again" and often thinks "that [his] existence could easily come to an end" (268). Lamenting that he has found neither purpose nor profession, he fears that he might have to "go away" without having "said what [he] has to say" (269).

Hessel also speaks in the novel of the thoroughly commingled pleasures of flirtation and flânerie. In the faces of female strangers he detects the memory traces of the women he has loved, "the half-open lips which one had regarded breathing in sleep" (297). The narrator also contrasts his own timidity and clumsiness with "Claude's" audacity: "I am always afraid when I follow a girl. And generally I give up easily. In any case, it's much more pleasurable to give yourself up to the movement of the multitude in the hopes that some woman or other might reward you with a glance" (296).

Hessel describes Roché, in contrast, as a much more practiced and confident seducer. While not "one of those whom one recognizes immediately as a seducer," Hessel writes, Claude's "sweetness and nonchalant air make him even more dangerous" (196).

It is also in *Romance Parisienne* that Hessel speaks of "the archaic smile of the marble statue," a moment picked up both in the Roché novel and the Truffaut film, where the fascination with the smile of the statue anticipates the friends' later fascination with the novel's Catherine. And we sense already Hessel's fascination with strong and capricious women. He speaks of a certain "Manon," who "lets herself be kissed and caressed, with a kind of sated smile, and who then quickly gets up and changes the game. It's a matter of permanent seduction, but no one ever ever gets anything" (284). And again in anticipation of the events and attitudes described in *Jules and Jim*, the narrator constantly struggles against any and all sense of sexual jealousy. In a passage that mingles voyeuristic pleasure with masochistic pain, and perhaps a soupçon of homoerotic identification, he speaks of watching

Lotte, a woman in whom he is interested, dance with another man: "I saw her dancing with a tall slender Latin who awakened in her, coldly but with great art, a purely sensual pleasure, excitement, desire, which provoked in her something she had not known previously, to wit voluptuousness without passion" (322).

But at the same time he regretfully censures his own feelings of sexual possessiveness while watching her: "Weren't my fears, in the end, nothing but jealousy? Didn't the petit-bourgeois in me aspire to keep the sweet prey for himself, to bring her into his lair, to be the first and only witness of her trembling metamorphosis?" (323).

For the narrator all feelings of jealousy are relativized, indeed, rendered grotesque and petty, by the historical context of a world war. Threatened by the excesses of hysterical nationalism, the narrator takes refuge in pacifist and internationalist values. An early avatar of the "make love not war" philosophy, the narrator writes: "[T]his conflict is alien to me. And if it costs me my life, and if I am to be counted among the thousands of involuntary heroes fallen on the field of battle, all that would touch me much less than what was the memory of a glimpse of a young woman" (323).

If Roché was a rake and a dandy, Franz Hessel in some ways seems the eternal child, who charms others through his spontaneity, sincerity, and guilelessness. If Roché was mysterious and elusive, Hessel was open-hearted, wearing his emotions on his sleeve. Within the triangle he was both the overarching protector and the child who needed protecting. And for a woman like Helen Grund, as we will see, he was in some ways the ideal lover/father—devoted, paternal, and attentive to both wife and children.[3]

CHAPTER NINE

THE PROTOTYPE FOR CATHERINE
HELEN GRUND HESSEL

W E CAN NOW turn to the third member of the triangle—Helen Grund (Hessel)—the model for Kate in the novel *Jules and Jim* ("Catherine" in the film as played by Jeanne Moreau). Helen was born in Berlin in 1886, the daughter of a banker whose avocations were music and painting. The son Ulrich Hessel describes his parents as follows: "My mother was vigorously anti-conformist. She rejected bourgeois morality, but within her anti-conformism she managed to find, if not a morality, at least a very rigorous sense of ethics. My father, on the other hand, even if he was capable of hard work—I see him again in his smoky room, where he stayed all day long—was a pure bohemian."[1]

Helen's other son, Stéphane, meanwhile, casts the following light on his parents:

> I considered my mother a veritable goddess. She was very brilliant, demanding, willful, a little authoritarian, with literary ambitions. She had a very beautiful writing style. But she preferred to sacrifice by bringing up the children and at the same time publishing as a serious journalist, in order to support the family. She had a good deal of admiration for my father but probably also considered him as someone who was not completely responsible. The literary character that she inspired in Roché's novel was not at all exaggerated in terms of her physical charm."[2]

At the time Franz Hessel met her in Paris in 1912, Helen was studying painting. Although she never exposed her paintings, she clearly had visual as well as verbal talents. A journalist and fashion writer, Helen Grund also kept an elaborate diary concerning the triangle. A multitalented individual—painter, dancer, writer—she was blessed with many famous artist friends. Much as Roché had introduced Gertrude Stein to Pablo Picasso, Helen had introduced the poet Rainer Maria Rilke to Walter Benjamin. Like Franz Hessel, Helen was well connected to the avant-garde movement. Alexander Calder's hanging steel shards, for example, were first called "mobiles" in the Hessel home, and even more specifically in the playroom of their boys, Ulrich and Stéphane.[3] In Paris Helen earned a living as fashion correspondent for the women's' supplement ("Fur die Frau") of the *Frankfurter Zeitung.* In her writing on fashion Helen went far beyond the superficialities of fashion journalism to forge a precocious version of what many decades later would be called a "cultural studies" approach. For her, fashion is "the plastic representation of the deepest human desire—for perfection. It is the proof that humanity should respect an ideal of grace and charm, just as an artist might admire her creation before her desire for perfection comes to trouble the enterprise."[4]

Helen Hessel, too, was fascinated by the phenomenon of flirtation. For her, Paris and Vienna were the world centers of fashion because they recognized the importance of feminine coquetterie. Fashion has a compensatory role for women because they are unfairly condemned by biology, in collaboration with social norms, to restrict their role to bearing children and to suffering, in some ways more severely than men, the slings and arrows of the ravages of time and corporeality. One of the admirers of Helen Hessel's journalism was Frankfurt School theorist Theodor Adorno, who recommended her writing to Walter Benjamin. Like both Roché and Benjamin, Helen had a life replete with unfinished projects: a comedy about Freud and Weininger; a short story about her affair with a man named Koch; and a five-act play (written after the war) called *Blut* (Blood), about the anti-Semitism suffered by a German professor (in short, a play about what might have happened to Hessel if he had not left Germany). After the war Helen also translated *Lolita* into German. Yet both Roché and Truffaut, symptomatically, play down Helen's intellectually productive side. And it is true that Helen never quite realized her artistic ambitions, partially out of confusion about her goals but also because of very concrete obstacles, not shared by men in the same way, such as her responsibilities as a mother (Roché, too, never completely realized his literary ambitions). While Helen speaks in her diaries of being a "mother above all," neither Roché nor Franz Hessel speaks very much about being a father.

When Helen first went to Paris in 1912 at age twenty-six, she became associated with a circle of artists who frequented the celebrated Café Dome in Montparnasse, then one of the favored watering holes of the avant-garde. There, artists from many countries became transfixed by her charm. As Franz Hessel put it: "Everyone loved her. Wherever she was, she was the center of attention."[5] By casting Jeanne Moreau for the role of Catherine in his film adaptation, Truffaut shifts the national balance of power toward the French side. Instead of two Germans and a Frenchman, it becomes a question of two French and one German (both Roché and Truffaut, interestingly, play down the Jewishness of Franz Hessel). At the same time, Helen's self-description in her journals as "allemande jusqu'à la moelle de mes os" (German to the very marrow of my bones) gives way to Truffaut's decision to make the character French rather than German. On the other hand, Truffaut can be said to be "faithful" to the prototype in that he now makes Catherine, within a kind of transposed nationalism, French to the very marrow of her bones, having her laud Napoleon, for example, and make obnoxious boasts about the incomparable virtues of French wines.

Truffaut cast Jeanne Moreau, who seemed to him to have played too many roles unworthy of her talents, because she was the greatest "amoureuse" in French cinema. Reportedly everyone—but most notably the producer, Raoul Levy; the actor Henri Serre; and the director, François Truffaut—fell in love with Moreau on the set, thus recapitulating the process by which Parisian artists and intellectuals fell in love with Helen on the "set" of Left Bank cafés. Truffaut and Moreau became friends when the director gave the actress a copy of the Roché novel. Moreau also brings to the film the intertextual aura of some of her previous roles, especially as the sexually liberated heroine both of Louis Malle's *Les Amants* and of Roger Vadim's *Les Liaisons dangereuses*, an aura further heightened by the paratextual buzz generated by her numerous real-life affairs.

According to Ginette Vincendeau, Jeanne Moreau, as seen by Truffaut, embodied the typical contradictions of New Wave portrayals of women, combining retrograde, even misogynistic, projections with a seductively modern allure. A kind of "muse" of auteur cinema, Moreau supposedly epitomizes the "antistar" who is "unphotogenic." (Given that spectators of both genders loved to gaze at Moreau, however, perhaps "not conventionally beautiful" would be more accurate.) Moreau formed the antithesis of the bourgeoises played by actresses like Danielle Darieux and Michele Morgan, which makes her perfectly suited to representing a taboo-breaking rebel like Helen/Kathé/Catherine. The fact that her eroticism tended not to be displayed directly but rather suggested, meanwhile, suited her to the sexually modest romanticism favored by Truffaut. Vincendeau places her in the tradition of the flâneuse, "[strolling] the fashionable European locations of the time: Paris, the Cote d'Azur, Venice, Rome, often to a soundtrack of cool jazz."[6] As the quintessential "modern woman" of the 1950s and early 1960s, Moreau incarnated and actualized perfectly the kind of woman a Roché, or a Truffaut, would be attracted to. But as Vincendeau also points out, Moreau's "'liberated' and anti-conformist heroines" are brought down, in the end, to an essentialized femininity, "testimony to our patriarchal culture's love of beautiful but deadly or damaged women."[7]

The novel and film's Gilberte, meanwhile, was based on Germaine Bonnard, a puppet maker, and Roché's regular mistress, the patient, long-suffering Penelope, who waited for Roché to return to the rocky shores of their relationship after his long erotic odyssey. Bonnard finally married Roché in December 1927, only to break with him in 1933. Bonnard was for many years Roché's refuge, his safe harbor, his maternal substitute. Yet in the novel *Jules and Jim* Roché very much underplays and undervalues his long-standing relationship with Bonnard, when he describes Gilberte as someone Jim "saw at intervals," a matter of "inclination, not passion, a lightweight love which he hardly noticed" (119). In Roché's journals she is variously called Meno, Menocha, Mno, Vieve, Lilith, "Moderation," and even "17," after the number of years Roché had spent with her at the time of the ménage with Helen (seventeen years seem a long time for a "lightweight" love). For Roché, Bonnard was his "secret garden, surrounded by high walls." But his journals, and the novel, never mention the various abortions that he asked Bonnard to endure. Roché writes in his journal that Helen was often jealous of Bonnard, but in fact Helen at times encouraged Roché to have the courage and honesty to assume his responsibility and marry Bonnard.

Bonnard/Gilberte's quiet but nonetheless crucial role in Roché's life, quite evident in the diaries, is not fully reflected in either the novel or the film. Of all the women in Roché's life, Bonnard was the most dramatically victimized by him, a fact that Bonnard herself became even more conscious of when she read Roché's diary account of their twenty years together. Shortly after Bonnard and Roché married, Roché met another woman, Denise Renard, who told him that she was desperate to bear his child. On the night after his mother's death, Roché made love with Renard for the first time, beginning an affair that was to be an affront to both Helen Hessel and Bonnard. Helen, who began the affair with Roché in 1920 and maintained it until 1933, finally refused to see Roché at all, referring to him only as "the liar." She also forebade her husband to see him. Indeed, Franz Hessel complained that "Helen's violence, and her revolver, always come between us." Bonnard, too, ultimately broke with Roché but refused to concede him a divorce. Bonnard had Roché's child on May 11, 1931, but for a long time Helen did not know about the son. When Roché revealed the existence of the child to Helen on July 15, 1933, Helen became furious and threatened Roché with a gun. Then she swore that she would never see him again, a promise that she kept.[8] Two countries were now littered with the wreckage caused by Roché's duplicity. All the utopias, both domestic and international, were coming to a bitter end.[9]

CHAPTER TEN

L'AMOUR LIVRESQUE

ALTHOUGH WOMEN WRITERS at the time were generally hemmed in by glass-ceiling constraints and masculinist prejudices, Helen Grund roamed the streets of Paris with another female flâneuse, German writer Charlotte Wolff; together they frequented the bars, dance halls, and arcades of the French capital.[1] Here, therefore, we must open a parenthesis concerning the very interesting figure of Charlotte Wolff. A middle-class Jewish psychiatrist, poet, and singer, Wolff (1904–1986) left Germany for Paris in May 1933. In Paris she lived with Helen Grund, beginning in 1933, a fact provoking speculation that they had an affair. Charlotte was also a friend of Walter Benjamin, with whom she shared an enthusiasm for things French. Indeed, she translated some of Baudelaire's poems into German. Wolff did pioneering research into issues of lesbianism and bisexuality—one of her best-known books is entitled *Bisexuality*—ultimately becoming a major influence on the German lesbian movement in the 1970s. Stéphane Hessel describes Charlotte Wolff as a "militant lesbian" who felt a Platonic passion for Helen. In her autobiography Wolff describes Helen as follows:

> Helen Hessel was the perfect example of an avant-garde woman. She could do everything and did everything well, whether working in the soil before the First World War or writing fashion journalism in the 1920s and 1930s, whether being the mistress of numerous men or simply mother and spouse. She enchanted both men and women in exactly the same manner. Her blue eyes, clear and cool like the lively air of a spring morning, her elegance and her confidence made her the prototype of feminine seduction. . . . She could as well write an essay as saddle a horse or drive a car. In love with danger, who did

everything passionately, whether lovingly or full of hatred, whether working or loafing. . . . I was fascinated by her and eagerly accepted her invitation to travel with her by car from Berlin to Normandy. She had rented with her friend Roché a farm in the little village of Sotteville. . . . I had no idea of what awaited me. Helen and Roché shared a room. The third week of our vacation, Franz arrived. One might have imagined that he would be jealous of his wife's lover, but in fact it seemed that Roché was his best friend. . . . This threesome seemed to be a fortunate constellation where neither love nor friendship had to take second place.[2]

Interestingly, Charlotte Wolff saw Walter Benjamin as similar to their mutual friend Franz Hessel, both in his lack of jealousy and in his having a possibly homoerotic side: "We were emotionally at ease with each other, as he, too, had a homo-emotional side. The way he spoke of his friend, the poet Heinle, could leave one in no doubt about his love for him. . . . He never experienced the torments of jealousy, either about his wife or his beloved Julia, who did not requite his love. . . . [T]he intimacy between his wife and his friend did not disturb his peace of mind; on the contrary, it brought the two men closer together."[3]

Wolff also gives her early impressions of Franz Hessel, comparing him to a gentle and smiling Buddha: "His large face, brown eyes, full lips, and serene expression combined eastern meditation with French gourmandise. . . . I called him Hessel, the taster, as he was an excellent cook. He was as cosy as a loving mother."[4]

Franz and Helen Hessel, in Charlotte Wolff's account, "replaced the Benjamins." But with the Hessels she could do wilder things, like watch the passionate dancing of same-sex couples. Franz had faith in Charlotte's literary gifts, and she enjoyed visiting him in his rather ascetic circumstances: "His room was like a monk's cell—bed, table, and one chair. That was the way servants were treated. Perhaps he was protesting to his wealthy parents about social injustice. . . . Things were different when Helen arrived from Paris. We sat around in the elegant living room, furnished in white, or lounged on easy chairs in her own large and thickly carpeted studio. She had the muscular figure of a young man, and breathed vitality and joie de vivre."[5]

But Helen and Charlotte really became much closer in Paris:

Helen and I were an odd couple of friends. I had always been attracted by her, not without fear of being suddenly rejected. But now I basked in her warmth. Her friendship and wish to see me settled in a new world was the rock to which I clung. [She and her son] loved each other like twins rather than mother and son. The boy had the wisdom one sometimes finds in the young who are well-loved companions of their elders. These two shared their lives in an almost obsessional concern for their mutual well-being. There seemed to be no secrets between them; they teased, talked, kissed, and scolded one another in turn.[6]

After Helen decided they should share an apartment, they finally moved in together in August 1933. They lived together in an apartment in the fifth arrondissement and talked a good deal, as Helen was in the process of breaking up with Roché. According to Stéphane, "Little by little, Helen was surmounting her anger and bitterness toward Roché and turning her energies toward work, writing, and meetings with creative people, where Charlotte Wolff becomes part of the scene. During my short stays in Paris, I would discover this strong and ardent personality, very svelte but with a very masculine voice . . . fascinating her partners with her luminous gaze."[7]

Charlotte noted in Helen the same lack of jealousy that she had noted before in Franz. When Helen's closest friend, Baladine Klossowska, began to be interested in Charlotte, Helen "showed no sign of resentment."[8] And Helen included Charlotte completely within her own artistic circles; through Helen, Charlotte met Thomas Mann, Aldous and Maria Huxley, Pablo Picasso, Man Ray, and Antonin Artaud. The two drew apart, however, when Charlotte began to sense that Helen had ambivalent feelings toward Jews. And the relationship ended when Helen made what Charlotte calls "an unmistakably anti-Semitic remark."[9]

All of these bohemian figures were terribly bookish. Rarely in history has there been a more bookish ménage à trois than that of Roché, Helen Grund, and Franz Hessel. "One has never seen [Roché and Franz Hessel]," Helen Grund Hessel remarked in her own diary, "without their diaries."[10] Seldom has a ménage generated so much writing, not only by others but also by the participants themselves. Like Roché, Hessel also wrote a novel about the romantic triangle—*Alter Mann* (The Old Man), written between 1933 and 1940 and published posthumously in German in 1987; it was translated into French as *Le Dernier voyage* in 1997. Like so much concerning Hessel, the novel almost did not survive, since the manuscript was thought lost until it was found by Ulrich Weinzierl in 1984. In order to speak about the affair in *Le Dernier voyage*, Hessel splits himself up into two personae, the elderly painter, flâneur, and former banker Kuster, and his son-in-law, Ernst. In a dialogue of innocence and experience Kuster initiates his son-in-law into the distilled and disillusioned wisdom of old age. At the same time, the old flâneur becomes fascinated with a woman named Doris, whom he sees as the paradigm of the "New Woman" of Weimar culture.

But it is the triangular relationship between Ernst and Lella and Claude, in the novel, that recapitulates, more or less, the Franz-Helen-Roché triangle. The narrator describes Lella/Helen as bronzed and agile, with a stormy temperament that experiences "mortal panic in the face of any form of resignation."[11] Alluding to Helen's popularity in Parisian cafés, the narrator tells us that at the Café Dome all the painters wanted to paint her. She was close to Claude yet independent of him. All three live the affair as a glorious experiment in a love transcending bourgeois mediocrity. Hessel tells the story through a distancing device. He has the old man Kuster read Lella's letters about her affairs with both Ernst (Hessel) and Claude (Roché). For Lella (Helen), Ernst (Franz) awakens in her all that is "obscure and dark," while Claude awakens "that which is luminous" (48). In the letters Lella speaks of the mingled pains and pleasures of her relationship with Claude, using the same liquid imagery that often characterizes, as we will see, Helen's intimate journals: "Days and nights pass and our dialogue never ends. Our fingers never stop touching. I hurt like someone who has just been whipped. It's a streaming in me, a river of blood and honey. . . . [E]ach part of me is as if pierced by rays or arrows."[12]

At times the narrator speaks of Lella's dreams of living with Ernst and Claude: "They are such good friends. A life as a threesome should be possible. But as soon as they begin to share this dream, it seems to her that they gang up against her . . . and when Claude stops seeming marvelous, she begins to find him so French, so logical, and then she longs to return to her sweet dreamer, with whom she began a quite different kind of game of life and love" (50).

Ever the understanding husband, the narrator praises Lella's intelligence and artistic talent and generously imagines both Claude and Ernst from Lella's perspective. Throughout, Kuster is characterized as having a Buddha-like calm, as if he were serenely contemplating life's weird vicissitudes from the other shore of death.

CHAPTER ELEVEN

THE POLYPHONIC PROJECT

ROCHÉ, FOR HIS part, kept a voluminous diary from 1902 to 1959, which ultimately produced some seven thousand pages of writing, contained in more than three hundred separate notebooks, only a small portion of which was published in 1990. After the last gasp of the ménage, Roché had the utopian idea of a collective "six-handed" novel, which would consist of the participants' different accounts of the affair, together with the others' reactions to these accounts. Although on one level Roché's project recalled the utopian dreams of the Athenaeum group, on another it formed part of the broad currents of artistic modernism, with its predilection for fractured and multiple viewpoints, a procedure found in Eisensteinian montage, with its clash of ideas, or in cubist ready-made collage, with its "dehumanized" multiplicity of materials and perspectives. Construing adultery as a mode of experimentation, Laura Kipnis has stressed the shared procedures of the sexual and artistic avant-gardes: "[Both rely] on improvisation and invention; poaching from established places; haphazardly borrowing, rejecting, or inverting its conventions on an ad hoc basis. Like previous bricoleurs and collage artists, [they produce] new forms out of detritus and leftovers; a few scraps of time, some unused emotions are stuck together to create a new, unforeseen thing . . . covertly transforming a vast social infrastructure of intimate relations from dyad to triangle, revamping its very contours."[1]

Roché dubbed the project registering this libidinous infrastructure "polyphonic writing." He was apparently unaware that the term *polyphony* had also been introduced, in exactly the same period, in Russia (by the literary critic/philosopher/cultural theorist Mikhail Bakhtin) and in Brazil (by the poet/novelist Mário de Andrade). For Bakhtin, the music-

10. Helen (foreground) and Franz Hessel at home. Photo courtesy
Carlton Lake Collection, Harry Ransom Humanities Research Center,
University of Texas at Austin.

derived trope of polyphony referred to the complex play of discourses
and voices in the work of Fyodor Dostoevsky. The concept called attention to the coexistence in a text of a plurality of voices that do not fuse
into a single consciousness but rather exist on different registers, generating dialogical dynamism among themselves. The definition bears

relevance, as I hope to show in subsequent discussion, to the orgy of écriture generated by the literature-inflected relationship of Roché, Grund, and Hessel.

The notion of polyphonic writing is clearly both alluded to and practiced in the novel *Jules and Jim* itself, although the word *polyphony* itself does not appear there. After their reencounter at the chalet in 1920, Jim and Kate take turns telling the story of the three friends (Roché, Franz, and Helen). Jim begins his story with "Once upon a time there were two young men."[2] When Jim finishes, Kate announces, "I'll tell you the whole story over again, just as it happened to me" (92), providing an instance of, if not polyphonic, at least antiphonal narration. At another point the narrator contrasts the style and content of the two diaries: "Kate read to them long passages of her diary of last year, from Jim's arrival to his departure for Paris. It was as intricate as a Hindu temple, a labyrinth in which it was easy to get lost. Jim's diary was as clear as a table of contents by comparison" (127).

Finally, Jules proposes a collaborative book about their triangular friendship: "If you wrote the story of your relationship—but wrote it separately and fully, you from your own irreducible point of view, Kate, and you from yours, Jim, and published them together, it would make a very unusual book" (127–128). Interestingly, the ever-retiring Jules does not include himself in the project, much as he often did not include himself in the actual relationships.

Roché had pursued the same idea of multivoiced contrapuntal writing earlier during his affair with the two sisters Margaret and Muriel Hart, and one finds traces of the project in the later novel *Two English Girls*, published in 1956 and filmed by Truffaut in 1971. Polyphonic forms of writing, then, are evoked both in *Two English Girls* and in *Jules and Jim*. When Jim observes that the Kate and Jules versions of the love story "didn't tally," the threesome agree that Kate and Jules "take up the story alternately." The proposal ends in an "entertaining joust between . . . two master story-tellers" (98). Here we find a kind of homology between sexual vanguardism—with its defiance of conventions, its multiple perspectives, its montage of moods, and its collaging of lovers—and artistic modernism. In a male-dominated milieu Roché, whatever his limitations in sexual terms, did at least want Helen's voice to be heard. In another sense, however, Roché's polyphonic project was designed to provide solace and artistic compensation for the ménage's affective failure in real life. The relationship could be made eternal only through the posthumous alchemy of art.

At the same time, the ménage itself did have a clear utopian dimension. The three participants shared some very fundamental values, notably their common desire to question certain bourgeois conventions, their eroticized appreciation of art, their nostalgic longing for lost childhood and innocence, their goal of transcending the pettiness of sexual jealousy, their tendency toward bisexual identifications, and their fascination with love and death. In cultural terms all the members of the triad aspired—and here they were typical of cosmopolitan European modernism—to move past what James Joyce's Stephen Daedalus called the constraining "nets" of language and nationality.

Language formed an important part of this attempt at self deprovincialization. The three principals cultivated a kind of linguistic "nowhere" (in Greek *u-topos* 'no place'), in that they were all trilingual, fluent in German, French, and English. Often they mingled all three languages in the same conversation, sometimes even within the same sentence. Responding to Jim's suggestion that the frontiers between languages be abolished, the narrator of the novel tells us that the threesome "made up some short poems in a mixture of three languages, just as things came into their heads, as in dreams. Jules and Jim invented a new continent of their own" (*Jules and Jim*, 132).

We see this same multilingualism, or *polyglossia*, in Helen's journals, where one of Helen's free-verse poems goes as follows (in the original):

> *Je te love,*
> *je te feel,*
> *je te like,*
> *je look at toi*
> *sans flinching.* (Journal, 541)

The novel also gives voice to cosmopolitan antinationalist sentiment by scrupulously avoiding the conventional names of actually existing countries ("France," "Germany," "Austria"), preferring instead paraphrastic circumlocutions such as "Jim's country" and "Jules's country" and even "Hamlet's country." In an age of armed and violent chauvinism they prefer identifications that are personal and literary rather than national and chauvinistic. Pan-Europeans avant la lettre, they all see their erotic and literary collaboration as an anticipatory exemplum of peaceful international relations. As cosmopolitan artists they prefigure John Lennon's song "Imagine," in terms of transcending a narrow nationalism, and John and Yoko's pacifist sleep-ins, in terms of anti-war protests with erotic overtones. For them, their collaboration symbolized the hope of peacefully transcending differences not only in national belonging but also in religious affiliation. An element of ecumenical and transnational symbolism thus infused their love, pointing to an implicit analogy between the attempt to transcend sexual jealousy between individuals on a personal level and the transcendence of envy and rivalry between nations on a political level, all to be evoked through erotic and literal écriture.

CHAPTER TWELVE

JULES AND JIM
THE NOVEL

Roché's *JULES AND JIM*, in this same vein, articulates the tensions between law and desire, between the wish to transcend jealousy and the will to power and possession. It conjugates the verbs *to love* and *to prohibit* in all their moods and tenses. A constant leitmotif in the novel has to do with the issue of playful rule breaking and the creation of new conventions. When Jim first introduces Jules to Lucie and Gertrude, for example, Jules, as master of ceremonies, proposes that "they abolish once and for all the formalities of *Monsieur* and *Mademoiselle* and *Madame* by drinking to brotherhood, Bruderschaft trinken, his favorite wine, and that to avoid the traditional and too obtrusive gesture of linking arms, the drinkers should touch feet under the table, which they did" (15).

Here the elegant, lofty etiquette of conventional decorum is parodied and transferred to what Bakhtin would call the "lower stratum." But in the process of discarding old conventions, these bohemians inevitably adopt new conventions, rules that will themselves ossify in their turn, becoming stodgy and oppressive. (The New Wave, by analogy, rejected the old conventions of the French "tradition of quality," while creating the new conventions of the existential New Wave art film, conventions that could in turn degenerate into hackneyed formulae.) Indeed, both the novel and the film are obsessed with rules and the breaking of rules, rules that are at once moral, artistic, and cinematic. Jim's rule about not staying the full night with his mistress Gilberte, rules of grammar and orthography (anarchists who "can't spell"), rules about footraces, rules about fidelity and friendship, rules about editing and mise-en-scène. At a later point, when Jules offers to remarry Kate, Jim observes that "it's a fine thing to rediscover the laws of human life; but how practical it must be to conform to the existing rules!" (158). The final sentence of the novel, picked up by the film, alludes to this same tension between law and desire. Jules would have liked to scatter Kate's ashes to the wind, but it "was against the regulations" (239).

On one level the novel *Jules and Jim* conveys the exhilarating possibilities of love beyond jealousy and bourgeois constraint. A constant motif is that people can have sex together, in varied combinations, but without bitterness or grudges: "She and Jim frequently saw Annie, without ill-feeling on either side" (112). Or again, here are Jim's thoughts about the web of sexual relationships in which he is enmeshed: "Given that there were four people variously joined together by love, was there any reason why the result should be discord? Kate wasn't betraying Jim by being kind to Jules. Jim wasn't betraying Kate by remaining fond of Gilberte. He felt no conflict inside him between them; they appealed to different regions of the heart. How he longed that Kate, too, would never feel any conflict in herself between him and Jules; and that Kate and Gilberte would never be enemies!" (121).

Yet Roché is clearly idealizing not only the real situation here but also his own behavior. Edited out of this erotic fresco are the various explosions of jealousy (on the part of all the participants), the many abortions, the financial resentments, the vindictive gestures, and the thoughts of suicide. In real life all these relationships left a terrible legacy of bitterness, especially on the part of the women whom Roché "deliciously seduced and conscientiously betrayed."[1] Roché deployed his understanding of women in order to manipulate them, juggle them, exploiting the tantalizing danger of getting caught in flagrante as an aphrodisiac. The very project of a polyphonic account of the ménage was designed to heal the wounds provoked by the triangle's failure in real life. The prototypes of both Gilberte and Kate, we remember, ended up rejecting Roché. Germaine Bonnard, Roché's mistress for thirty years and his first (secret) wife, refused to see him during the last thirty years of his life, and Helen Hessel not only refused to see him but also forbade her husband to see him. Nor is it simply a question of "hoggamus, higgamus, men are polygamous, higgamus, hoggamus, women

11. The etiquette of the encounter. Source: Photofest.

monogamous." While the novels, as well as the diaries, reveal that the women, as well as the men, exercised sexual agency, that they, too, were audaciously experimental, they were also, in the end, more humane and responsible than the men.

This other, dystopian side of the picture is also occasionally underscored in *Jules and Jim*, expressed in metaphors evocative of mathematics and exchange. Jim and Kate frequently quarrel about the "equations" of love. In terms of relationships, does Gilberte "equal" Jules, or does she equal Albert? A related idea is the desire to "get even" or be "even Stephen." By sleeping with Albert, Kate imagines that she wipes out, in the logic of the sexual vendetta, the traces of Jim's infidelity: "So now everything's right between us, Jim: we're quits" (125). Another, more commercial, expression of this mathematical language is the idea of "paying for" one's infractions. Desire descends into the world of the commercial tally. And in this sense Jim (Roché) reverts to the disenchantedly cynical common sense of his mother: "His love for Kate had shot across the sky of his life like a dazzling comet. Now, he visualized it sometimes as a kite tangled in overhead power-lines. He still said, 'It'll all work out somehow,' but his mother, who knew little of both Gilberte and Kate, said, 'Nothing works out and everything has to be paid for'" (216).

At times paranoia enters the picture. Surreptitiously reading an entry in Kate's diary, Jim thinks he discerns the phantom shape of a rival, and perhaps projecting his own unfaithful behavior onto Helen, he wonders, "How much more is [Kate] hiding from me?" (141). In a spirit of boomerang moralism the Don Juan begins to wonder if his lover Helen is a despicable "Dona Juana" not worthy of trust. Reading a novel that Kate had given him, Jim notes that she underlined a passage about a woman who gave herself, in her imagination, to a man in the next cabin. (The issue is picked up in the form of dialogue in the Truffaut film.) This apparently banal erotic fantasy inspires an orgy of moralistic righteousness on Jim's part: "Jim was struck, as if by a confession; for this was Kate's way of exploring the universe, and was bound to be carried out in practice as well as thought. He had the same lightning curiosity himself. Perhaps everybody had. But he controlled his own, for Kate's sake. Whether she controlled hers, for his sake, he was not sure" (220).

These reflections, coming from a man who never restrained his own erotic curiosity, who was one of the major Don Juans of the twentieth century, who was clearly what contemporary therapeutic jargon would call a "sex addict," would seem to embody an extreme form not only of the "double standard" but also of what Sartre called *mauvaise foi* (bad faith). One wonders if Roché ultimately did not like women, whether he was not abusing them for some obscure reason, perhaps having to do with his attitudes toward his own "phallic mother."

At another point Jim exploits the image of Kate's infidelity (imagined or real) to justify further infidelities on his part, infidelities that take very aggressive forms, to the point even of planning to sleep with Kate's sister Irene, as Roché almost did with Helen's sister Bobann. Here sexual revenge becomes a form of didacticism gone awry, of Jim's showing, almost pedagogically, what the pain of jealousy feels like: "And, now that he thought of it, what a marvelous revenge he could take on Kate by sleeping with Irene! What a dagger he could drive home where it hurt most, to make her realize what it felt like, and to cancel the memory of Harold's exploring hands!" (142).

But after sensing Irene's hesitancy, Jim abandons the plan. In the language of war and peace and diplomacy the narrator tells us, "Peace

was made between them without Jim having carried out his retalia-
tion" (143). (Interestingly, Kate is more severe with her sister than with
Jim about the contemplated infidelity.)

At times, the relationship between Kate and Jim becomes hugely
destructive and even self-destructive. Eros suffers the undertow of
Thanatos. Kate speaks repeatedly of doing something "irreparable."
When Jim tells Kate about his plan to have a child with "Michèle"
(probably code for Denise Renard), Kate laments the lost possibility of
their children and then turns on Jim: "Her face was turning pale and
her eyes hollow; she was becoming a Gorgon. Each saw in the other
the murderer of their children. Kate said softly: 'You're going to die,
Jim. Give me your revolver. I'm going to kill you, Jim'" (227).

Even Kate's final act as a kind of suicide-driver, driving herself and
her lover off the bridge into the Seine, constitutes her last, lethal flirtation with the "irreparable." In historical fact, the suicide-driver passage "condenses" two facets of Helen Grund Hessel's real life: first, her
various threats to shoot Jim, and second, a February 1930 incident when
Helen provoked an automobile accident in the Place Denfert–Rochereau
in Paris, after driving erratically, as if in a trance, for several hours. But
of course, in another sense Roché is unfair to Helen (Kate) since Helen
Grund, although she did admit to threatening Jim, never did actually
murder either him or herself. Indeed, it is symptomatic that the only
part of the novel that departs dramatically from fact is precisely the part
that vilifies Kate/Helen.

CHAPTER THIRTEEN

FROM NOVEL TO FILM

WHEN THE NOVEL *Jules and Jim* first appeared, in 1953, it received very few and generally lukewarm reviews. It was only Truffaut's praise for the book in a 1955 review in *Arts* that called renewed attention to the novel. Roché thanked Truffaut for the review in a letter and later visited Truffaut and saw *Les Mistons*. (Roché spontaneously penned a very favorable review, meant for *Arts*, but Truffaut could not publish it since it would seem like favoritism, since he was the official critic for the journal.) Ultimately, Truffaut's adaptation turned the novel into a best seller, translated almost immediately into English, Spanish, German, and Italian. As noted earlier, *Jules and Jim* represents that relatively rare case in which a film adaptation saved a relatively obscure novel from oblivion. But Truffaut also rescued some of Roché's other writings. After Roché's death, his widow, Denise, asked Truffaut for advice about what to do with her husband's intimate diaries, many in the form of agendas, which registered his amorous exploits from 1901 to his death. Truffaut had thousands of pages typed up for future publication. According to Carlton Lake, Truffaut kept a copy of Roché's journal in his office, and "hardly a week passed that he didn't dip into one part or another, just for the pleasure."[1] While directing *Jules and Jim*, Truffaut had access not only to the diaries but also to earlier drafts of the novel, and he made those materials available to his screenwriter, Jean Gruault. Although the point is admittedly speculative, I would suggest that the diaries had a subtle impact, even at times an unconscious impact, on the very mise-en-scène of a whole series of Truffaut films, most obviously on *Jules and Jim* and *Two English Girls* (in 1971) but also on *The Man Who Loved Women* (1977), which can be seen in some ways as a filmic recapitulation of

Roché's life as a Don Juan, with which Truffaut was familiar thanks to having read the diaries. (We will return to *The Man Who Loved Women* at the end of this text.)

François Truffaut described his first response to the novel *Jules and Jim* as a "coup de foudre" (literally "bolt of lightning" but figuratively "love at first sight"). What most moved him were the relationships between the characters: "In reading *Jules and Jim*, I had the feeling that I had before me an example of something the cinema had never managed to achieve: to show two men who love the same woman, without the public being obliged to make an affective choice between the characters, since it has been led to love all three of them equally."[2]

In a review of Edgar G. Ulmer's film *The Naked Dawn* (1955) Truffaut compared the film to *Jules and Jim* in that it showed how two friends and their shared girlfriend love each other tenderly "thanks to an aesthetic morality constantly reconsidered."[3] Truffaut also loved the sonorous alliteration of the title's two *J*s. He appreciated as well Roché's sly, understated style, where the emotion derives from lacks and ellipses and from all that is left unsaid. For Truffaut, Henri-Pierre Roché was a writer stronger even than Jean Cocteau because he "managed to achieve the same kind of poetic prose, but through a less extensive vocabulary, forming very short sentences made up of everyday words."[4] In the film Truffaut sought to create the cinematic correlative of Roché's spare, indirect, oblique, "telegraphic" style. What for Roché were verbal excesses to be excised from the written manuscript became for Truffaut the filmic and rhetorical excesses to be avoided in the film. Truffaut even emulated the self-effacingly offhanded modesty of Roché's style by asking cinematographer Raoul Coutard to adapt a documentary style that would tone down the beauty of the cinematography: "If at any moment one becomes aware of the beauty of an image," Truffaut said, "the film is spoiled."[5]

In his comments on the novel Truffaut reveals himself to be a shrewd analyst of literary style. The key to Roché's style, for Truffaut, is understatement and indirection. Studying Roché's actual manuscripts in order to explore the novelist's process of creation, Truffaut was impressed by "the enormous percentage of words and phrases which had been crossed out."[6] This quality of understatement bears, first of all, on the issue of sexual representation. Although Truffaut

12. Truffaut with Jeanne Moreau, the Catherine [Helen Grund] character in *Jules and Jim*. Source: Photofest.

admired the work of Henry Miller, Roché's style is the polar opposite of Miller's brutal explicitness. In Roché the "coucherie" is between the lines rather than between the sheets. Using minimalist quotidian detail, here, for example, is how Roché evokes a brief idyll of cohabitation and lovemaking: "Jules' two pillows lay side by side on his bed these days, and the bed smelt good."[7] But quite apart from sexuality, Roché generally prefers to quietly evoke rather than name, suggest rather than state. Although Roché is in many ways the polar opposite of a writer like Hemingway, the two writers nonetheless share their deceptively simple "tip of the iceberg" approach. It is as if Hemingway had been retrofitted with a less macho, more refined and intellectual sensibility. Take, for example, the following description of Kate and Jim's visit to the coastal town of Landes:

They ate dozen upon dozen [of oysters], washing them down with a light white wine which seemed quite harmless. Kate, thirsty, for once drank more than Jim.

"Go steady on the wine, Kate."

"Don't worry, Jim."

With their packs on their backs they set out through the town. Kate began singing loudly. It was nice to hear, but it woke people up; Jim told her so and she thanked him sincerely, but began a moment later. . . . The man and his wife were proud of the effects of the local wine. (199–200)

The passage elicits, even screams out for, the word *drunk*, but the light comic touch depends for its effect on the word never actually being used. Nor is Kate's behavior ever explicitly qualified as "impulsive" or "irresponsible"; it is left for the reader to make such judgments.

Given the differential powers of film and novel in terms of sexual representation, the Truffaut film, perhaps inevitably, performs a sexual mainstreaming of the Roché book.[8] And here a technique of understatement serves Truffaut well. Jules's visit to a prostitute, for example, is rendered as nothing more than an opened door and a stockinged leg, plus the narrator's "Jules decided to visit the professionals." Perhaps worried about film's capacity to literalize and embody sexual activity, Truffaut makes the film much "tamer" than the Roché source novel and infinitely tamer than the journals. The novel and the journals give us a real ménage, with three characters actually sleeping together at the same time, literally in bed together, and watching each other make love. The film, in contrast, offers what amounts to serial monogamy. The adaptation also edits out the gay and lesbian scenes mentioned both in the novel and in the journals, the visits to the places where "men danced with men," for example. The only trace of such homoerotic matters is the narrator's comment that "some thought [Jules and Jim's] relationship abnormal." The film also bypasses the Roché passages involving drugs (ether) and nude bathing. But all this "cleaning up" did not prevent the film from being banned for spectators under eighteen (in France), or from being temporarily banned (in Italy), or from being condemned by Catholic organizations or censors in many countries. In Alberta, Canada, for example, the film was condemned as "degrading and offensive due to its emphasis on excessive promiscuity in sexual relations."[9]

Truffaut's adaptation of *Jules and Jim* brilliantly demonstrates the capacity of adaptations to exercise creativity rather than servility. It illustrates the contention, on the part of some theorists, that adaptation ideally consists of a reading of the novel and a writing of a film.[10] It illustrates Truffaut's claim that adaptations can do the "same thing as the novel, but better." Rather than "copy" the novel, Truffaut applied a kind of electroshock to it, exploding it into discursive fragments and shards to be reassembled and recontextualized and collaged together with "alien" materials from other sources. Not only does the film show modernist artists and "modern" men and women, but it also practices modernist techniques. Adaptation for Truffaut is a recombinant practice; he is less interested in being "faithful" to the novel per se than in drawing creative energies from a larger transtext that includes not only texts, such as other novels and films and plays, but also artistic practices, such as the avant-garde penchant for devices such as montage and collage. For Truffaut, adaptation is a recombinant practice of freedom. By reorchestrating preexisting texts, he "auteurs" the novel, imposing his authorial signature.

We detect this recombinant quality in the many scenes in the film that scramble and recontextualize the events and dialogue from the book. As Carole Le Berre puts it: "This work of displacement and montage, whose material expression is the remontage of the text performed with Jean Gruault 'with glue and scissors,' and which turns the film as it is written into a vast moving puzzle, is pursued by Truffaut as he manipulates Roché's text by rewriting the commentary, placing next to each other sentences that had been separated or far from one another, transferring a phrase linked to one character in the book to another in the film, or changing the sequencing of the text."[11]

The two separate elements of (1) the two men going to a Scandinavian play with Magda and (2) Kate's leap into the Seine, for example, are reconfigured in such a way that Kate's leap into the Seine is triggered by Jules's misogynistic reaction to the Scandinavian play, which he interprets as an indictment of women in general. Elsewhere Truffaut picks up a miniscule detail in Roché's text, for example the mention of three friends playing at throwing darts, which comes fairly late in the novel, and recuperates that detail for the opening credit-sequence montage. Elsewhere the language changes its discursive status; passages written in the free indirect style, designed to communicate a character's inner thoughts, are rendered as direct dialogue. Jim's inner thoughts about the need for amorous pioneers to be courageous and generous, for example, are transformed into direct, dramatized dialogue between Jim and Catherine.

One chapter in the novel, entitled "The Crows," anticipates certain images associated with the work of Truffaut's beloved master, Hitchcock, and specifically *The Birds* (1963). Hunting in the Burgundy countryside, Jules and Jim note a flock of crows "soaring and wheeling overhead" (74). In a great "whirling disc" the flock forms a "vortex near to the ground, about to dive on Jules." Jim imagines "the crows [enveloping] him, and getting pecked in the eyes." But what is more interesting than the incident itself is its conclusion: "Jim was stirred, as if by some symbol which was beyond his comprehension" (74). Truffaut, in the adaptation, omits the avian reference but keeps the concluding phrase, while placing it in an entirely different context. The very same phrase is used at the moment when Catherine disguises herself as a young man, "Thomas," and confronts the "test of the street" and where the voice-over narration comments that both Jules and Jim "were moved, as by a symbol that they didn't understand." The emotion generated by the incident of the crows in the novel, where the sexual overtones are subdued, is transferred to an entirely different incident. It is thus given a specifically sexual content, having to do with Catherine's androgynous nature, at once male and female. (Certain analysts of *The Birds*, we are reminded, have seen the avian pecking as sexual in nature, a punishment for the "desire that speaks in Melanie's look.")

Truffaut performs a number of "operations" on the source novel to make it more acceptable and "readable" for a mainstream film audience. First, he reduces in number the proliferating lovers in the novel (and even more in the journals) to a manageable minimum. The figure of Albert in the film, for example, "condenses" Catherine's various lovers in the novel and Helen Hessel's innumerable lovers in real life (and in the memoirs). This condensing operation is even more striking in the case of Kate. The novel's cornucopia of women characters (at least forty) is reduced, basically, to Catherine and Gilberte. In the novel entire chapters are devoted to the characters Lucie, Odile, and Magda. In this sense the scripting and filming process can be seen as the progressive elimination of Catherine's women rivals (or, in a more feminist light, her potential allies). Catherine herself forms a centripetal amalgam of the traits of many of the novel's characters. It is as if she "inherits" their various traits. She is of aristocratic and peasant ancestry (like Odile in the novel), she illuminates books (like Gertrude), and she is an "apparition for all men" (like Lucie). Catherine has Gertrude's sensuality, Lucie's poetic sensibility, Odile's strong-willed temperament. She gets her vitriol from Odile, her fondness for bicycles from Lucie. Collapsing multiple characters into the single figure of Catherine has the effect of heightening our sense of her as a composite and heterogenous figure, riven by contradictions and ambiguities. She is character as collage.

Truffaut also streamlines the plot. The novel (and the journals even more) proceed through systematic amorous discontinuity and rupture. Love is continually disrupted by narrative turnabouts, missed rendezvous, fresh liaisons, bursts of anger, fortuitous temptations, and unexpected obstacles. The film, in contrast, foregrounds only the missed rendezvous in the café, the confusion about the letters, and Catherine's false pregnancy. The film also elides the European travels, for example, to Berlin and Venice, which form an important part of the book. (Some of the omitted materials—the trip to Germany, and Jim's love affairs with two women friends of Jules—formed part of the original script but were never filmed.)[12]

The film also interjects "alien" intertextual materials, many added during shooting. And here Truffaut shows again that adaptation can be an exercise in invention. For the New Wave filmmakers and theorists, films were "written" with what Alexandre Astruc called "le camera-stylo" (the camera pen). For the New Wave directors and theorists, films were written not so much in the sense of being scripted as in the sense of being improvised during the actual shoot. As Carole Le Berre points out, Truffaut "rewrites" the film during the process of making the film by "modifying, cutting, displacing, and filling in the blanks" of the script.[13] Le Berre cites as examples virtually all the bits of "stage business" invented to physically occupy the three characters—the playing of dominoes, the fights with broomsticks, the bicycle rides,

Catherine weeping in Jules's arms—in short, many of the scenes that "furnish" and give texture to the narrative.

Truffaut lifts from the novel *Two English Girls* the passage where Jim cites his professor Albert Sorel advising him to "[t]ravel, write, translate . . . [to] learn to live anywhere . . . [because] the future belongs to the curious." Capricious like his character Catherine, Truffaut also indulged his own whims by including such deliciously extraneous invented materials as Thérèse's cigarette-steam engine, Albert's slide show, the "Scandinavian" play, and the song "Tourbillon de la vie," whose theme of amorous whirlwind provides a musical mise-en-abîme of the film as a whole. Truffaut takes from Joshua Logan's *Bus Stop* (1956) the self-serving mathematical sophistry of Catherine's claim to Jules: "You haven't known many women, I've known lots of men. . . . [T]hat averages out." Truffaut also absorbs certain imagistic leitmotifs from the novel: the emphasis on water (Catherine's jump into the Seine, her leap into snow, the car's plunging into the river) and fire (the vitriol, the cremating of Jules's and Catherine's bodies).

While literature need not be unduly concerned with costs, locations, and production values—a novelist can conjure up space travel or the Battle of Waterloo without spending a penny—the cinema requires money, equipment, and the proverbial "cast of thousands." In adapting Roché, Truffaut confronted the inevitable problems typical of costume dramas and period pieces. Had he known just how complicated costume dramas were, Truffaut once remarked, he would have set the film in the present (Paul Mazursky did just that in his mediocre remake, *Willie and Phil*). To evoke the period of the story, Truffaut deploys a series of evocatively minimalist techniques: locations (cafés, châteaux), costumes (old-fashioned bathing suits), period posters, works of art (for example a chronological sequence of Picasso paintings), literary references (the "Scandinavian" play), and archival footage.

Although the action of the novel begins in 1907, the year that Roché and Franz first met, the film begins in 1912, bringing the events closer to World War I. In a case of thematic "amplification," the film pays much more attention to the war than does the book. The novel's simple line "the war broke out . . . [and] Jules went to the Russian front" becomes in the film a veritable essay on the inane brutality of warfare. Truffaut also adds Jim's visit to a military cemetery, with its endless columns of tombstones. The anamorphic stretching of archival footage of trench warfare, generated by the screening of 16-mm materials in the wide-screen Dyaliscope format, makes the soldiers, as Truffaut himself suggested, look like crustaceans crawling mindlessly over ragged rocks. The novel's brief aside that the two soldiers would probably never meet on the battlefield becomes, in Truffaut's hands, the heart-wrenching opposite: the friends worry that they might accidentally kill each other in battle, thus underscoring again a pacifist dimension only latent in the book. There is constant talk of trenches and the wounds of war, reminding us of the role played by World War I in catalyzing a pacifist and international feeling among so many modernist artists. The spectator becomes acutely sensitive to the effects of war on the male consciousness. Thus Truffaut's antiwar feelings in the 1960s are made to resonate with the antiwar feelings of the historical avant-gardes of the 1920s and the modernist movement that has often been seen as emerging from the ashes and ruins left by the First World War.

This pacifist impulse in the film is rooted, furthermore, in Truffaut's own biography. Apart from the fact that Truffaut grew up during the most catastrophic war of all time—World War II—and that he made *Jules and Jim* a scant fourteen years after the end of that war, Truffaut also doubtless had another war on his mind—the war in Algeria that raged from 1954 until 1962. Truffaut made *Jules and Jim* during the period of Boris Vian's antiwar song "The Deserter," which says, in effect, that "Monsieur President, I just received my draft notice, but I'm not going to go to war. I was not put on Earth to kill innocent people." We recall that Truffaut was himself a deserter from the French army and that he signed the famous manifesto of the 121 denouncing the war in Algeria, all of which doubtless strengthened the pacifist feelings expressed in the adaptation.

While novels such as Doctorow's *Ragtime* have the capacity to mingle "documentary" materials with fiction, the filmic medium enjoys a unique feature not available to a verbal medium—the capacity to deploy actual archival footage, which congeals past time by registering the lived look and texture of a specific historical period. Thus Truffaut uses a wide variety of archival materials—footage of troop movements, trench warfare, shots of the Eiffel Tower, the Paris metro—to evoke the World War I period, and he uses newsreel footage of Nazi book-burnings to evoke the rise of Nazism in Germany. Truffaut integrates the two types of material—staged and documented—through sound effects (explosions, trains), period music (tinkly piano à la silent cinema), and offscreen voice-over commentary. Skillful movement matches "cover" the differences between the two types of footage. One battlefield segue, for example, deploys smoke to camouflage the transition from archival footage of bomb explosions to a shot of Jules writing letters in a bunker. Truffaut even integrates material from fiction films, for example, the studio-lit shot that seems to be pilfered from *All Quiet on the Western Front*. The war, backgrounded as a vague threat in the novel, comes to occupy the foreground of the film. It is this use of archival footage and contemporaneous reenactments, above all, that give us the sense that we are observing characters who are living in the early decades of the twentieth century and not in the 1960s of the film's production. Since those shots of Paris and the subway in the 1920s are obviously real, we subliminally reason, then those characters must be real as well.

CHAPTER FOURTEEN

DISARMING THE SPECTATOR

IN MAKING HIS filmic adaptation of the emotionally and sexually charged materials of the novel (and the diaries), Truffaut was understandably concerned about the reaction of the general public to his bohemian threesome. Here we must be mindful not only of the important shift from a verbal to an audiovisual, multitrack medium but also of a difference in context. While an erotic novel like *Jules and Jim* would be read by hundreds or at most a few thousand people, a film would be seen by hundreds of thousands. And if the original ménage took place during an experimental and avant-garde period, the beginnings of the New Wave coincided with the relatively conservative postwar period of "les trente glorieuses." Although France is often stereotypically portrayed as a libertine and sexually emancipated country, Truffaut was very much aware that the France of 1961 was a country where divorce and contraception were still illegal and where attitudes, including sexual attitudes, remained fairly conservative, especially in the provinces.

The opening credit sequence of the film, in this sense, constitutes a tour de force of affective rhetorical persuasion. (Scorsese once said that he would give anything to have filmed the first ten minutes of *Jules and Jim*). The film begins by exploiting a device—acousmatic speech (that is, a heard voice whose source is not shown)—available only to film. We hear a female voice reading a poem, taken, as we have seen, from *Two English Girls*, which goes as follows:

> *You told me I love you*
> *I told you "wait"*
> *I was about to say "take me"*
> *but you said "go away."*

The screen remains dark while we hear the (as yet) unidentified voice, which we later realize to be that of Jeanne Moreau/Catherine. The technique is disorienting since we cannot see or identify the speaker. The words of the poem itself set up the theme of melancholy misencounters in love, anticipating all the mishaps and misunderstandings in the film: the love letters lost or crossing each other like ships in the night, the missed rendezvous in cafés, and the various other examples of aborted communication. The poem also exemplifies the fabled "bittersweet" quality that characterizes Truffaut's films. The poem's disenchanted air alerts the spectator that the film will offer some cheerful and amorous scenes but that the story will not necessarily end happily. At the same time, a gendered narrational shift takes us from the voice of Catherine (Moreau) as invisible female narrator to the voice of an equally invisible male narrator (Michel Subor).

The opening sequence is shrewdly calculated to disarm any early 1960s spectator who might be judgmental about a ménage à trois. Truffaut skillfully blocks and brackets any conventional, moralistic response. He achieves this, partially, by introducing the overarching theme of play. The spectator, it is implied, should not take all this too seriously—it is only a game, play, art; and art, as a special, privileged, inconsequential sphere of life, is not subject to the conventional "regulations" of bourgeois morality. The jaunty carousel music further underscores the ludic theme, since we associate the circus and carousels with childhood and the pleasure principle. The first shot of Jules and Jim taking costumes out of a trunk, as David Davidson points out, further underlines this playful attitude, as the pair seem to be trying out new costumes, new roles, new relationships, just as Truffaut is trying on new styles and genres, in this case his first period piece. Life is portrayed as a carnival, a playful masquerade. The gesture also constitutes a self-referential device, reminding us that we are about to see a costume drama, in which actors try on roles and don old-style clothing.[1]

We then see various shots of Jules and Jim at play. At a gateway each insists the other enter first, the kind of over-polite exchange seen in silent-period comic shorts and a reminder to us of the prankish incidents—for example "the waterer watered"—typical of the early Lumière films. In short, Truffaut gives us exactly the kind of mute filmic vignettes that the characters' prototypes might actually have

13. The centrality of games. Henri Serre (left) and Oskar Werner
in *Jules and Jim*. Source: Photofest.

seen in the early decades of the century. In fact, the whole credit
sequence displays many of the salient features—nonsynchronous dialogue, accompanying nondiegetic music; and comic episodes—typical
of a miniature silent film. Thus the segment as a whole "signifies" the
silent period, exactly the period in which Jules and Jim grew up and
became men. The film medium and the characters are suggested, as it
were, to have come of age together.

The credit sequence shows the two friends to be immensely creative.
Like the characters in a musical comedy, they transfigure the materials of everyday life, transforming utilitarian instruments (brooms) into
props (swords) for artistic performance. Like silent comedians, they
transmogrify the quotidian, turning everyday life into art. In appearance they constitute a version of the classical comic duo, usually based
on physical contrasts such as fat/skinny or tall/short. In the novel these
contrasts are stated even more strongly. With the friends' first encounter,

Roché describes Jules as "short and plump" and Jim as "tall and thin."[2] In the film their body language betokens their personalities and prefigures the future. Jim dominates Jules in the broom fight, forcing him back, foreshadowing a future in which Jim plays the more active role while Jules is more passive, at times even masochistic. A close shot of an hourglass sets up the theme of passing time, while a shot of a Picasso painting (*The Embrace*) suggests not only the love theme but also the perennial trope of art as triumphing over time by providing a factitious immortality, a favorite theme in the essays and speeches of André Malraux at the time of the film's making. A shot of a guitar-playing man (whom we subsequently learn is Albert) introduces a sister art form—music—reminding us again that the film is about the arts and about artists, about music, painting, literature, and cinema.[3]

The credit sequence provides an aesthetic matrix; it plants the narrative "seeds," as it were, that will sprout only later. It offers a "montage of attractions," a promise of the pleasures—games, musical performance, romance—yet to come. It is as if Truffaut had provided a trailer for the film within the film itself. A quick montage of shots of anonymous women, followed by a close shot of Catherine, subliminally signals the fact that the men's dalliances with other women will ultimately be abandoned in the name of Catherine. She first appears in a relatively close shot, much closer than those framing Jules and Jim. Her name credit also comes first but not her image. Despite the lack of a female name in the title, the film seems to be telling us, Catherine will play a major, even indispensable, role. She is shown from the outset as the active principle, the catalyst, the instigator. The two men appear together, but she appears alone; it is as if the two men need to join forces to equal her in strength. At the same time, the film's title, and the men's togetherness, prefigures the overall trajectory of the film, where male friendship proves more resilient and trustworthy than heterosexual love. They are Don Quixote and Sancho Panza; Catherine, as Dulcinea, is a subordinate figure. The final shot of the overture sequence, showing Jules and Jim foot-racing along a wooden bridge, anticipates a later footrace, with Catherine, on a closed industrial bridge with chain-link fencing. The footrace introduces a slightly discordant note: games, while innocent and childlike, also involve intense competition, winners and losers. And at times players cheat, as Catherine does in the race that comes later.

At the same time, the opening sequence constitutes a glorious demonstration of one of the concerns of the *Cahiers* critics and of the New Wave: the theoretical issue of "cinematic specificity," the question of the resources available to the film medium but denied to literature. While analysts of adaptation often stress what has been "lost" in the transition from novel to film, they sometimes forget to note what has been gained. Better stated, the sequence shows off film's capacity to amplify what is only latent in a verbal medium like the novel. It evokes the various sister arts—painting, music, theater—of which film is the synthesis and culmination. In his novel Roché deploys style and diction to shape our mood. But in the film the cinematic techniques themselves—the hyperrapid editing, the brightly lit shots, the clear focus, the bouncy music—evoke joy, energy, happiness, creativity, molding an impression of open-air jouissance. Although a bohemian lifestyle and sexual freedom have been evoked, no morbid chiaroscuro suggests a gothic or puritanical attitude toward that lifestyle. The filmic style is whirlwindlike, rapid, fluid, as if the film were rushing toward its real subject, in this case Catherine, or better, the relationship between Catherine and the two men. It is as if the narrative were starting "in flight," only then descending, slowing down, and "landing" in the diegesis proper.

Multidimensional in its effect, the credit sequence on the one hand painlessly provides a substantial amount of expository information: the silent-period setting, the social identity of the major (and even some of the minor) characters, the artsy environment. We are clearly thrust into the presence of an avant-garde milieu, inhabited by bohemian artists, from whom one should not expect strait-laced behavior. The sequencing of shots—which presents first Oscar Werner and Henri Serre, then Jeanne Moreau, and then the child Sabine Haudepin—subliminally suggests a whole narrative trajectory from friendship to romance to procreation. But the dizzying montage gives us too much information to assimilate. The spectator is left morally off balance by the whirlwind of images, rendered malleable and ready to accept and even love characters who might not normally have been accepted at the time of the film (or even now in the time of "family values"). As many critics have pointed out, the technique itself induces a kind of moral-emotional flexibility, even vertigo, in the astounded spectator. The basic procedure is to place all the events under the sign of homo ludens, of play and games. The film will be a kind of game, and games are innocent by definition, yet games also provoke emotions and can have serious consequences. The overture sequence anticipates the ludic spirit of the film as a whole, where the characters—like their historical prototypes as they portray themselves and one another in their journals—constantly play all sorts of games: costume dressing, dominoes, the village-idiot game, horse and rider, scavenger hunts, foot-racing, fencing, boxing. Like children, the characters see life as play. And art, like this film, is simply another form of play.

The opening sequence anticipates the various stratagems deployed in the film to win acceptance for the characters: the unsensational treatment; the lack of explicit depiction of sexual activity; the narrator's cool, neutral tone. If the narrator can accept these characters, the spectator implicitly reasons, why shouldn't I? The acting, too, is offhand and understated; the moving scene where Catherine and Jules cry together was actually improvised rather than planned. Truffaut also uses contrasting characters to show Catherine, and the ménage, in a more favorable light. Against the backdrop of Jules's and Jim's prior aimless wandering between one-night stands, Catherine represents a relative stability, even if only as part of a ménage. Jules and Jim and Catherine together form a kind of family, albeit an unconventional one. Furthermore, the film repeatedly draws contrasts between Catherine and even more "promiscuous" foil characters, most notably the flapper-like Thérèse, who leaps like a grasshopper from man to man on a nightly basis, and Nicole, cruelly proffered as "objet de sex à l'état pur" (a pure sex object). Jules and Jim and Catherine are presented as the courageous pioneers of an alternative lifestyle. Given the sympathetic portrayal of the three major characters and their relationship, the spectator hopes that their experiment will succeed, hopes that they will be generous enough to meet the emotional challenges confronting them.

Truffaut also deploys narrative voice-over with great skill. The male voice-over obviously relays the implied-to-be male narrator of the novel, reinforcing the gendered storytelling of the source text. *Jules and Jim*, as the director himself once remarked, is probably the only New Wave film to use voice-over commentary so abundantly.

(Here Sacha Guitry's *Roman d'un tricheur* is clearly a partial source.) One of the features that Truffaut found attractive in the novel was its sense of a serene distance toward events that were lived passionately, a distance that is in part a result of the time elapsed since those events. The narration often helps convey this sense of distance. Truffaut's narrator often uses the French imperfect, which shapes a feeling that we are looking back at typical behaviors and activities, without judgment. One third of the words of the film are offscreen narration, mostly from the Roché novel itself but also a small proportion written in the style of Roché by Truffaut and Gruault. Throughout, the offscreen narration operates as a kind of discursive gearbox regulating narrative speed and density. Some passages from the novel were included simply because Truffaut found them very beautiful yet impossible to simply film. Thus the voice-over articulates the hard-to-visualize emotions from the novel, for example, the filmic narrator's observation that "Jules and Jim were moved [by Catherine's Chaplin-like transvestism] as by a symbol which they didn't understand."

At times the voice-over spotlights a single subjectivity. After Catherine's sudden leap into the Seine, for example, the film's narrator tells us that the incident "made a strong impression on *Jim*" (emphasis mine). In this sense the film gestures toward Roché's project of polyphonic writing in that the voice-over adds a distinct narrative voice not strictly subsumable into those of the characters. Elsewhere, the narration assures a quick, stenographic summary of an evolutionary series of events, as in the observation that "happiness fades quickly." The narration also plays with tense and voice, and with direct and reported speech. The past tense of the voice-over narrator's "Jim had asked" modulates into the directly synchronous speech of "Who is Albert?" We discover again film's capacity to conjugate many tenses simultaneously: the present tense of the moving image, the past tense of some of the commentary, and so forth. Each filmic track, in short, can have its own tense and mood.

Jules and Jim also sometimes fosters deliberate temporal imprecision. We are not certain about the duration of the threesome's vacation in the Midi or how much time elapsed between Catherine's pistol-wielding threat against Jim and the later, apparently friendly and nonchalant, encounter in the cinema. Despite the narrative passage of some seventeen years during the course of the film, Truffaut does not have his makeup artist artificially "age" the actors. (Interestingly, this process of artificial aging finds no equivalent in written fiction, where the author ages the characters verbally, simply by describing them as aged.) Jim shaves his mustache and Catherine dons spectacles, but that is the extent of the changes. Rather than "age" the actors, Truffaut evokes the passage of time through references to the history of painting, notably through the chronological series of Picasso paintings linked successively to impressionism, cubism, and papiers collés. The allusion to Picasso, although nonexistent in the novel, seems especially apt when one remembers that Roché was a friend of Picasso's, that he owned Picasso's paintings, and that he had often watched Picasso at work painting in his atelier.

The film partially constructs itself through the play of broader intertextual reference. Some of these references—to Lumière and silent-era slapstick in the credit sequence, to Chaplin and *The Kid* later—are specifically filmic. Other references are less to films per se than to filmic techniques. Deeply knowledgeable about the history of film style, New Wave film directors like Truffaut often resuscitated "obsolete" techniques such as the iris-in or masking for poetic effect, much as novelists like Cervantes and Henry Fielding resuscitated archaic literary devices such as the epic simile. For example, Truffaut exploits the archaic device of "masking"—a device familiar to film scholars from the silent film epics of D. W. Griffith—to isolate Catherine and Jules during their first meeting in a café. Even the choices of location can gesture toward an intertext, as when Truffaut stages a chance meeting between his characters at "Studio des Ursulines," a theater famously associated with the avant-garde cinema generally and specifically with the scandal provoked by Buñuel's *Un Chien andalou* in 1928.

Literary intertextuality also pervades the film. The "Scandinavian" play, which one imagines to be by Ibsen or Strindberg, provokes a strong reaction on Catherine's part, for she is moved by the heroine's freedom-loving and life-inventing power. The reference is apt since Scandinavian theater of the period was renowned for its modern liberated women characters such as Hedda Gabler and Miss Julie, even when the dramatists treated those characters misogynistically. Other references are exclusively verbal, as in the repeated comparison of

Jules and Jim to Don Quixote and Sancho Panza. Even costumes and landscapes can evoke literature: Jim at one point dons an expansive cape, for example, evoking Byron carrying the "pageant of his bleeding heart" across the landscapes of Europe, and scenes set by foggy lakes conjure up the intertextual memory of Lamartine's "Le Lac," and the "lake country" poetry of Wordsworth.

Speaking more generally, Truffaut adroitly weds technique and theme in ways that remind us of Deleuze's claim that the cinema has a philosophical dimension in that it generates concepts, not in language but in blocks of movement and duration. At the same time, Truffaut was very much molded by Sartrean ideas, and the New Wave has sometimes been seen as the cinematic expression of postwar existentialism. The film's free, improvisational style, in this sense, demonstrates the idea of "existence before essence," where the flow of filmic energy is not channeled into the canonical vessels. Few Truffaut films offer as many cinematic "flourishes" or stylistic effects or poetic outbursts of lyricism. The characters' game of searching for "relics of ancient civilization," for example, "authorizes" Raoul Coutard's close-to-the-ground handheld camera to sniff around the foliage for strange (planted) objects. Often, the effect depends on a move from the verbal to the visual register. The narrator's claim that the "characters soared high, like birds of prey," for example, "triggers" soaring aerial shots over the landscape.

Jules and Jim renders appreciative homage through style to what Truffaut called the novel's "aesthetic moral ethic which is constantly under review."[4] Oxymoronically fusing the ethical and the aesthetical, the film registers this theme of freedom and creativity not only on the more obvious verbal level, as when Catherine praises the heroine of the play for "[inventing] life at every moment," but also, and much more interestingly, on the level of mise-en-scène. The idea of freedom is rendered cinematically, through Coutard's antiacademic cinematography, through the film's sudden, impulsive swish pans, through 360-degree pans (for example the pan that circles along with Thérèse and her cigarette steam engine), and through dazzling aerial shots that engender a feeling of flight and "what it feels like to be free." We are reminded of Pier Paolo Pasolini's notion of "free indirect discourse" in the "cinema of poetry," where a character becomes an alibi for stylistic virtuosity on the part of the author.

In *Jules and Jim*, for example, the film becomes imbued with the anarchic spirit of its characters, and more particularly of Catherine. The filmic editing consistently associates Catherine with fragmentation and discontinuity. The "modern" woman is rendered through "modernist" montage. Interestingly, this fragmentary technique is anticipated in the novel itself. While Roché's term *polyphony* evokes the aural notion of multiple voices, his novel also practices a visual polyperspectivalism, a multiplicity of "points of view," at times even in the most literal sense. Here is Roché's account of the encounter of the two friends with the "archaic smile" of the statue whose appearance anticipates that of Catherine: "A toy steamer took them to the island; they hurried to their statue and spent an hour with it. It was beyond even what they had hoped. They lingered around the goddess in silence, gazing at her from different angles; her smile was a floating presence, powerful, youthful, thirsty for kisses and perhaps for blood" (72).

The film renders this floating gaze through rapid and multiangled shots moving toward and around the statue. (We are reminded of Alain Resnais's art documentaries, such as *Guernica*, in which the director brings painting to life through zoom-ins and selective framing, creating a dialogue, as it were, between the various figures in the painting.) The film's broken, disruptive editing renders the pivotal moments linked to Catherine: the men's first anticipatory glimpse of the statue; the "mismatched" shots of the first meeting between Catherine and Jules and Jim; the four "miscut" shots of Catherine's plunge into the Seine; and the three jarringly discontinuous shots of the final, fatal plunge into the river off a castrated bridge. It is as if Catherine's actions and image were being envisioned through a cubistic multiplicity of contradictory angles. We are reminded of Bazin's critique of the unhealthy fragmentation that he sees as inherent in montage as opposed to the healthy integrity of mise-en-scène. In fact, Catherine is consistently associated with a discontinuity that is occasionally celebratory but more often threatening and "dehumanized" in an aesthetic sense.

Many sequences in the film exemplify this happy marriage of filmic technique and thematic leitmotif. One sequence set in the chalet picks up on a frequent theme in the intimate diaries: the valiant attempts by the characters to dominate and transcend their own feelings of jealousy. Roché notes in his *Carnets*: "an effort to not be jealous of Franz; I don't want to be jealous" (220). Or again, when Roché observes Helen sitting on Franz's knees, giving him an endless kiss: "I leave them for a moment and find them doing the same thing. I'm happy for Franz, but I have to transcend the malaise that I feel" (338). Truffaut captures exactly this conflict between high principles and the lower passions in the chalet sequence where Catherine leaves her lover Jim in a rocking chair downstairs, in order to cavort with Jules upstairs, right above Jim, who overhears their raucous laughter. A crane shot takes us from Jim downstairs, trying to read and concentrate and forget Catherine, up to Jules and Catherine upstairs in bed. In other words, Jim tries not to succumb to his jealous feelings, which he regards as beneath him and unworthy of their friendship, but the crane shot suggests that his mind keeps "craning up," as it were, to the space of Jules and Catherine. (The novel, interestingly, placed all three characters on the same floor.)

Or consider the presentation of Gilberte and her small apartment. The novel portrays the relationship with Gilberte as a "tacit alliance against passion," where she and Jim made love in a "tiny flat" but basically led "separate lives" (119). Jim refuses to stay overnight with Gilberte because such a practice, for a self-respecting bohemian like Jim, would constitute an irremediable "fall" into the mundane obligations of conventional marriage. Gilberte is rendered as subdued and confined, often sick and reclining, her lack of energy a foil to Catherine's boundless dynamism. The mise-en-scène of the film renders Jim's perspective on these encounters by framing them through the bars of Gilberte's metal bed, itself enclosed within a suffocatingly narrow room. In sum, the staging itself conveys the implicit "norms of the text," translating Jim's view of marriage and monogamy as a claustrophobic prison.

The sexual politics of the Truffaut film are in some ways more masculinist even than the sexual politics of the Roché novel. Roché himself, as we have seen, was an inveterate Don Juan, whose intimate journals inform us about his various wives and mistresses and about an almost daily regimen of outside liaisons and prostitutes. The typist asked to type up Roché's diaries, Truffaut tells us, refused to finish the job because the "unconscious cruelty" of Roché's "stories of interchangeable women" made her sick, "leaving her dizzy."[5] Yet in the novel and the film Roché's Don Juanism is projected not onto Jim, the character based on

Roché himself, but rather onto Catherine, the character based on Helen Grund Hessel. Furthermore, although the real-life Helen Grund had sometimes threatened Roché—he speaks of their "revolver nights"—she never did actually kill him. Yet both novel and film turn Catherine into a kind of suicide bomber, wielding an automobile as a lethal weapon.

In fact, the finale constitutes one of the major ways the novel departs from historical fact. In real life Franz Hessel was the first of the trio to die, followed by Roché and then Helen, but in the novel (and film) it is Jules alone who goes on living. For Roché, this posthumous rewriting of the factual record probably constituted a kind of guilty homage to Franz Hessel, who had died in extremely painful circumstances a short time before Roché's first draft. At the same time, this rewriting "kills off" Helen, who had rejected Roché as "the liar," while rendering Helen as a killer, within the sexist context of a clichéd "hell hath no fury like a woman scorned." Indeed, Roché noted in a June 1944 diary entry that he had decided to rewrite the real ending, inventing a new one by having "Kathé and Jim die before Jules' eyes."[6] In this way Roché was underscoring the tribute to his recently deceased friend but also committing an injustice against Helen. Although Helen did in fact threaten violence, the more important point is that her subjectivity is more or less elided.

These choices must also be contextualized in terms of some of the parallels between Truffaut's own life and Roché's. Truffaut's biographers report that at the time of the filming of *Jules and Jim* Truffaut was still married to Madeleine Morgenstern but was also involved in a love affair with Liliane David.[7] In short, Truffaut himself was living a triangular situation but hardly the experimental, utopian triangle portrayed in both novel and film. It was rather the classic wife-plus-lover on the side—the schema later portrayed with such frosty distance in Truffaut's *The Soft Skin*. Nor were the New Wave directors, in the period of the film's making, amicably sharing women with their friends. In a letter from 1961, the year of *Jules and Jim*, Jean-Luc Godard wrote the following letter to Truffaut: "There is no more friendship between [the New Wave directors]. Each of us has gone to our own separate planet, and we no longer see each other in close-up but only in long shot. Every day the women we sleep with separate us more than they bring us together. It's not normal."[8]

Setting aside the vaguely homoerotic overtones of the Godard quotation—that is, the suggestion that men should be brought together through "their" women—the more important point is that Truffaut, in Roché's wake, chooses to portray Catherine as the one person in the triad not equipped for the challenge of reconciling freedom and fidelity. She is the one who "cheats," not only in footraces but also in love. The point is heavily underlined in the veritable sermon that Jim flings at Catherine on the occasion of their lachrymose rendezvous in the country mill, where he accuses her of "exploring the universe" through adultery, and she responds by waving a gun at him. According to Jim, Catherine believes that only one person should be faithful in the couple—the other one. Given what we know about Roché's (and Truffaut's) innumerable affairs, this scapegoating of Catherine as promiscuous constitutes a rather extreme case of *mauvaise foi*. While both novel and film question conventional morality, in sum, the dumb inertia of the sexual double standard still reigns supreme in both texts.

Truffaut's Catherine is a fraught, ambivalent, deeply ambiguous character. Truffaut's published correspondence bears the traces of his own ambivalence: there he sings the praises of Jeanne Moreau as an actress but calls the character a *poule* (whore). In 1978 Truffaut said in correspondence that he made the film, but without being conscious of doing so, as a tribute to his mother, as a way of pleasing her and winning her approval, a way of "showing that [he] understood her."[9] As a character, Catherine is on the one hand free, dynamic, protean, creative, and a cause of protean creativity in others. (In this same spirit of a relative approval of the mother figure, in *Amour en fuite* (1979) Truffaut has a former lover of Antoine's mother describe her, approvingly, as an "anarchist.") Jeanne Moreau's performance, especially, makes her a luminous and charismatic screen presence. Catherine in the film is a catalyst for movement; she realizes her prototype's ambition of making men move and dance to the wand of her desire. Like Thérèse, she is the locomotive, and the men are the caboose. It is she who proposes most of the activities in the film—the cross-dressing test, the trip to the beach, the footrace. Jules calls her "a queen," and like a queen she commands the direction and speed of the movement of others. She is the primum mobile of the narrative, but the men are the conductors of the narration.

14. Catherine on the brink. Source: Photofest.

On the other hand, Truffaut's Catherine is capricious, even egomaniacal. As someone craving perpetual attention, she embodies the venerable sexist trope of the narcissistic, self-regarding, "high-maintenance" woman. She incarnates what Harold Bloom calls the "Sphinx as the central image of woman's solipsistic self-absorption."[10] Associated with nature (the eternal feminine), she is described by Jules as an (ultimately destructive) "force of nature." While her prototype was a highly successful, self-supporting journalist, painter, and illustrator, the Helen portrayed by both Roché and Truffaut is stripped largely of these talents and achievements. At one point in the novel Roché even attributes a cannibalistic or vampiric discourse to Helen: "I'm in the very middle of your own red heart, Jim, and I want to drink and drink and drink" (*Jules and Jim*, 109). Catherine is the "femme fatale" mentioned in the "Tourbillon" song. Her presence triggers a discourse of male victimization, whereby she is transformed into the offended goddess or murdering woman found in other Truffaut films such as *La Femme d'à côté* (1981), *The Soft Skin*, and *La Mariée était en noir*

(1968). At the same time, Catherine incarnates that other avatar of the femme fatale—the siren. The siren lures men into the sea, where they drown, and it is no accident that Catherine lures Jim to a watery death, imaged in the unforgettable frozen frame splash/crash of the finale of the Truffaut film.

For Catherine especially, but also to some extent for Jim, a couple must generate children, since children provide the raison d'être of the couple. Artistic creativity is not enough; procreation is the litmus test of love. This bohemian triangle/trinity is, ultimately, both eugenic and Catholic. Despite its portrayal of Catherine as an active and in some ways sympathetic figure, the film in the end associates her with a whole gallery of antiwoman myths and archetypes: Eve the temptress, Pandora and her box, the Sphinx and her mystery, the Sirens and their song, the "femme fatale qui fut fatale." Thoroughly archaic prejudices lurk just under the surface of the portrait of this thoroughly "modern" woman. And the portrait seems especially retrograde when one remembers that the book was published, and the film released, in the same postwar period that had brought to public consciousness a new feminist discourse and a new genre of independent woman, exemplified by writer/activists like Simone de Beauvoir, whose classic *The Second Sex* had been published more than a decade earlier, and described by novelists like Françoise Sagan and Christianne de Rochefort, and performed by actresses like Brigitte Bardot and Emmanuelle Riva.

But in the end the film, like the novel, is not really about Catherine. Although the film begins with Catherine's voice-over poem and ends with her death, ultimately it is not her story but that of the two men. Ironically, Truffaut's progressive downplaying of Catherine recapitulates the same process that occurred with Roché's novel. A preferential option for the story of male friendship is reflected in Roché's diary entries. In a December 15, 1942, entry Roché notes, "I have begun to write with great passion the story of my friendship with Franz."[11] In another entry Roché writes that the story is becoming less and less the "story of Helen" and more and more the "story of me and Franz."[12] As the doubly male title of both novel and film suggests, it is ultimately a male story, with little place for Catherine's subjectivity. The real issue is how Catherine is seen by the two men. They admire the statue that resembles her, as they admire her. But she is an image, one that "moves" in both senses of that word. Ultimately the film revolves less around her goals and subjectivity than around a mobilized scopophilia of male desire. Furthermore, the film's Catherine has herself internalized the male gaze. Portrayed as male-identified, she expresses much less solidarity with women than with men, unlike her prototype, who, as we will see in our own analysis of Helen Hessel's intimate diaries, was quite capable of bonding with women, sexually as well as emotionally.

Truffaut portrays Catherine's male counterparts, meanwhile, as practicing an effortless solidarity with other men. Unlike her they do not seem competitive or jealous. (Indeed, Truffaut chose relatively unknown actors precisely to avoid any feeling of a competitive battle royale between stars.) Although there are contrasts between the two men—Jim is mobile, Jules sedentary; Jim is active, Jules passive— both are distinctly not macho; Jules, especially, is infinitely patient, wise, and long-suffering, much as the real-life Franz Hessel, from all accounts, seems to have been. Indeed, it is noteworthy that the various written accounts of Hessel tend to appeal to images of religious serenity; he is repeatedly figured as "saint," "monk," or "Buddha."

Consistent with the film's title, which excludes Catherine from the charmed circle of male camaraderie, both novel and film ultimately privilege male friendship over heterosexual love or reliable conjugality. The novel is perhaps even more clear about the theme that friendship perseveres even when relationships with women do not. Indeed, the novel echoes with homoerotic overtones in its evocation of two men who are in love but not necessarily sexually, as in the following passage: "He was reunited with Jules in Jules's own city. Their old, uncomplicated relationship started up again instantly. It would have been beyond Jim's powers to say what Jules meant to him. In the past they had been nicknamed Don Quixote and Sancho Panza. When he was alone with Jules (just as it used to be when he was alone with Kate), time disappeared for Jim. The most trifling thing became completely satisfying. . . . [Jules] energized all Jim's sensibilities" (161). It is not surprising, in this context, that other observers concluded, as the novel tells us at the very beginning, "that their relationship must be abnormal" (9).

The final chapter of the novel tells us that Jules and Jim, over their twenty years of friendship, had "never quarreled" and that it was dif-

15. The threesome at the beach. Source: Photofest.

ficult for Jules to "think of a couple who accepted each other as whole-heartedly as he and Jim" (237–238). All of which raises the question whether the men in the novel (and in life) were not ultimately connecting with each other through the women, something that Roché made explicit in a letter to Franz Hessel. "Making love with [Helen] is a little like making love with you."[13] (We will return to the homoerotic theme when we examine Roché's diaries.)

The film alternates two kinds of time—a magical, idyllic time of childlike play, on the one hand, and moments of rupture and threat, on the other: the sudden departures of Jim or Catherine, the eruption of war into their peaceful lives, Catherine's sudden slaps and outbursts. The film's style mirrors this narrative alternation by creating a cinematic oscillation between nervous, jumpy, quick-edited sequences, on the one hand, and slow, mise-en-scène–based sequences on the other.[14] Indeed, the film features a wide gamut of editing strategies, moving from extreme discontinuity (the deliberately misedited shots of Catherine), to extreme continuity, for example, the five-minute single-shot sequence in which Catherine tells Jim her version of their relationship. In a certain sense Truffaut offers a filmic version of Roché's polyphonic writing, not so much in the sense of the multiple perspectives of characters but rather in the sense of a multiple-speed, polystylistic approach to telling the story. In historical terms the film "darkens"—with the advent of World War I—then cheers up, and then darkens again with the Nazis. In terms of the three principals' relationships the movement accelerates and then slows. Overall, the film moves from the rapid montage of the overture sequence to the more deliberate pacing of the later sequences. It is as if the film itself ages as it goes along, slowing down in pace alongside the aging characters.

There can be no deep accounting for the uneasy, ambivalent, spellbinding fascination of *Jules and Jim* without delving into the profoundly mythic undercurrents in the film, its way of touching on themes with deep, millennial resonances within the culture. The first of these themes has to do with the Western theme of the *liebestod*, of love and death and impossible love lived as pathos (etymologically "to suffer"), love of the neurotic and self-destructive type so brilliantly anatomized in Denis de Rougemont's proto-Lacanian classic *Love in the Western World*. (Truffaut often said that he was fond of films about "les amours impossibles"). In *Love in the Western World* de Rougemont traces the occidental fixation with love and death to the medieval myth of Tristan and Isolde as a story of love that thrives on obstacles and taboos. Romance comes into existence only where love is fatal, frowned on, socially proscribed, doomed. For this reason it can only be fully realized in death, through suicide pacts and tragic misunderstandings, à la Romeo and Juliet. Jim and Kate, the novel tells us, "thought of death as the fruition of love, something they would attain together; any time, perhaps even tomorrow" (*Jules and Jim*, 117).

Picking up on the theme of gender-blurring so frequent in the diaries, the film also touches on another myth, that of the androgyne, the sexually ambiguous figure who was neither man nor woman. The androgyne, a favored motif in the avant-garde art of the period, found not only in the hermaphroditic paintings of Magritte but also, for example, in the androgynous boy/girl figure run over by the automobile in Buñuel's *Un Chien andalou*), also asserts its presence in the film. Franz, in this sense, has androgynous qualities. He demonstrates a long-suffering passivity of a kind stereotypically associated with women. Many critics have pointed to the sexual indeterminacies in the film—Catherine's cross-dressing as a Jackie Cooganish "man"; Jules's gender confusions in French, mistakenly using the masculine *fou* for Catherine—which point to a certain sexual ambidextrousness. All of this is uncannily appropriate to the artistic representation of a triangle that was triply "bisexual," conjugating Roché as a feminine dandy, Franz as womanly in his (stereotypical) domesticity, and Catherine as a kind of phallic woman and avenger.

Another, less mythic, appeal of the film is to a kind of social utopia sometimes found in the history of the novel as genre, that is the doubleness and class tension that pits romance, with its courtly, medieval overtones, against the novel, with its middle-class world of work and aspiration. *Jules and Jim* offers a twentieth-century version of romanticism through its sensitive, curious, artistic characters, who collectively form an aristocracy not of blood but of sensibility. The characters live largely in their imagination, not needing to worry terribly about such vulgar concerns as earning a living. Their conversation is full of wonderfully carefree nonsense—"If it rains, we'll go to the beach" or "I'm writing a novel, where insects are characters." They can follow their whims to pursue a statue's archaic smile in an Adriatic island. Their life is relatively "unencumbered," to use Henry James's description of romance; it is life lived as errant desire, as erotic flânerie.

Within this romantic milieu the film offers a chaste, nonpornographic sexual utopianism, characterized at its zenith by multiple loves without competition, generosity instead of jealousy. In its utopian moments the film portrays a generous pursuit of reciprocal pleasure in the autonomous Republic of Love. This transcendent idea of unpossessive love characterizes not only Jules, Jim, and Catherine in their best moments but also some of the minor characters. The transcendence of jealousy is symmetrically extended outward, on both sides of the gender divide, whereby Albert, as Catherine's unjealous lover, mirrors Gilberte as Jim's unjealous lover. One wonders, however, what the film (and the novel) would have been like had the events been presented from Gilberte's, or even Catherine's, point of view. And the communicative transparency and apparent lack of jealousy clearly involve an element of idealization, one rudely questioned not only in Helen Hessel's and Roché's own diaries but also a few years later by Truffaut himself in *The Soft Skin*, where the husband philanderer is not at all a contemplative Buddha like Jim but rather a harried philanderer, anxious, fearful of being discovered, and where the "other woman" is impatient and dissatisfied, and the abused wife ends up murdering the husband. (While in real life murderers are overwhelmingly male, in Truffaut's films, symptomatically, they are almost invariably female, reflecting perhaps both guilt and resentment toward women.)

During the planning of *Jules and Jim* Truffaut expressed ambivalence about the novel's ménage à trois. On the one hand, he thought of it as "un pur amour de trois" (a pure love of three people). On the other hand, he confessed to his American friend Helen Scott that "*Jules and Jim* will be a . . . demonstration through both joy and sadness of the impossibility of any amorous combination outside of the couple."[15] The finalized film conveys the same ambiguity. Ultimately, *Jules and Jim* supports the ménage through its details and atmosphere and texture but condemns it through its narrative structure. The transcendent aspirations of these sympathetically portrayed pioneers of love and friendship keep running up against real-life obstacles—their own possessiveness, the temptation of competition, the will to power and vengeance. All three of the principals admit that they were often jealous, and Catherine, during her disenchanted rendezvous with Jim, takes off her makeup in front of the oval mirror, revealing wrinkles and lines. Whenever they resort to a language of numbers or mathematics—"When I'm 32 and you're 29, but when I'm 40 you'll want a woman of 25, and I'll be alone"—we know things are not going well. Jim tells us that Catherine has contemplated suicide. The amorous Icarus has been burned by the sun. The final sentence of the voice-over narration, just after Jim and Catherine (like Roché himself in real life) have been cremated, gives a sense of the ontological limitations inherent in the battle between law and desire: "Jules wanted to mingle [Jim's and Catherine's] ashes, but it was against the regulations." How one experiences *Jules and Jim* depends very much on what the spectator chooses to take away from it—whether the affirmative texture of the ardent love and warm camaraderie shared by the threesome or the dull force of the "regulations," the psychic and societal obstacles to the fulfillment of the film's erotic utopia.

16. The face of disillusionment. Source: Photofest.

The publication of the novel *Jules and Jim* did lead to a kind of reconciliation between Roché and Helen. In the October 31, 1957, entry in Roché's diaries he describes a letter, probably from Helen, that he disguises to hide from the potentially jealous eyes of his wife, Denise. In cryptic terms Roché reports that Helen speaks of "our love/life," saying that she is now free from jealousy, and full of affection for her lovers and for her family. A relieved Roché concludes, "She loves *Jules and Jim*."[16]

And in a relatively rare instance of a situation in which a real-life prototype for a filmic/literary character was able to react to the portrayal of her own character, Helen Hessel was able to see the Truffaut film. In a letter to W. A. Strauss (September 4, 1964) she writes, "I was the young woman who jumped into the Seine for spite, who missed the rendezvous, who married her dear, generous Jules and who went through the ecstasies and disasters of a lost and crazy love. Yes, she even took a shot at her Jim, all that is true and experienced."

In a January 30, 1962, letter Helen Hessel also wrote to Truffaut himself:

At 75 years of age, I am what remains of Kathé, the awesome heroine of Pierre Roché's novel *Jules and Jim*. You can imagine my curiosity as I waited to see your film. On Jan 24, I ran to the cinema. Seated in the dark theatre, after noticing the disguised resemblances, and some more or less irritating parallels, I was soon swept away, seized by your magic power and that of Jeanne Moreau in resuscitating something that had been lived so blindly. That Pierre Roché knew how to tell the story of our threesome, while keeping quite close to the actual events, is not miraculous. But what disposition, what affinity, made it possible for you to make palpable the essence of our intimate emotions? In this sense, I am your only legitimate judge since the two other witnesses, Pierre and Franz, are no longer there to say their "yes" or "no."[17]

Hessel's letter concerning the film casts an uncanny light on the issue of "fidelity" in adaptation. Rather than a question of fidelity to the novel, here the question becomes one of fidelity to the feelings of the prototypes of the characters. The real-life model for the filmic character confronts her specular simulacrum and passes judgment on the adequacy of the portrait. As the prototype, she who had been both the subject and object of real-life infidelities, she becomes, in a certain sense, the empowered arbiter of the film's "fidelity," not to the novel this time, but rather to lived experience.

CHAPTER FIFTEEN

POLYPHONIC EROTICISM

A STUDY OF THE various journals, letters, and novels dedicated to the three-way affair can enrich our discussion of both novel and film by offering clues to what Roché left out of the novel and what Truffaut left out of the film. One point of difference is absolutely crucial. Jules's prohibition to Jim in the film—"not this one, Jim"—is often read as a demand that Jim not "steal" Jules's girlfriend, but seen in historical and autobiographical terms, it means that they will not "share" this one. The film also implies that the triangular relationship had no precedent in their lives. The Truffaut film gives us the impression of a single ménage, to wit the one involving Jules, Jim, and Catherine. But all the evidence from the diaries and the biographies suggests that both Roché and Hessel had participated in many other ménages, even before they became friends. Roché had begun the practice of sharing women with other friends, such as Jouanin and later Marcel Duchamp in New York (with Beatrice Wood). Franz Hessel, too, had been involved in ménages even before his friendship with Roché. In 1904, two years before he met Roché Hessel engaged in a ménage with Franziska zu Reventlow and the Polish painter Bogdan von Suchocki. Indeed, Henri-Pierre Roché's diaries show that Roché and Franz Hessel had a long history of sharing women, which began with a ménage with the painter Marie Laurencin in 1906. After becoming Laurencin's lover, Roché encouraged a "friendship" with Franz. A November 26, 1906, entry speaks of a triangular encounter:

> Franz's room. He, Flap [Laurencin] and I. . . . Flap . . . begins to rummage through Franz's closet, shows off his neckties, and makes us laugh. Tea. Flap dances, shows her lovely legs, lets down her hair,

throws herself across Franz's big bed. On each side of her, at a distance, Franz and I stretch out and each of us takes one of her hands. She and Franz sing softly to each other. . . . With her eyes fixed on Franz, Flap moves closer to me, and the movements of her hand ask for caresses. I caress. First her arm, then her leg, then her thigh. Darkness is falling. They continue to sing. My finger reaches her sex, closed then suddenly half-open, and Flap, still singing, trembles a little. My caress is light.

I get up to leave. Finally, she looks at me. Her expression frightens me. I leave them together for the evening.

Or again, a December 13, 1906, entry reflects some of the tensions and awkwardness of sharing:

On Franz's bed. Franz, Flap and I. They are a delight to look at. We talk. It's almost unreal. Franz finishes my sentences. I finish his. They play cat and mouse. Franz is the cat. Flap's hand the mouse and my vest the mousehole.

Flap leans back against me. I growl a few indistinct words into her shoulder and my arm slips around her waist and brings her mouth over to mine.

Franz is now on the chaise longue. My mouth brushes up against, then nibbles at, Flap's. Our lips dance back and forth. She bends into me. "I love you," she says. Franz excites her but doesn't take her. I pick up Flapo like a little child and set her down on Franz.

She doesn't move; her face is flushed, as though she were sulking.

In a November 22, 1906, diary entry, long before Roché's affair with Helen, Roché calls Hessel his "charming co-caresser." It is hard to resist the speculation that the two men were not also, in symbolic terms at least, caressing each other. Indeed, many of the diary entries glow with a kind of apparently transphysical yet homoerotic desire. When Laurencin and Roché are together, they both miss Franz; indeed, Roché writes (December 20, 1906): "I miss Franz, especially when I'm with Flap." Indeed, in a letter, Laurencin alludes to a certain homoerotic current coursing through all these relationships. "Franz is in love with you

[Roché]," she complains, "and all the other men are in love with one another, which leaves me out in the cold."[1]

According to Roché's biographers, Franz and Henri-Pierre shared absolutely everything: "their pipes and their wallets, their books, their reflections, their experiences, their trips, and their women . . . from prostitutes . . . to women artists (Marie Laurencin), to French women friends of Roché's, to foreign women . . . to Hessel's German women friends."[2] In his journals of 1906, the year he met Franz Hessel, Roché wrote, "[Franz] and I have the same taste in women, but we desire different things from them and not for a moment do I think there has been any rivalry between us." Franz Hessel, meanwhile, passionately despised jealousy, even as he suffered from its pangs. As he puts it in his novel *Romance Parisienne*, "I have never stopped hating and despising jealousy, that hideous grimace of love, even though I am feeling it now" (285). It is against this background, and only against this background, that Hessel's/Jules's interdiction against Jim becoming erotically involved with Catherine (a moment privileged in both novel and film) gains its force and meaning.[3]

Both Roché and Hessel were writing in the wake of the sexological work not only of Freud but also of Otto Weininger (*Sex and Character* [1903]), Havelock Ellis (*The Psychology of Sex* [1897]), Patrick Geddes (*The Evolution of Sex* [1889]), and Charles Albert (*L'Amour libre* [1902]), not to mention the sexually audacious work of literary naturalists like Emile Zola. Indeed, Claude, in *Two English Girls*, gives Zola's sexually explicit *Germinal* to the two sisters in order to further their sexual education. Much of the sexological work of the time had to do with nonnormative forms of sexuality. In this sense the various diaries also reveal a certain homoerotic undercurrent, largely downplayed in the novel and even more in the film. The real-life Helen reveals in her journals that she practices a blasé, unprogrammatic lesbianism. She makes love to women, she writes, but unenthusiastically, "only to make them happy" (*Journal*, 389). Characteristically, she uses the pretext of homosexuality to perform one of her many sexual (verbal) inversions. In an imaginative transgender and gender-bending twist, she claims to her two male friends that she is in fact a male homosexual who wants to make love with both of them. "Do you two want me?" she asks. "Let me know, so that I can learn love as the true man that I am" (*Journal*, 390).

In Roché's case seduction plays a role not only within his hetero-sexual amours but also within his male friendships. Roché's affairs with women are implicated, invaginated as it were, within his friend-ships with men. That the real-life Roché maintained an intense rela-tionship with his mother—a crucial theme in the journals as well as in *Two English Girls*—while also leading a polyandrous and dispersive Don Juan–like existence further complicates the portrait of Roché's erotic imaginary. What we find with Roché is a kind of homoerotic Don Juanism, that of men pursuing and sharing women but where the pursuing together is as important as the object pursued. At the same time, the narrator's words about Jim's relationship with his mother, in the novel *Jules and Jim*, evoke the unstated pact that existed between the pair, a pact necessarily fatal to any prospective permanent hetero-sexual relationship: "He never wanted to marry any of the girls she chose for him, and she had never approved of any of those he would have enjoyed being married to" (216–217). Thus a mother preternatu-rally faithful to one man—her husband, Pierre—brings up a son con-stitutionally incapable of fidelity, and perhaps even love, toward any one woman.

CHAPTER SIXTEEN

SEXPERIMENTAL WRITING
THE DIARIES

THE CASE OF *Jules and Jim* complicates the issue of the filmic adaptation of novels, since we are dealing not with a single source but rather with multiple sources alongside the novel, in the form of the letters and diaries, some of which François Truffaut read. The diaries form a glorious mélange of exalted romanticism, linguistic experimentation, and accounts of the everyday business of living. Many features prominent in the journals of Henri-Pierre Roché and Helen Hessel leave only minor traces in both novel and film. For example, the journals reveal a certain obsession with eugenics. Even though the prototypes were generally on the left and even flirted briefly with communism (while at the same time being naïve and relatively apolitical), they share a eugenic concern with "perfecting the race," an idea often associated, ironically, with the "scientific racism" of the Nazis. Roché, who refers to his own spermatozoa as "my children," constantly speculates about the genetic and procreative potentialities of his sexual partners, that is, their capacity to generate beautiful and intelligent children. The Truffaut film, for its part, retains only minimal traces of these ideas, most notably in Jim's and Catherine's obsession with a potential child as a kind of validation or blessing on their love. In the film Jim jokes that their hypothetical child would combine the parents' genetic features, notably "skinniness" and "migraine headaches."

The prototypes' journals and diaries reveal what we know to be often true, that individuals, especially artistically inclined individuals, tend to regard episodes in their sexual lives as epoch-making world-historical events. The diaries create a special atmosphere of *folie à trois*, of a world apart, a vertical realm at once resonantly spiritual and passionately physical. The diaries also speak of real-life events not treated directly in the novel or film. The novel, Roché's journal, and Helen's journal all refer to an incident in which Helen felt an impulse to play the toreador in front of a moving train, as if the train were an angry bull, jumping out of the way only at the last moment, a performative acting out that brings with it the intertextual memory of the finale of *Anna Karenina*. In his version Roché reports that "Franz groaned indignantly, much as he did the day Helen jumped into the Seine." Helen describes the incident in her own usual disruptive, fragmented, and in this case even cinematic, style:

> The train visible in the distance. A need for danger.
>
> I place myself between the rails.
>
> See the sky above. Superb, cold stars. Beautiful, intact solitude—the locomotive's two eyes grow bigger.
>
> Franz: "Lukschen, come back." A plaintive voice, a discouraged command.
>
> In order to be admired by Pierre, I have to throw myself on the ground. The train passes above me and I get up safe and sound.
>
> . . . My eyes fixed on the locomotive's two eyes—the sound of being out of breath—. Pitiless power—come destroy me—finally—in love—fascinated—stay standing without moving—catch the blow and depart into nothingness. (*Journal*, 233)

There are many ways to "read" such a passage. On one level it provides a clever twist on the *liebestod*; Helen tests and provokes love through the threat of provoking her own death. We also see Helen's theatrical propensities; she is ever performing for the men, provoking them in a sadomasochistic manner. We sense a complicity between the exhibitionist and the voyeur. But at the same time, this complicity takes place within a context in which Helen refuses to be taken for granted.

In *Against Love* Laura Kipnis laments the ways that Weber's "work ethic" has come to penetrate the realm of sexual affection to the point that "we've been well-tutored in the catechism of labor-intensive intimacy." The rhetoric of the factory, she complains, has become "the default language of love."[1] The members of the Helen-Franz-Roché ménage, in contrast, saw love under the sign of play. They were creatively perverse, even theatrical and flamboyant, in their performance of everyday amorous life. Renewing contact with the lost paradise of childhood playfulness, they were inventive in their erotic games. In their journals they imagine themselves playing a wide repertoire of roles, some involving transgender transformations (Helen pretending to be a gay man), or the violation of kinship taboos (Helen pretending to be Roché's son), or chameleonic changes in profession (Helen as a nurse taking care of the sick child Roché). All these cases, interestingly, involve Helen performing roles for the men. At times Helen fantasizes an incestuous relationship between siblings: "If I were your sister," Helen tells Roché, "I would defy the law and love you" (*Journal*, 69). Helen also imagines being a whore in Marseille, with him as her pimp (*Journal*, 72). Here, as elsewhere, their libidinous imaginary is deeply entangled in the titillating power of the taboos being defied; the Law, in the Lacanian schema, nourishes Desire.

The theme of women assuming multiple roles in men's lives is often echoed in Truffaut's films. Jules says of Thérèse that "she was both my mother, and my little daughter." In *Two English Girls* Muriel writes to Claude: "I am your wife. I was your sister, your friend, everything you'd want." Rejected by Thérèse, in *Jules and Jim*, Jules says of her that she "was a little bit my daughter, and a little bit my mother." In Truffaut's *Domicile conjugal* (1970), as Wyatt Phillips points out, Antoine tells his departing wife, Christine, that she is his little sister, his daughter, and his mother; she sarcastically replies: "I'd have liked to be your wife too." And in *Love on the Run* (1979) Liliane tells Christine that Antoine "needs a wife, a mistress, a little sister, a nanny, and a nurse" and that she "cannot play all those roles at once."[2]

In the diaries the couple's play is entangled in the web of gendered social and sexual relations. Helen exalts the blurring and shifting of sexual distinctions, a release from the boundaries of socially imposed gender roles. "In so far as I can remember," Helen writes in a letter to Roché, "I have never accepted, never played the role: woman" (*Journal*, 517). Or again, she writes of her inability to have orgasms through masturbation: "I suffer from not being able to orgasm. If I were a man, I would go to a bordello" (*Journal*, 498). It is in this same spirit of gender reversal, of the "unruly woman" and the "woman on top," that Helen fantasizes having Roché adopt her name: Pierre Roché Grund (*Journal*, 489).

We also see Helen's penchant for role playing in her reaction to seeing a lion and a lion tamer at a circus. She instantly imagines herself as a lion: "I put my big, fat, beautiful paws around you, and hit your grumpy face. . . . I sit on your back and jump up and down. I try to make you fall on your side. I bury my nose in your ear and roll around in front of you so you take me in your open arms. And then you give in, just as you've taken me in your big paws, and hold me against you. Pierre, Pierre. I'm drunk with desire, to play with you" (*Journal*, 491).

At another point, Helen's wide-ranging empathy—what the German romantics called *Einfühlung*—roams beyond human beings toward another animal species: "We are in the prairie, three or four sheep. A desire to be on all fours and say 'baaah'" (*Journal*, 303). We are reminded of the empathic projections expressed in the letters of poet John Keats, imagining himself a sparrow, "pecking around in the gravel."

Lacan famously defined *love* as "giving what one does not have to someone who does not want it," and some of Roché's poems suggest a kind of vicious circle or Zeno's paradox within love, implying an impossibility of fulfillment:

> *The more I take you*
> *The less I possess you*
> *The more I take you*
> *The more jealous I become*
> *The more jealous I become*
> *The less I love you*
> *The less I take you* (*Carnets*, 58)

Roché's gift for metaphor sometimes takes surprising turns. Admiring Helen's capacious "deep throat" talents for fellatio, Roché compares her to "an agile sword swallower." Helen's journals, meanwhile, offer a different perspective, the filmic countershot, as it were, of the same sexual act, in an account at once more mundane and more poetic. Finding fellatio "delicate, difficult work," she worries about hurting him, since "he's afraid of teeth" (140). At the same time, she kisses him like "a madwoman": "His cock in my mouth. It's big and strong. It rapes my mouth. I don't want it. I hurt him. He advises me: 'gently.' His children [semen] flow, urged, as if by sighs, into the depths of my throat, into the heat, into the center. I have the impression that I'm drinking egg, mystery, the invisible, the future" (*Journal*, 43).

Both Franz and Helen emphasize what they call "lovesleep," the oblivious, somnolent calm that follows in the wake of the storm of passion. Helen writes: "His arms around me. No desire to move. Complete forgetfulness—of the battle. Tranquility, equilibrium of our breathing" (*Journal*, 64).

At times the formulations verge on the mystical and the oceanic, as when Roché exults that lovemaking turns them "into a single bloc of glorious, illuminated flesh" (*Carnets*, 218). Or, again, with echoes of Dante's "love that moves the stars," the following passage: "we are the universe, the milky way, and all the stars, all turning and moving. We move softly in our sleep without letting go of each other. Vertigo of the sky. Pure and incredible intoxication" (*Carnets*, 22). But whereas Roché speaks of oceanic astronomy, Helen speaks as the bard of reciprocal and mutually incorporative love. While Roché concentrates on his physical sensations, she stresses his individual emotional importance to her: "It's too little to say: I love you," she writes concerning Roché; "it would be more precise to say: you give me everything I need. . . . You make me happy, you give me strength, joy, you shake me, calm me, and you move me entirely. . . . I don't even dare to think that you don't love me, any more than I would think of becoming blind or losing my mind" (*Journal*, 553). Or again, "Ever since I have loved you, I have done nothing which did not have you as the goal" (*Journal*, 555). Helen calls Roché "My love, my buddy, my brother, my genius, my mouth, my eyes, my longing, my work, my lion," and, playing with the rules of grammar and syntax as she plays with the rules of love, she adds: "my in-the-arms, my rolling-over-you, my wash-the-God. I-fuck-the-God, I-play-with-the-God" (*Journal*, 498).

What interests Helen is the dissolution of the very distinction between self and other, between inner and outer; there is no longer inside and outside but only a kind of Chagalian invagination. The emphasis is on the breaking down of walls or the transcendence of the boundaries of the self, on fusion and melting into one another, on not being able to tell where one body ends and the other begins. Helen emphasizes what Bakhtin would call the "in-between" of persons, the dissolving of the walls of skin, the permeable membrane that separates selves, the mutual ingestion of lovers. Helen sees sexuality as "situated," an "ecological" sense of the importance of the environment of eroticism. Profoundly relational, Helen reminds Franz, "Everything I do is in relation [en rapport in the text] to you. I am happy" (*Journal*, 493). For Helen, sexuality exists in relation to the general existence of the body, in relation to other persons and to the larger field of the common social life.

Both Roché and Helen anthropomorphize Roché's penis, conceiving it as an unruly creature of independent will, a miniature adolescent or "mischievous little boy." At one point Roché tells his diary that his naughty puerile organ "had never been so young, so gay, so swollen with sap" (*Carnets*, 106). Reacting to Man Ray's photos of the naked Helen and of himself, Roché finds it all "terrifyingly beautiful" (*Carnets*, April 13, 1923). Relentlessly phallocentric, the epistolary lovers worship at the shrine of male tumescence. (Ideas of phallus worship, we recall, were common in Germanic avant-garde circles.) Literalizing the notion, they refer to Roché's penis as "God"—a resurrected divinity in the wake of the Nietzschean "death of God"—where the uppercase *G* presumably precludes any polytheistic pantheon allowing for rival gods ("Thou shalt have no other gods before me").

Nor is there any reciprocity here; Helen's sex never becomes a "Goddess." Helen speaks of "The God who mounts, who seeks his way, touches me, finds me, enters me, fills me, takes me, leaving all spaces filled" (*Journal*, 244). Both Roché and Helen recognize a certain rebellious, Luciferian desire for autonomy on the part of Roché's "God." Helen writes, "He speaks of his penis with infinite respect, confidence, and friendship, although he is angered at times by an independence that he must also humbly acknowledge" (*Journal*, 60). But Helen also shows a woman's skeptical awareness of the fragile, ephemeral nature of male tumescence. Conscious both of the power and the vulnerability of the male organ, Helen writes: "Men have the 'advantage' of this arm which can punish, which can deeply wound a woman (the God that does not budge). But they have the disadvantage of not being able to cheat [that is, fake orgasm]. I remember that I used to always think, very vainly, that I could raise up God whenever I wished, but [this experience] corrected my error. . . . Poor men. Dependent. We have to give them a lot of confidence" (*Journal*, 176).

But in the end Helen believes in her God and His wonderful works: "The God was entirely inside me. But how can I do otherwise. The God wants to enter and I want to receive him. That's it. It's simple, and healthy, and beautiful" (*Journal*, 387).

In the journals Helen shows herself capable of an overpowering and total love that mingles the mundane and the sublime: "I love Pierre's [Roché's] every little gesture. It's a joyous event to see him spit out apple pits" (*Journal*, 473). At other times Helen's love is anguished, conflicted, passionate, even despairing. She writes to Roché: "I am yours. I want to love you, not belong to you. Help me, Pierre, I am suffering. I love you." At times, the mingled feelings expressed in her journals anticipate the oxymoronic love/pathos not only of *Jules and Jim* but also of films like *Hiroshima mon amour*, which yoke pleasure and pain, desire and death.

Interestingly, Helen Hessel's journals and letters treating the first period of the ménage (1920–1921) were published almost simultaneously with Roché's in 1990/1991. It was as if the couple were being reunited postmortem, through the publication of their love letters, thus instantiating the romantic liebestod trope of a love realized, like that of another literary Catherine (with her stormy Heathcliff), only "beyond the grave."

CHAPTER SEVENTEEN

SEXUALITY/TEXTUALITY

RARELY HAS SEXUALITY been so intermingled with textuality as in the intimate journals of Roché and Helen. Love writing here becomes a form of "sympoesis," a way of shaping a shared dominion where passion holds sway. Their "lovers' discourse" is richly embroidered with classical literary references. Franz, after all, had reminded Helen that she "shouldn't always mix the Greeks up with [our] affairs" (*Journal*, 107). But speaking more generally, Helen and Roché see sex itself as languaged, as what Roland Barthes calls a "fait langagier." This idea is of course not new; it is implicit in the old trope of "the language of love" and of love as the "universal language." In *A Lover's Discourse* Barthes speaks of the "language-nature of the amorous sentiment" and "the endlessly glossed form of the amorous relation."[1] Barthes compares language to a skin that we rub against others: "It is as if I had words instead of fingers, or fingers at the tip of my words."[2] In an earlier relationship Violet Hart had used similar words in a letter to Roché: "This paper is your skin—and the ink my blood—pressing hard so that the marks can never be rubbed out."[3] But for the amorous triad of Franz, Helen, and Henri-Pierre, not only is eroticism linguistic, but language is erotic. The eroticism of language and the language of eroticism, then, have mutual intercourse, while metalanguage leads to autoerotic jouissance: "language experiences orgasm upon touching itself."[4]

In this spirit the prototypes were all extremely inventive in their amorous discourse. At one point the threesome react in horror at what strikes them as a terribly brutal American expression for making love: "screw" (visser). In preference to such crudeness they deploy a special code shared only by themselves. "Spend" (in English in the original) refers to orgasm; "la petite femme" (the "little woman") refers to the woman's sex; "little man" is the penis; "touch little man" is masturbation; "unwell" means "menstruating." The entry for August 21: "Nuit Luk et moi—nus—bonheur—sp. et sp, et k.p.h. et t.p.h. et k.p.f. et grand amour" can be translated as: "Helen and I nude, at night, happiness, double orgasm, fellatio and masturbation and cunnilingus and great lovemaking" (*Carnets*, 313).

Language penetrates eroticism and sexuality in countless ways. It is no accident, perhaps, that so many erotic films begin with the reading of a book or that so many paintings and lithographs feature a woman, a book dropped to the floor, and a rapturous expression.[5] For our literary lovers, language informs sexuality at every point, in the eroticizing power of the spoken word, within the "speech act" of seduction, in the erotic effect of reading (the libidinal "pleasure of the text"), in the conversations that lead to or accompany their sexual activities, in the "para-linguistic" groans, moans, and sighs that provide the sound track. In the various intimate journals of the principals the word is present in every erotic encounter, even silent ones, if only in the form of "inner speech." Even their masturbation comes accompanied by inner speech, of remembered or anticipated verbal fragments; their monologues, like those of Dostoevskian characters, can be oriented to the other, to a hoped-for or remembered "responsive understanding."

The erotic journals of the principals suggest that if language constantly permeates sex, one can also regard sex itself as a kind of language. Within the body, transmitters speed across synapses, neurons signal, and messages race from the erogenous zones to the brain and back again. Even corporeal secretions are communicative, constituting transmissions from the inner self to the outer body and to the other. The body in arousal exhibits indexical signs of desire; it sweats, it stretches, it reaches out, it opens up, it lubricates and makes way for erotic dialogue.

The eroticism of the diaries, like that of the cinema, is "multitrack," taking verbal, tactile, olfactory, and visual form. Love in the journals of Helen and Roché speaks in the monologue of masturbation, the dialogue of the couple, or the polylogue of the orgy. In their case sex at its worst becomes an exercise in power, a clash of languages and mistranslations of linguistic and gestural codes, an epidermic juxtaposition of monologues, dialogue gone awry. Sex at its best in the journals is a communicative utopia, a boudoir carnival characterized by "free and familiar contact" and transindividual fusion.[6]

But sex and words are also linked in another, more direct, way in the journals. In the epistolary equivalent of phone sex, Helen experiences an orgasm while writing. Both Helen and Roché speak of the episode. In the July 16, 1921, letter, Helen writes to Pierre:

> Pierre, I want you to take me and kiss me. I want your lips on my eyes. I want my head on your chest, my ear hearing your voice inside your chest resonating "Luki." I caress you, the God in my mouth. My tongue caresses you—I adore your come which fills my throat. Come in my mouth, please. Right away. Pierre, do it quickly, lift me on top of you. . . . I want to take you. . . . I roll on you, I am both you and me as I adore you. Oh, Pierre, I just came while writing you. (*Journal*, 563)

In a complementary shot-countershot of perspectives Roché relates the very same letter in his journals, describing it as so "explosive with love, with her account of (my imagined) caresses, that she comes to a climax just as she signs the letter, with her penmanship reflecting her coming . . . her signature fainting and falling like our bodies after orgasm" (*Carnets*, 288).

Hardly all sweetness and light, the Helen/Roché relationship, as expressed in the diaries, sometimes becomes a naked power struggle, a Titanic battle of egos. At times, she describes Roché's discomfiture: "He looks embarrassed, nervous, unsure of himself. I look at him without pity. I've won. He's weaker than I am. A proud feeling of victory" (*Journal*, 56). For Roché, Helen has natural charismatic authority, reminiscent, perhaps, of that of his mother: "She is a born leader: she assigns joy and order around her" (*Carnets*, 34). Helen, meanwhile, is nothing if not self-critical about her "human, all too human" personality. She admits to a spoiled, narcissistic side, which she attributes to the fact that "I've always been spoiled, my mother in-law admired me and did everything I wished, my father adores me, and the same adoration transpired at school and with my friends in Berlin. I need that, I love that, I work for that, I am just a poor beast if people don't love me, don't spoil me. . . . Sometimes that also disgusts me, but what can I do?" (*Journal*, 150).

For Freud, narcissistic spoiling can become a self-fulfilling prophecy, in that spoiled people exude a confidence that draws others to them, who spoil them in turn by living up to their narcissistic expectation of being spoiled. Helen confirms the Freudian view that narcissistic women fascinate because "it is as if we envied them their power of retaining a blissful state of mind—an unassailable libido-position which we ourselves have abandoned."[7]

The diaries on occasion also betray an intermittent element of sadomasochism, of a clawing sexuality with a hard, cruel edge. Truffaut once revealed, as I pointed out earlier, that the secretary whom he asked to transcribe Roché's diaries desisted from her task because she was nauseated by Roché's "unconscious cruelty." But we learn from Helen Grund's journals that she, too, could be despotic and vindictive. Lying alongside Pierre, Helen weeps as she reads about Penthesilea, the mythic queen of the Amazon. She identifies with Penthesilea but only, she clarifies, with the Penthesilea "after she has devoured, torn, raved, and drunk the blood of Achilles" (*Journal*, 298; emphasis mine). "Only Penthesilea's destiny," she tells her diary, "can satisfy me" (*Journal*, 299). Helen's consciously cruel capriciousness "answers" Roché's unconscious cruelty.

The violent transports of the lovers sometimes seem a quieter, more domesticated, version of Georges Bataille's accounts, for example in *The Story of the Eye*, of ritual, orgiastic transgressions, which mingle intense pleasure (at the exceeding of boundaries) and intense anguish (at the realization of the force of the norms). Helen and Roché do not offer us, of course, that sublime or transcendental pornography where saint meets voluptuary in a world that celebrates all the "excesses" that gleefully perturb the orderly round of respectable activity: childbirth, copulation, defecation, regenerating filth, and orgiastic excess. Yet at times, their transgressive écriture does occasionally display a kind of isomorphism between the violation of sexual taboos and the violation of discursive norms. But in their writing, this notion of parallel transgressions is not so much theorized as it is simply lived and enacted.

But what is finally so striking and unusual in this amorous triad is not so much its audacity or its synthesis of the erotic and the transgressive, by now banal, but rather the much more unusual conjunction of the erotic with the familial and the domestic and the quotidian.[8] And in this context it is worth reflecting on the complexly woven relationship between Franz and Helen. According to Manfred Flügge's account, Franz told Helen, when he put the wedding ring on her finger, that the ring was a "symbol of [her] freedom."[9] But Helen simultaneously appreciated and resented Franz's lack of jealousy. She accused him of being lazy in love and disliked his way of making her do all the work in the relationship. At the same time, she despised the dull, monotonous drone of bourgeois marriage. She seemed to both need and despise domestic stasis. She therefore sought out temptation and risk, anything that might upset a tiresome equilibrium.

Truffaut's *Jules and Jim* conveys a sense of something we discern in all the various accounts of Helen Hessel, including her own: her uncensored, impulsive, whimsical spirit, her fondness for what Gide would call "des actes gratuits." At once masculine and feminine, charming and outrageous, Catherine charms through her spontaneity. In her journals Helen describes herself as divinely capricious: "I went to the hairdresser and asked him to whiten my hair. He thought I was crazy but I explained to him that I wanted to transcend all vanity and coquettishness, which exist only to make possible flirtations and easy liaisons" (*Journal*, 469). Truffaut also picks up on another aspect of Helen's self-portrayal in her journals, one especially apt for cinematic amplification, to wit, her view of herself as a catalyst for movement: "I would like to move (and make move) all men. Become a great spectacle. And women too. I look at Fanny. She is desirable too" (*Journal*, 48). Or again: "I have the mission to trigger movement ("mettre en movement" in the text) in all those who meet me, even if only for a little while. I have no time for idylls or rest" (*Journal*, 150). At a dance hall Helen and her woman friend Sauermann enter into a playful competition to see which of them could "move the men's penises more quickly while dancing" (*Journal*, 322; emphasis mine). Truffaut translates this idea of "making others move" through his mise-en-scène: in the film Catherine literally triggers and anticipates movement. She prods men to follow her, by leading them on her bicycle, for example, or by inviting Jim to run after her, or by proposing, and then just as suddenly initiating, a footrace.

Helen's journals also register another salient feature conveyed by the Truffaut film: her sudden changes of mood. In the journals, the tender and loving Helen will suddenly turn into a cruelly aggressive Helen, who speaks of "a need to be alone, to be naughtily malicious [méchante]" (*Journal*, 116). This capricious unpredictability doubtless forms part of her charm for some men, who feel challenged to domesticate her, to tame her as if she were a lioness. Playfully sadistic, Helen enjoys "confusing and disorienting" her lovers. At other times she expresses a kind of pansexual desire: "I feel like going in the street and making love with all those who desire me" (Roché assures her that she'll find a dozen candidates right away). Or, on another occasion, at a café: "I do the rounds of the cafés. To choose a man for the night" (73). Nor does class snobbery restrict her desire. In a Lady Chatterley–like passage she notes: "A chauffeur with a tire under his arm—a young man—looks at me with amorous admiration. I like him. He's clean and strong. I look at him with pleasure. Our eyes remain fixed on each other. I'm ashamed. I'm full of love—it's spilling out of my eyes. Either I love Pierre or all men. If I can't love Pierre, I must love the mass of men" (*Journal*, 269).

For Helen, love is like a contagious fluid or energetic wave that spreads outward centrifugally from those who love, leaking out into the atmosphere. While she and Pierre chat with the maid, Helen notes that the maid has become "wrapped in the atmosphere of our love" (*Journal*, 271). At another point Helen fantasizes about sex with strangers on a train. Sharing a compartment with four men, she fantasizes: "I could easily kiss all of them in turn" (*Journal*, 131). At times Helen becomes whimsically self-destructive, with a wish to do something "irreparable." This self-destructive impulse goes as far as narcissistic self-mutilation. Against the expressed wishes of both Franz and Henri-Pierre, she has a doctor perform a painful operation that sews up her sex, refashioning her as a "sixteen year old girl" (*Carnets*, 363).

Interestingly, both Roché and Helen speak little of Franz Hessel in their diaries. They call their gentle patriarch, quite appropriately, "Father." Roché describes Franz as a "specialist in unhappy love" (*Carnets*, 125). Even Franz describes himself as unworthy of love, as if an adherent of the Groucho Marxish option of refusing to join any club that might accept him: "knowing myself as I do, I shall never be able to forgive any woman for loving me" (*Jules and Jim*, 37). For Helen and Pierre Franz becomes the stable backdrop figure, the taken-for-granted guarantor, the axiomatic support on which everything else is premised, an anchor and source of stability that "enables" and "authorizes" their playfully dangerous flirtations. Franz is both the father who protects and the eternal child who needs protection. (As Hessel's sons seem to have realized, men who want to remain children do not necessarily make the best fathers.) Franz plays the innocent to Catherine's imp. As a wealthy man Franz also provides a kind of financial security for Helen. In her appreciations of Franz, Helen stresses not so much his intrinsic qualities as what he provides for her in emotional terms. His attractiveness for Helen has to do with the fact that he granted her more freedom than she had ever enjoyed before. Thanks to Hessel, she is richer and freer within marriage: "He is so lazy, so heavy, so untouchable, in the end, that he excited me enormously. I had become accustomed to being always attacked—brutalized. He left me so much space for taking the offensive. Up to then, I had only known the defensive position. I liked his way of letting himself get caught up in things. His grand and loving indulgence toward me and toward everyone. He is what I would call amusing and somehow 'large.' The ideal man to marry—the suffering of marriage reduced to a minimum" (*Journal*, 303).

Unlike the jealous husband of conventional lore, Franz even defends Helen's lovers. When she criticizes Roché, for example, Franz upbraids her: "you're wrong . . . he's suffering" (*Journal*, 362). But at times Helen also resents Franz's lack of jealousy, regarding it as a form of indifference, a sign of lack of love and concern.

CHAPTER EIGHTEEN

THE GENDERED POLITICS OF FLÂNERIE

I N HER DIARIES Helen often spoke of her wanderings around the city. It is highly revealing to regard Helen's strolls around city streets in the context of the politics of flânerie. Anke Gleber and other feminist critics have underscored the strongly classed and gendered nature of flânerie. Working-class women who used the streets to get to work were not seen as artistically inclined flâneuses; only bourgeois women were, and they only rarely. But even the bourgeoisies were severely hemmed in by all kinds of restrictions. A quiet but nonetheless overpowering social normativity, enforced within the politics of the everyday, dictated that women lacked any right to stare, scrutinize, or watch, and women flâneuses like Helen Grund and her friend Charlotte Wolff were rare indeed. Female walkers in the streets were likely to be taken not as flâneuses but rather as "streetwalkers." The other side of the axiomatically patriarchal "a woman's place is in the home" was that "a woman's place is not the street." As Adrienne Rich points out, "Characteristics of male power include the power of men . . . to confine [women] physically and prevent their movement by means of rape as terrorism, keeping women off the streets; purdah; foot-binding, atrophying a woman's aesthetic capabilities; haute couture, 'feminine' dress codes; the veil; sexual harassment on the streets."[1]

To compensate for their exclusion from the streets, according to Gleber, women "project all their endeavors into their domestic interiors and become—unwillingly—complicitous with their exclusion from exteriority as well as from new directions of technology, production, and perception."[2]

For Gertrud Koch the aim of the sanctions on women strolling in the streets, rather like the aim of the veil, "is to remove women from the voyeuristic gaze of men." The converse prohibition against women being free, unharassed spectators in the movie theaters "denies the voyeuristic gaze to woman herself."[3] And as Gleber points out, men still habitually "check out" women, "in a casual yet consistent cultural ritual that continues to make women's presence in public spaces a precarious and volatile one."[4] These perennial pressures even today provoke various defensive ruses for contemporary women flâneurs: the exaggeratedly purposive walk, the off-putting walkman or cell phone, the blank, neutral expression, the strategically chosen dog or male companion.

Women like Helen Hessel and Charlotte Wolff, for their part, dared to be flâneuses, both together and with their male friends. Wolff herself comments on their historically precocious utopianism: "Who were we and all those other young women of the twenties who seemed to know so well what we wanted? We had no need to be helped to freedom from male domination. We were free, nearly forty years before the Women's Liberation Movement started in America."[5]

But Wolff's portrait of freedom is perhaps idealized. Given the overarching patriarchal domination in social life, it is not surprising that Helen's intimate diaries expressed envy not of the penis per se but rather of male power and prerogatives. The diaries reveal a frustrated desire for sexual agency. A constant leitmotif is the idea "if I were a man." If she were a man, she tells Roché, she would be like him (*Journal*, 34). Reading Roché's book about Don Juan, with Roché at her side, Helen writes: "If I were a man, I would be like [Don Juan]." And trumping even Roché's machismo, she adds this zinger: "Perhaps even better" (*Journal*, 92).

At other times the in-some-ways-male-identified Helen seems happy to be "just one of the boys." Walking in the street hand in hand with both husband and lover, she describes their alliance as follows: "I walk between them. Their friendship unites them. I take Pierre's hand. And Franz's. I don't separate them; rather, their friendship detours through me" (*Journal*, 433). (One of the most popular posters and stills drawn from the film *Jules and Jim*, interestingly, showed Catherine flanked by the two male friends.) This unity also extends to any potential children generated by these relationships. Given this all-embracing cross-gender complicity, any conceivable child emerging from the diverse relationships becomes in a way the child of all three "parents":

> Helen: "I'm pregnant, Pierre. What should we do?"
> Pierre: "Let's talk about it, with Franz if he wants to.
> Helen: "Naturally. It's his child too. He protected our love."
> Pierre: "No, on the contrary, he forbade us to have a child."
> Helen: "That doesn't count. The child belongs to all three of us."
> (*Journal*, 338)

But while Franz is usually obliging and self-sacrificing, at times Helen and Roché must minister to his needs as well. Helen writes to Roché: "'Father' needs us. Don't delay. The situation is confused, not desperate by any means, but still. . . . He's such a marvelous being—like a book dead or asleep, maybe you can wake him" (*Journal*, 483).

CHAPTER NINETEEN

COMPARATIVE ÉCRITURE

I N THE PUBLISHED journals Helen Hessel and Henri-Pierre Roché, in keeping with the idea of "polyphonic writing," constantly comment on each others' diaries, making stylistic suggestions and thematic observations, sometimes disputing the interlocutor's account. Their journals reveal two quite different literary styles. Roché especially is fond of oxymoronic expressions—"refreshing crises," "beautiful perils"—that evoke his addiction to danger as an aphrodisiac. The exchange of commentaries on the intimate journals also highlights some of the contrasts between their personalities and literary style. In the novel Roché's narrator describes Helen's diary as intricate and labyrinthine, and Roché's as flat and clear like a "table of contents" (127). While Helen criticizes Roché's mania for noting exact dates, Roché criticizes Helen's penchant for vagueness and imprecision.

Roché's journals take the form of daily notebooks: he records the books he has read, the plays he has seen, and above all, the women he has seduced. As a Robinson Crusoe of love, Roché inventories his conquests and orgasms in a kind of ledger book of passion. Roché applies a Protestant-style work ethic to sexuality: "Love," he writes, "is in a way my work."[1] Much as Crusoe chronicles his accomplishments in his journal, or Benjamin Franklin chronicled his efforts at self-improvement, Roché registers his progress in the art and craft of seduction. Roché's concerns are genitally focused, concentrated on the erotic telos, on the "Big O." Relentlessly priapic, his life seems to flow outward from his penis, which is never far from his mind. He is preoccupied with the mechanics and the pyrotechnics of lovemaking, while Helen is more interested in lived duration, concerned with savoring the experience, not destroying it through a technical analysis that "murders to dissect."

Unlike Roché, Helen frequently reports looking at herself in the mirror, describing herself variously as "tired" or as "beautiful like a diva." "Looking at myself," she says, "I find myself pretty and made for love" (*Journal*, 321). Helen's remarks illustrate Bakhtin's oft-repeated insight that we are never really alone, that we are always in dialogue with others, even when regarding ourselves in the mirror, for we are even then always already seeing ourselves through the eyes of imaginary others.[2] When Helen envisions herself psychically, without a mirror, she finds herself "all right," but when she looks in the mirror, she sees herself—quite improbably from the photographic evidence—as the "ugliest woman of all the women she knows" (*Journal*, 17). Elsewhere she directly challenges the mirror: "The mirror lies. In truth, behind the ugliness, I am beautiful" (*Journal*, 171). At the same time, her diary entries illustrate the salience of theories concerning the female internalization of the male gaze, whereby women are prodded to submit themselves to the mental self-scrutiny of a "Judgement of Paris," where men reign supreme as the ultimate judges in a beauty contest. Thus Helen critically scans her own appearance, to the point that it becomes unclear whether she is comparing herself, to her own disadvantage, to other women or simply internalizing the imagined negativity of a fantasized male gaze or both at the same time.

We find this same ambivalence about her body in an episode with Roché where Helen exposes her nude body at the window. Helen sums up the exchange in her diary:

> Helen: "I am ashamed of all my imperfections. I hide them from you."
>
> *Drying myself, I go to the open window. Nude. Visible for any passersby.*
>
> Pierre: "But you also show them [your imperfections] to complete strangers." (*Journal*, 183)

With Helen, self-confidence waxes and wanes with the moment: He [Roché] takes off my trousers. He looks at me. I am painfully conscious of my ugliness. A feeling of inadequacy and of being a fraud" (*Journal*, 42).

Interestingly, Helen is attuned as well to a more general specularity and circulation of looks and "looking relations"; she is a veritable analyst of the gaze. She describes herself watching Roché looking at himself in the mirror, for example, something Roché himself never finds worth describing. In a case of what Bakhtin might call "excess seeing," she is even more aware of what he looks like as he regards himself than he is himself: she tells her diary that Pierre regards himself with a "mother's tenderness" (*Journal*, 210). At times she abstracts or distances herself from her own regard, feeling "as if my own eyes looked at me from behind my head" (*Journal*, 330). Elsewhere, she reflects on the interchanged looks between the two of them, detecting a "guilty look" on his face or finding herself suddenly frightened by a harshness in his regard. At another point Helen deploys an analogy to convey her feelings. She tells her diary that she and Roché "look at each other like adults who are moved by the joy of children" (*Journal*, 299). At times she even imbues the regard with a kind of hallucinogenic, supernatural power. Describing a shared moment in a café, she writes: "I stare at Pierre. We look at each other. As I feel his eyes running over me, our table slowly rises, closer and closer to the ceiling. If I don't look away, we will break through the ceiling and rise into the sky—and the waitress will be scandalized. I close my eyes to ease the shock as we come back to earth" (*Journal*, 308).

For Helen, their mutual looks convey a preternatural identification one with the other. She tells Roché, "Pierre, you are like me—when I look at you, it's as if I were looking at myself, but transformed into a tall and slender man" (*Journal*, 101). She is always conscious not only of her own looks but also of the "looks" of others, the kind of thing that Roché would never find worth saying unless it were a prelude to sex. At the same time, Helen constantly senses the silent weight and subtle pressure of the male regard; she feels, almost telepathically, the laser-like gazes of a whole series of men bearing down on specific points in her body—on the nape of her neck, for example, or on her back. At times, she is discomfited by this male regard and at times flattered by it: "It's so easy to make me happy. Almost any man who gets excited [while watching me] can have that effect" (48).

In aesthetic terms Roché's style is straightforward, while Helen's is both quotidian—she constantly tells her diary what she is wearing, for example—and experimental. Her writing is also more technically "advanced" and avant-garde than Roché's, as when she gives us the equivalent of a Joycean Molly Bloom–style interior monologue:

> How strong and brutal he is. He manipulates me like an object, pulling my head backward. His knees hurt my hips, he shakes me, I feel my bones. I'm suffocating, there's no end to it. He's above me, with his Jupiter head—I find him again, recognize him—I scream out with pleasure—me—a spring—flowing out of a mountain. We fall from the mattress. Splendid. Two machines of incommensurable power, equal. Eyes wide open. His God takes off into me as if it were on wheels. He strikes me, opens me up wide, runs all around me. I no longer wonder if I love him." (*Journal*, 59)

Or again, Helen offers a mode of language—fragmentary, associative—reminiscent of what Russian writers like Bakhtin and Eisenstein called "inner speech": "Next to Pierre. No light. God doesn't move. We can sleep. Fear of sleeping and then waking. Die Hindernisse nehmen (jump over obstacles) and make love, me and Pierre. . . . Sometimes my body almost says yes—I make an effort. It's dark. Rely on experiences. Imagine something—the expression on his face, his hair messed up, a crazy desire to look at him. That's it—dry, hard, local—carried away, hurts me—need to finish him, quickly with my mouth, to run" (*Journal*, 75).

The pair also draw in their writing on different stocks of images. While Roché's imagery is about divinely hard erections, Helen's imagery tends toward the fluid and the aquatic. She stresses the inner body, the surge of blood, the way desire resonates through her anatomy. She compares the desire she feels to a seed growing inside her. Often her metaphors emphasize liquidity—her desire "flows" toward Roché (*Journal*, 186). Fluid imagery also flows through her dreams: "I dreamt: I cut a vein in my neck. The blood runs along my body and under the earth in a stream with a swift current which flows in a specific direction, like a cable, and knows that it runs toward you. And she sings: 'you, my liveliest movement I flow in you'" (*Journal*, 565). In Helen's discourse passion "floods" and "spills." It radiates heat and expresses itself in vibrating flutters of energy.

17. Helen Hessel au naturel. Photo by Man Ray. Source: Man Ray Trust.

Helen stresses a kind of libidinal multiplicity and decentering; the geography of pleasure is seen as ranging within and over the entire body. Her approach is multisensorial, synesthetic. Despite her obsession with "le regard," Helen at times dehierarchizes the senses, implicitly overthrowing the primacy of sight (and thus of voyeurism), frequently appealing to the relatively neglected senses of smell, taste, touch, and hearing. In this sense Helen's thought accords very well with the feminism of Luce Irigaray, who relativizes the status of vision in favor of other, neglected senses. More than the other sense organs, Irigaray writes, "the eye objectifies and masters": "It sets at a distance, maintains the distance. In our culture, the predominance of the look over smell, taste, touch, hearing has brought an impoverishment of bodily relations." Male sexuality, for Irigaray, contributes to the "dis-embodiment" and "de-materialization" of eroticism. Male sexuality becomes privileged both because it operates visually and because the male sex is visible.[3]

Roché's prose is more instrumental, teleological, moving like a locomotive toward the final terminal of the "spend." We are reminded of Shakespeare's summing up of an experience with a prostitute in his sonnet: "an expense of spirit [for the Elizabethans, semen] in a waste of shame." Helen, in contrast, registers the random flow of thought and the slow passage of time in an impressionistic stream:

> I wash in my bedroom.
> Come back.
> Pierre is in bed.
> In his arms.
> Our little bed.
> A desire to have a room for us.
> God who stands up.
> Pierre Pierre.
> His fingernails on my back.
> My room. Injection. (Journal, 156)

Helen's view of sexuality is, above all, paratactic, a leveling vision of minglings and juxtapositions. Helen rejects what might be called the "monadization" or "diadization" of eroticism. For Helen, sexuality is not alienated from reproduction, from the progression of genera-tions; it always exists in relation to the general existence of the body and in relation to other persons. Whereas Roché tends to see sexuality exclusively as a "genital act," Helen sees it as a broad, multicentered canvas, a crowded space teeming with vital activities. For Helen, no conceptual hierarchy places copulation, or orgasm, at the summit of importance. In this sense she stands somewhat outside of what Stephen Heath calls "the sexual fix," the modern idolatry of sexuality as the imperious raison d'être of human existence.[4]

While Roché's écriture offers an idiosyncratic amalgam of relentless physical desire mingled with strangely abstract ideas, Helen's memoirs offer a surprising amount of medical, gynecological detail about such things as menstruation, abortions, sperm counts, and medical procedures. She is in this sense fascinated by what Bakhtin saw as the transgressive, self-transforming body. For the Bakhtin of *Rabelais and His World* the key elements of the body are those points at which it outgrows itself and transgresses its own limits, those places where the confines between bodies and between the body and the world are overcome, where there is interchange and inter-orientation. The body's central principle is growth and change; in exceeding its limits the body expresses its very essence.[5]

Helen's writing, in this sense, is extremely imagistic and sensuous. It is as if her body were a shifting series of vortices of energy, the site of radical differentiality. She is especially attentive to the phenomenology of her own sensations: "I'm floating, I'm gliding, his arms around me" (*Journal*, 378). Caressing her own hair, she writes: "I touch it, pinch it with my fingers, since only my fingers can telegraph whether my hair has felt something, as my ears witness the different sounds my hair makes" (*Journal*, 423). She even offers her hair a tongue-in-cheek ideological gloss, dubbing it "Free hair, socialist hair, independent hair" (*Journal*, 423). At times she expresses a solitary, autotelic self-delight: "I take off everything, walking around completely nude, slowly . . . Eve in paradise. I stretch out on the grass. The sun burns my face. I open my mouth to swallow the rays. I open my legs to let the sun enter" (*Journal*, 87).

Unlike Roché, who focuses more on sex and the hunt, Helen describes the nuances of mood and ambience. For example, she dedicates close attention to the kinetic and kinesthetic sensation of enjoying a wide repertoire of dance fashions—fox trot, waltz, polka, and so forth—seeing movement, in a quasi-utopian fashion, as collective jouissance: "Music. Everyone reunited under the authority of rhythm—all the movements conditioned by the movements of others—the unity of the couple—the four feet adjusting to one another, understanding one another, the tension derived from the consciousness of being watched, to be visible. It's beautiful" (*Journal*, 324).

At times, Helen's writing has a cinematic feeling, as when she describes their parting in a railroad station:

> *Our lips united—pain—which passes quickly.*
> *A whistle—wheels which turn.*
> *Finally, how beautiful to see the train begin to move.*
> *I wave to him, I see his arm waving to me. We're still facing toward*
> *each other—there, the wheeled caterpillar turns—I don't see him any*
> *longer. I turn on my heels.* (*Journal*, 477)

Alongside its mundane concreteness, Helen's style also reflects a level of theoretical ambition generally lacking in Roché. Lovemaking, for Helen, is at once theoretical and practical, a form of creative labor: "Vision theory: women and men who simply love, who give themselves without thinking about it, without a plan, without reserve, are seen as guilty beings, asocial, lazy, people to be punished. . . . The great artists of love perform important social work. They instinctively know after their first experience that human beings have more need to love than to be loved. Especially men" (*Journal*, 135). But men invariably disappoint Helen, whether through laziness (Franz), or through blind selfishness (Roché), or through lack of theatrical imagination (the case of another lover, Thankmar Munchhausen), or through the lover's sabotaging of her own desire for love (the case of the perpetual suitor Koch) (*Journal*, 135). Anticipating the feminine disenchantments of the age of *Men Are from Mars, Women Are from Venus*, Helen speculates that "there are (perhaps) only one hundred men in the world with the necessary force and will to really make themselves really lovable" (*Journal*, 135). Helen even theorizes the etiology of the exhibitionistic practice of some couples who socialize their desire by making love in public. (We are reminded that another German, Wilhelm Reich, was also theorizing sexuality, and especially "polymorphous perversity," in this same Weimar period.) "Here it's no longer a matter of taste, but of absolute power. One needs to have a natural disposition, but training is most important. Such people will be polygamous out of duty and always disappointed, more or less. If two such people find each other, their only pretext for complete happiness would be to let their love be seen, to show their perfect play to the world. Only that could save them from continual polygamy" (*Journal*, 136).

At another point, Helen spatializes her love relationships in the relational form of graphs, plotting herself as a "knot" joining various human "threads" (husband, lovers, children, relatives, friends) more or less distant in space (see *Journal*, 138).

In exaggerated form Helen and Roché wrestle with perennial dilemmas shared by millions of people, between the desire for intimacy and commitment and the desire for sexual freedom, between comfortable routine and the frisson of novelty. In this sense both Helen and Roché resist what they see as the numbing confinements of marriage. Although Helen and Pierre enjoy playing with the idea of being a normal couple—with children, in the same bed, the worker coming home from work every night—it is only that: play. Helen describes Roché, meanwhile, as detesting marriage because he doesn't want to take the trouble of being faithful or of being united in a single, common goal, to nurture love within a publicly associated "kind of society" (*Journal*, 468). But Helen, too, resists the "narrowness" of marriage. In this sense all three members of the ménage seem like harbingers of the sexual counterculture of the 1960s, the movement that tried to live creatively and polymorphously, outside of the system of conjugal regimentation.

Helen and Roché also differ in their concepts of jealousy and fidelity. While Roché is quite shameless, preoccupied only with not getting caught in his duplicities, Helen is more likely to speak candidly about her own feelings of guilt or shame and to worry over exactly how honest she should be with her lovers. Helen has the "honesty" to confide to her diary (and thus indirectly to Roché and Franz, in the cases where the two men read her diary) exactly when she has lied or dissembled: "I said yes," she tells her diary, "but I thought no" (*Journal*, 26). Or again: "I feign indifference" (13). Caught up in another love, she wonders if she should lie to Roché: "I'm ashamed. I'm afraid of seeing Pierre again. What should I tell him—there's nothing to tell him. Just that we kissed a bit. Faithful? Yes, I've been faithful. Have I cheated? Not at all" (*Journal*, 471). Responding to his betrayals, she at times threatens eye-for-an-eye erotic vengeance. "When I said I wanted your God to be mine alone," she writes Roché, "that's exactly what I meant. If you give it to another woman, I will not allow myself to love you before I make love with some man or other" (*Journal*, 555). Here we sense an element that often erupts in both the novel and the Truffaut adaptation, a kind of uncompromisingly harsh mathematics of sexual revenge, the tit-for-tat cuckolding of "nous sommes quittes" (Now we're even-Stephen).

Roché, meanwhile, is a compulsive flirt—in contemporary terms, a "sexaholic"—*even* when he is in love. We sense in Roché the absent center and perpetual flights of Don Juanism, the metonymic slide from one evanescent desire to another. As a romance junkie, Roché has an agenda-driven (and a full-agenda-ed) notion of "infidelity." Within his self-serving view the mere act of sexual intercourse does not actually constitute infidelity. Nor is it for him only a Clintonesque matter of oral sex not constituting "real sex." For Roché, even full-bodied inter-course does not constitute infidelity. Infidelity becomes serious and real only when one gives oneself up with total passion: "When I made love without passion, with a pretty pleasure with Bigey, for example, I did not feel like I was being unfaithful to Luk [Helen]." To a point Roché is consistent, since he acknowledges that "we are jealous about what women feel, not what they do" (*Carnets*, 124). At the same time, Roché applies a double standard, becoming jealous if anyone other than Franz touches Helen. At times, Roché's brutal selfishness can astonish, for example when he asks one of his many occasional lovers (Wiesel) if "[she] would be ready to raise a child generated by [himself] and another woman" (*Carnets*, 76). Symptomatically, Roché transfers this idea to Kate in the novel: "[Kate] asked whether Lucie would be willing to bring up the child she was going to have with Jim" (*Jules and Jim*, 135). Only very rarely, when he is himself made jealous, does Roché retrospectively imagine with any sense of reciprocity the suf-fering and pain that he might have caused others: "I feel in my heart a pain analogous to that which I must have caused for Mno [Gilberte, that is Germaine Bonnard]" (*Carnets*, 409).

Helen demonstrates a vigorous, quasi-feminist sense of personal independence. At the beginning of her relationship with Roché she writes, "I would hate to be tied to him, or to anyone. My joy works within myself" (*Journal*, 40). In stereographic notations she warns herself not to be weak: "To fight against amorous dependency toward Pierre. Not to authorize desire for him. Seek financial independence" (*Journal*, 78). Helen does not want to "love any single individual, or force [herself] in a single direction." Rather, she prefers to "spend myself in all directions" (*Journal*, 48). Her rejection of any form of dependency is total: "It's horrible to be dependent on another, to become all languorous in that person's absence. I know many women like that. I despise them. Something in me doesn't want it. I want to be myself and I fight like a bull against this languor" (*Journal*, 145).

At times Helen's search for independence mutates into a fantasy of erotic domination. In what she labels a "vision," she imagines herself reigning like a sultan over a veritable harem of servile men. Here we are reminded of Jules's description of her, both in the novel and in the film, as a "queen." In her fantasy, when she shouts "Enter!" twelve naked men enter the room. As they walk, she coolly examines their penises. When she says "Dance!" they dance. With the first one who dances, "his penis flaps against his legs and his stomach, always in rhythm. I choose him as the first. Later we'll see about the others. There are two or three who excite me, or perhaps all of them. I cannot let any of them escape" (*Journal*, 84). The fetishistically numerical aspect of the account anticipates Catherine Millet's erotic memoir, published some eight decades later.

While Roché in his diaries sometimes seems calculatingly evasive—he deploys coded references to hide certain liaisons from the jealous eyes of potential lover-readers—Helen is relentlessly honest, even when she is confused or incoherent. We sense this honesty in the exchanges of letters concerning a frequent cause of tension between them: Helen's pregnancy and Roché's reluctance to take up responsibility for the resulting baby. She writes to Roché that she demands his wholehearted participation:

> I don't have the right, I don't want it, I don't dare, I'm revolted by the idea of having a child which you do not wish with complete generosity and simplicity. . . . Reserves, conditions, precautions insult me, annoy me. . . . [T]hey are bourgeois and mediocre. I married and divorced Franz with a laugh. If for you these formalities are important from an "exploratory" point of view, for me they simply avoid

annoying situations. Family, authorities, etc. It seems to me stupid and cruelly démodé that you haven't married 17 [Gilberte, i.e., Germaine Bonnard]. . . . I want to act in open daylight, say everything publicly . . . not take a false name in a hotel. I refuse to do things in hiding. If that's a "sacrifice" for you, I don't accept it. (*Journal*, 596)

Learning of his cool response to her pregnancy, Helen regrets, in a December 12, 1921, letter, having imagined their child "with so much love": "You didn't know how to nurture my imagination, which was ready to think your love for me sufficiently strong to sweeten and soften pregnancy, which, to say the truth, is quite unbearable" (*Journal*, 599).

Helen suffers from the fact that Roché's letters concerning her pregnancy contain only "more or less hidden 'nos' and conditional 'yesses.'" Disappointed to find herself pregnant in the "least desirable of circumstances," she asks (in a December 13 letter) for a commitment, on Roché's part, to share responsibility for the new life they have created. Nor does she see abortion as a solution; for her, it would be an "ugly murder." And in the end she pleads, "Write me, speak to me. Dare to say everything." And in a letter written just two days later, she insists on the heavy responsibilities of parenthood: "A baby is as real as anything can be, a baby which, through the very fact of growing up, has a continual need of things that have to be paid for with money, work, and time. But the word 'responsibility' frightens you" (*Journal*, 598).[6]

When Helen realizes that Roché will not be forthcoming, she decides to have an abortion: "Let's not speak about it anymore, I'll put everything in order. I don't scold you. Be happy . . . make her [Bonnard] happy. I say that as a selfish wish, so that the death of the child will not be in vain" (*Journal*, 607). Thus, in an ultimate transcendence of jealousy, or perhaps in a parting aggression, she asks Roché to forget her and embrace her long-standing rival—Germaine Bonnard.

A later moment in Roché's life yields a veritable paroxysm of well-deserved and long-delayed comeuppance. Like a highflying Icarus, or like Claude's falling off the swing in the opening sequence of Truffaut's *Two English Girls*, he is brought down to earth with a thud. That is the moment, on July 15, 1933, when Roché, simultaneously involved with Germaine, Denise, and Helen, reveals to Helen that he has had a child with Denise. This is the moment when all the implied performative promises of the speech act of seduction—tacit promises of love or marriage, of commitment and offspring—are revealed to be hollow. When Helen tells Germaine about the child, both Germaine and Helen decide to break off with him, this time definitively. Helen returns to Franz, and Roché to Denise. Although Roché had always tried to convince himself that everything was simple, things had ended badly. Helen ended up calling him "the liar" and refused to see him. He also reads Germaine Bonnard's diary and discovers that she finds him impossible to live with, and Bonnard repeatedly tells others that her epitaph would read: "Her husband killed her."[7] Such are the "blowbacks" of amorous imperialism.

CHAPTER TWENTY

TWO ENGLISH GIRLS
THE NOVEL

A S POINTED OUT earlier, *Two English Girls* was based on Roché's memories of a triangular relationship between himself and two English sisters, Margaret and Violet Hart, a liaison that lasted, in one form or another, from 1899 to 1914. (Interestingly, all three members of this earlier ménage had been orphaned of their fathers.) In a short essay, perhaps intended to be a blurb for the book, Roché epitomized the novel as follows:

> My eightieth year is approaching. Decrepitude? Perhaps, but I hardly notice it. What a panorama! What sweet breaths of wind at this summit. One has one's whole life before one, like a nearly perfect sphere.
>
> Here is one of the games I play every morning before going to sleep.
>
> In parallel, I focus on a period of my life and I let it gently unroll each evening, like a film in episodes.
>
> . . . the facts: two English sisters, between eighteen and twenty. Muriel and Anne, and myself, Claude, French, eighteen years old, all three of us full of ideas, rather advanced ideas for 1899, making up a trio of friends, studying, playing, traveling together without flirtation. Two years flow by.
>
> We innocently scandalize the sisters' little English town and the mother of the two sisters asks me to cease my visits. I cannot stay away, especially from Muriel, whose hand I ask in marriage. A cold Puritan, she firmly says "No" but she offers to continue to

be my sister. I try out this possibility. Anne helps us. Three months later our mothers intervene, for the sake of "our health." We agree to separate for one year. I am sure that Muriel will never love me, and I commit myself to study and celibacy, a choice which moves Muriel towards a "Yes."

After a great deal of traveling hither and thither, Anne and I take up with each other again. One beautiful day in Paris she lets me cover her young breast in her hand. Later, by a Swiss lake, although she is still half a boy, she lets me take her . . .

At a distance I love both of them. Muriel tells Anne that she is in love with me, and Anne says that she and I have been lovers. After a year Muriel returns to give herself and to take me. . . . We think of marrying. But race, our ways of life, religion, studies—and the Channel—hold us back, and become obstacles. We love each other, but, in spite of ourselves, we pull back. . . . Four years later Muriel marries an "ordinary" Englishman.[1]

Roché based *Two English Girls* on his own recollections, on his letters and diaries, and on the letters and diaries of the two sisters, which he held either because he had received them directly at the time or because Margaret Hart gave them to him subsequently (especially in the case of unsent letters). Thus the resulting text was a kind of "documentary novel." Yet while the novel seems to consist of authentic and unrevised materials, Ian MacKillop points out that, in fact, almost all the materials were slightly rewritten and partially reinvented. Roché's first (literary) "adaptation," then, preceded Truffaut's cinematic adaptation. Violet Hart herself, furthermore, distinguished between the diary entries meant for a wider audience and those meant for herself alone, since "I would not write with the same absolute freedom unless I knew this was for myself alone."[2]

A kind of bildungsroman à trois, the novel charts the intertwined sentimental educations of three young people. Roché's preparation for writing the book included character sketches of the three principals. Anne is described as "independent," "curious," "sensual," and "a sculptor." Muriel is described as a "prophet," blessed with a pious altruism, but also as an actress performing in multiple arenas. Roché/Claude describes himself as a quick learner, "modest" yet "ambitious." At times the writing fractures into what Derrida would later call "split writing," within which the diaries or the letters of the protagonists are set side by side on the page. (We are reminded both of Roché's polyphonic project and of the modernist fondness for collage.) At the same time, the text also has a collective, transpersonal, and even cross-cultural thrust, especially in its repeated contrasts between Victorian, puritanical England and sophisticated, libertine France, as well as between English people and French people generally. The novel contrasts two national styles and ways of life at a time when the two countries were seen as polar opposites to the point that a conjugal alliance between a French man and an English woman, for example, was seen as so audaciously *outré* that it was called "a mixed marriage," as if it were a question, to use Roché's terminology, of two different "races."

The novel and the various diaries concerning Roché's relationship with the two sisters form a rich archive of commentary concerning international cultural exchange at the turn of the century. Roché constantly contrasts the free libidinous ways of the French with the committed austerity of the English, French mendacity with English honesty, French nonchalance with English seriousness, French inefficiency with English productivity. On meeting Anne for the first time, Claude becomes curious about her English homeland, with its paradoxical combination of "personal modesty with national pride, conformity and Shakespeare, the Bible and Scotch whiskey."[3] Anne admits that the English are less lively and open than the French but insists that they are also full of fantasy ("fantaisistes") in their own idiosyncratic way. For Claude, the two "races" have opposite concerns; the English are preoccupied with ethics, the French with aesthetics.

The triangular relationship takes place against the backdrop of international tension. Rumors of a possible Anglo-French war, linked to inter-European imperial rivalries in Africa, were then very much in the air. An element of what would later be called "(trans)national allegory" thus pervades *Two English Girls*, as it does *Jules and Jim*. Both novels purvey the same conjugation of transnational friendship on a personal plane and international conflict on a geopolitical plane. In both, love is implicitly proffered as an alternative to war. Yet at times love itself looks like war by other means. The pan-European theme that pervades not only *Jules and Jim* but also the journals and novels of Helen Grund and Franz Hessel emerges in *Two English Girls* in an offhand and facetious manner, as when the two sisters refer to Claude, because of his wide knowledge of European literature, as "the continent." "A good continental," Muriel reminds Claude, "should notice when his insular interlocutor is tired" (140).

Like the Helen Grund–Franz Hessel–Henri-Pierre Roché ménage, the similarly transnational threesome of Henri-Pierre, Violet, and Margaret shared the practice of diary writing. Roché read Margaret's journals for 1902 and thought of writing a novel based on the journals of all three participants. Asking Margaret for her letters, Roché appeals to her sense of civic virtue: "the story of our difficulties may prove helpful to others," the line that Truffaut uses as a preamble for his adaptation. In a sense Roché was already conceptualizing something like what he later called "polyphonic writing" vis-à-vis the Hessel-Grund-Roché ménage. Pierre even broached, with Margaret in England, the subject of a possible analytical history of their relationship. As "peaceful collaborators"—again the phrase carries overtones of international diplomacy—he would write one volume, while Margaret would write a companion volume. She would be entrusted with the English translation and furnish an appendix of fragments or case histories. Pledging to write with complete honesty, Roché would write "in order to be contradicted," avoiding dogmatism and hypocrisy. His goal would be to "study the moral, intellectual, social and sexual relations between Man and Woman."[4]

The novel *Two English Girls* went through an interminable process of revision. Roché contemplated many possible titles, including *Two English Girls, Two Sisters, Anne and Muriel, A Puritanical Girl,* and *The Great North.* (The complete original title was *Deux sœurs, ou: Two English girls et le continent* [Two Sisters, or: Two English Girls and the Continent].) The original title's indeterminacy—encapsulated in the *or*—mirrors the indecision, not only between possible titles but also between various women, that marks Roché's life as a whole. Roché first thought of writing the novel in 1903, when he asked Margaret for the letters he had sent her. But he had to organize all the letters in his possession and translate them into French. Then he had to tidy up the language, increasing the precision without altering the spirit. Roché also effects a change in genre. Margaret saw her own journal as a kind of "dream work," belonging to what she called the "vie irréelle." (We are reminded of another, roughly contemporaneous, English writer, Virginia Woolf, and her attempt to register the flow of fantasy and consciousness.) On the title page Margaret wrote to an imagined reader: "Private—Do not forget that much of this belongs to the life of the imagination."[5] At times, relying on memory or using creative license, Roché created new letters, some written in English. In fact, nearly every piece in the mosaic, as Ian MacKillop points out, was "carefully rewritten and interspersed with inventions."[6] In preparing for the novel, Roché wrote up a three-column set of character sketches:

ANNE	MURIEL	CLAUDE
Independent, Diana-type. Comrade. Friend. Curious: a bit sensual. No question of children. But sculpture. Wants Claude to make her a woman Idealist for her sculpture	Divided—alternate type: "prophet." Altruism. Pious. Redhead (father). Pride. anger. Born Writer. Realist, mystical. Intelligence. Napoleonism. Actress. Given to multiple domains.	A modest master. But: learns, writes. Quick angers and indignation. Ambitious for his work.

In generic terms the Roché novel formed an oxymoronic mélange of the old-fashioned and the experimental. It was old-fashioned in that it invoked two of the most venerable of literary genres—the diary/confession and the epistolary novel. Combining the traditions both of Rousseau's autobiographical *Confession* and of Samuel Richardson's melodramatic novels *Pamela* and *Clarissa*, Roché's novel presents a multilateral exchange of letters: Claude writes to Muriel, Muriel writes to Claude, Claude writes to Muriel and Anne, Anne writes to Claude, Claude reports Clair's memories. At the same time, what appears through the interstices of the letters and diaries together is a plural novel of development or maturation, one with three parallel and evolving voices. The novel is also audacious in attempting to orchestrate disparate and contradictory voices. The special challenge for Roché, rooted in the reality of a transnational and in some ways Platonic set of relationships, was to take characters who rarely shared the same space, who enjoyed an abstract, literary love, who communicated with each other through letters and with their own selves through their diaries—and somehow manage to create the sense of urgent flow associated with a direct narrative presentation of events, while also remaining more or less faithful to the historical record. The novel proper is preceded by Muriel's letter to Claude (June 9, 1901), in which she proclaims her mystical faith, shared with her sister, in completely monogamous romantic love:

> I believe that for each woman there has been created a man who will be her spouse. Although there may exist several men with whom she might have a peaceful, useful, and even an agreeable life, there is only one who can be the perfect mate. This perfect mate might die. He might never meet his mate, or even be married to someone else. In that case it is better for the woman that she never marry. . . . That is how we think, Anne and I, ever since our childhood. For my part, I will probably never marry, because I have a task before me which I can better carry out alone, but if God had me meet my man, then I would marry him. (unpaged)

The passage already foreshadows both the self-effacing solidarity and the intellectual affinity between the two sisters and the complex contradictoriness of Muriel's personality. Muriel states confidently that she will not marry, yet she also will marry. Her task requires her being alone, yet for each woman there is destined a man created to be her mate, and so forth.

An impossibility of fulfillment, a kind of *promesse de malheur*, seems to be inscribed into Muriel's contradictory aspirations. But the character of Claude, too, is "born" under the sign of frustration and failure. The book's plot begins, revealingly, with a kind of Icarus story, an account of a giddy Claude falling from a garden trapeze, all recounted in a somewhat telegraphic style: "the doctor declares: 'Broken ligaments. Six weeks in bed. Possible lifelong weakness in the legs.' My vanity is punished. I've broken my best part. I return to Paris, sick, I go to bed and start reading excessively" (13).

For Roché, reading and, later, writing become a soothing balm for the "falls" and failures of life. The novel telescopes the narrative by dispensing with descriptive physical detail and stressing instead what most interests Roché—the characters and their sensibilities and relationships. The beginning of the novel is a wonder of rapid and efficient exposition. Within the highly condensed space of the three initial pages, two of the principals—Anne and Claude—have met each other, spoken about their tastes and values, and decided together that Claude will visit Wales. The first few pages inaugurate many of the leitmotifs of the novel. One leitmotif concerns the theme of mimesis and imitation, as when Anne tells Claude that the slightly older Muriel is her paradigm and role model. Claude first sees Muriel as an image, in the form of her portrait as a thirteen-year-old girl, graced with a look that mingles duty and humor.

The novel constantly thematizes the subject of vision, thus providing fodder for a reflexive dimension in the Truffaut film. Arriving in Wales, Claude is at first constantly deprived of any view of Muriel, since she is in her room, and he is denied any view of her eyes; because of "a problem," she hides them from sight. Here we find an early instance of what will become a major theme in the novel—the notion of perturbed or problematic vision. As if in literal respect for the expression "love is blind," Muriel is shown as blinkered, without sight.

Struck by Anne's beauty, Claude experiences a Stendhalian shyness as he represses an impulse to take her hand: "I dreamed of taking her hand. In my head, I hear an imaginary, distant voice, Anne's voice saying 'So . . . kiss me quick'" (19–20).

The undercurrent of eroticism at this point is both pulsingly insistent and continually repressed. Every meeting is chaperoned, mediated and supervised by another human presence, whether that of one of the sisters or of the mother or of the neighbor, Mr. Flint. Claude is surprised that the two sisters and their two brothers—the brothers are excised from the film version—practice a kind of innocent nudism: they bathe in the nude but at two hundred meters distance from one another, with the rule that whoever looks will be "disqualified." Despite his own desire to look, Claude obeys this peculiarly English code of "forced honesty" (21). At the same time, Claude records his observations concerning the appearance and behavior of the two sisters—for example his appreciation of the nape of Muriel's neck and her way of swiveling her hips ("which would have been provocative in another woman, but not in her" [22]). Gradually, the three become inseparable. Claude appreciates their lack of vanity, their sense of fair play, and what he sees as their very English refusal to speak ill of others. The three friends dream of visiting Paris, and through a magical filmlike mobility, they actually arrive there. As they admire the "spine" of Notre Dame, Claude wonders: "Will I love Muriel one day?" They revel in the vibrancy of Parisian streets and cafés. And Claude in his journal throws off casual pearls of associative non sequiturs: "One day when we had read too much and it was raining . . . " (201).

We then move to Muriel's diary. During the same visit to Notre Dame, she wonders not whether she will love Claude but whether "she *merits* a friend like Claude" (italics mine), thus unknowingly illustrating Claude's thesis that in England everything revolves around ethics. Interestingly, the diary even includes Muriel's analysis of her own diary. Reading again her own speculations about the nature of her future relationship with Claude, she notes, "I see in this diary entry an intense friendship, a bit of romanticism, but not a trace of what I would call love" (32). The threesome resume their reading sessions, and Claude remarks that "sometimes I feel like touching their hands" (37). At times, tensions disturb the idyllic picture. Claude says of Muriel, "She finds me spoiled, an only child, and typically French. I find her brutal and too sure of herself" (39). On a country hike, in the company of Mrs. Brown, during a rainstorm they huddle together to play the "pressed lemon" game, which consists of rocking shoulders and arms together, an innocently flirtatious moment picked up in the Truffaut film. Claude writes about the episode in his journal: "I've spent months next to her, always trying to avoid touching her fingers, or to look at her hands and here she is pressing against me with all her strength. . . . I can't believe it. She is elastic. Her temples form pearls. I don't dare to breathe in her aroma" (41). Mrs. Brown cuts off the flirtatious frictions with a curt, "That will be enough" (41).

In his diary Claude also tells of his erotic adventures apart from the sisters—adventures not taken up in the Truffaut film. One such adventure involves a fortuitous encounter with a Spanish woman, Pilar, whom he first meets in the Burgos cathedral during Mass. In a scene reminiscent of the sacramental pornography of certain Buñuel films— for example, the opening sequence of *El*, set during a Catholic mass, where the protagonist falls in love with the heroine's feet—with their characteristic conjugation of eroticism and religiosity, Claude glimpses a beautiful woman at prayer, observes her taking communion, and follows "the flesh that prays" into a dark niche of the cathedral. The woman takes the initiative by taking his hand. Claude writes metaphorically of his own desire: "The Mediterranean swells within me." In bed later, they discuss their earlier sexual experience: "'It's my first time,' I say. 'Is that possible?' she asks laughingly. 'Until I was eleven I believed that if the naked statues of women in the public parks were lacking a little masculine penis, it was due only to the modesty and discretion of the sculptors. Later, in the painters' ateliers, I saw nude models, and I almost missed my imaginary women.' 'And me?' Pilar asked. 'You have what it takes'" (47).

Their encounter thus takes place under the sign of fetishism—the "I know, but nevertheless" of Claude's speculations about women's hidden penises. In a variation on the same theme Claude wonders if Muriel and Anne belong to the same species as Pilar. "Would they be capable of the same abandon? . . . [T]hey belong to another planet, to which I shall soon return, where what I lived here is excluded" (47).

Much of the conversation in *Two English Girls* touches on an issue that we have encountered before: the possibility of enjoying a love perturbed by jealousy. When Claude suggests that "it's good that some human beings go beyond the law," Muriel responds that "in that case one has to be ready to sacrifice oneself" (233). The remark anticipates Jim's postménage reminder to Catherine—included in both novel and film—that pioneers must be "humble and selfless." In Spain Claude meets a Spanish gentleman who believes in open marriage, open at least as far as the man is concerned. Claude asks how he would react if his wife lived by the same rules. The Spaniard responds that it is only Claude's Frenchness and his youth that blind him to the pleasures of a perfect Spanish marriage: "I adore my wife, the rest means nothing, and the possibility that you evoke could never happen" (50). On the same trip, Claude researches provincial bordellos, where his intercourse with the prostitutes is exclusively verbal. The madam compares her social role to that of a mayor or general, who contributes to public health and the well-being of marriages, in an institution where one finds "neither diseases nor scandals" (54).

In London Claude enjoys the soapbox oratory of Hyde Park. He admires the majestic cupola and the thick tables and comfortable armchairs of the British Museum and—in a very French appreciation of the user-friendly codes of British (as opposed to French) libraries— the "generosity of the catalogues and the lack of formalities" (59). He sees George Bernard Shaw, wearing his world-famous sarcastic smile, at the Fabian Society, but in general he finds the English "argumentative"—a surprising accusation for a Parisian—as well as "scornful, insensitive, and lacking in imagination" (60). Back in Wales Claude has a long conversation with Mrs. Brown, who worries that the activities of the threesome might provoke gossip in the town. Although the two daughters strike Claude as reserved and puritanical, their mother speaks of their "advanced ideas," of which she herself does not approve. The mother reports that Anne has told her that a romance might grow between Claude and Muriel, an announcement that comes as a revelation to Claude himself. He writes in his diary: "I never even dreamed she could love me. Whence my inaction. Mrs. Brown has unknowingly opened up a breach—I rush into it. I throw myself toward Muriel. I risk everything" (69).

But when he declares himself in a letter, Muriel's response is brutal:

> *Your letter is terrible.*
> *You don't know me.*
> *I love you as a sister, and even then not always.*
> *Dissipate your romantic vision.*
> *I love little and I love few. I am rough and rude.*
> *Anne and my brothers are sufficient for me.* (73)

As the queen of ambivalence, Muriel writes to her sister that she could imagine herself loving Claude but that the idea of Claude's loving her was "out of the question." Here again Muriel inscribes an axiomatic unrealizability into any potential relationship, perhaps because of suspicions about Roché or perhaps because of a conviction that such a relationship could never last. In another letter to Claude, dated four days later (January 28, 1902), she makes the following contradictory pronouncements:

"I love you, but not with love." . . .
"I played at imagining that I might perhaps love you." . . .

"Before Mother and before God: I don't have love for you." . . . "I wanted to see you . . . before receiving your letter. Now, I am afraid of you. I was at ease with you. I love you more absent than present." . . .

"Am I brutal? Repeat: 'She doesn't love me. I don't love her. We are brother and sister.' . . . I have no heart: that's why I don't love you and would never love anyone."

At the same time, in letters to Anne, Muriel reveals her passion for Claude: "It has happened to me that I would enjoy crying out, all alone in the woods, 'Claude, I love you.' And then the same evening, kneeling at prayer, to say: 'My God, I don't love him'" (76–77). The two sisters and Claude become thoroughly intertwined in their shared confidences. Anne writes to Claude that Muriel is incapable of measuring her own feelings, and Anne encloses Muriel's letter to her for Claude's perusal. In another letter (February 5, 1902) Anne reminds Claude of the biblical words concerning another set of sisters: "And Jacob labored and waited seven years for Rachel, because of the love he bore her."

The diary entries of the three principals mingle hyperventilating romanticism with down-to-earth pragmatism. In a kind of amorous narratology Claude charts the possibilities in terms of how their stories might actually turn out. In telescoped language Claude lists four possible outcomes with Margaret: (1) Goodbye; (2) Friends; (3) Uncertainty; and (4) Marriage. But he also expresses his doubts about the conventional trajectory of courtship: "male pursuit, desire increased on capture, followed by its decline and the end of curiosity."[7] And anticipating future tensions with Helen, Claude finds the idea of children completely irrational, an idea whose absurdity he characterizes in a mathematical formula: "We are two—we want to become one—we become three."[8]

Meanwhile, the friendship of the threesome progresses, as they reveal more and more about their feelings and experiences. Claude speaks in his diary (and tells the sisters) about a certain Thérèse, a circus performer who migrates to Montmartre from the provinces and who sleeps casually with a series of men who put her up for the night (96). (As we have seen, Truffaut borrowed the Thérèse character for *Jules and Jim*, where he emphasizes her high-velocity, trainlike recounting of her whirlwind marriages and affairs.) The two sisters are amazed that in France a woman can pursue her fantasies without suffering negative social consequences. But Claude's desire, as befits the art collector that Roché also was, is always filtered through the aesthetic: "Between the columns, struck by the sun's rays filtered through a stained-glass window, her beauty becomes unbearable" (98). He asks Muriel, for the first time, in elliptical language, "Muriel, would you like us one day?" With the generosity typical of Roché's characters, sister Anne, on learning of this other "us," responds: "I am happy. I think of you two." But Claude must also consult a less generous participant in the schema, the grand and pitiless surveyor of the whole erotic scene: his mother. He writes to her: "I love Muriel. I was waiting, before I told you, for a little hope. I only have a little. We will see each other more. I think this news will give you joy. . . . Muriel resembles you" (99).

The fact that Claire replies through a telegram suggests a kind of panic in the face of a possible commitment to Muriel on Claude's part. Note the urgency of her response: "Your health insufficient to found a home. You are two idealists. Come. Claire" (99).

Meanwhile, Muriel is shocked when she comprehends the true nature of Claude's earlier liaison with Pilar: "Your confession gives me extreme pain. If someone had said that about you, I would have sworn on the Bible that it wasn't true. . . . It's a shame that I'm English. If my mother and brother knew about it, they would rather see me dead than see me as your wife. . . . Expect nothing from me" (101). In an attitude that combines a severe Puritanism with a kind of proto-feminism, Muriel sees Claude as having "committed a crime against a woman" (102). The rigidity of her attitude is explicable, in part, by the tenor of her times. The Victorians, as we know, equated abstinence or sexual control with moral and religious purity. They contrasted pedestaled and restrained women with potentially dissolute and degenerate men. Anne's reaction, for its part, is no less harsh. For her, Claude has "committed what I was taught to be one of the worst things on earth" (106).

Despite Muriel's dramatic ultimatums—"Explain nothing. I can not listen"—she continues to speak ambivalently, hinting at a love that careens between joy and malaise. She reports that she often imagines telling Claude, "Leave!" but then quickly adds "and take me with you!"

Her discourse is marked by the grammatical signifiers of ambivalence, especially modals and conditionals: "If I had understood earlier, there would have been nothing between us" (102; italics mine). A few hours later she writes, "So I didn't really know you at all. My great affection, my hesitation was based on a mirage. You are dead inside of me" (102). But her feelings change from moment to moment, and an hour later she claims to be split into two: "I am half against you, and half with you" (104).

Such is Muriel's revulsion at Claude's liaison with Pilar that she cannot even bring herself to write the word *affair*, calling it instead a "thing:" "I should understand—or condemn you without any appeal. I became your sister only because I believed, in my way, that you were pure. I will never find that thing good. It's a precipice" (103–104).

Conjecturing that Claude might have left Pilar pregnant, she instantly identifies with Pilar and demands that Claude assume any potential paternal responsibilities. She speaks of their love in the language of loss, and even of death, and then, in words that Truffaut will transfer to Catherine in *Jules and Jim*, she invokes a kind of seesaw of love, a zero-sum game in which one must be up and the other down: "We shouldn't suffer at the same time; when you stop, I'll begin" (105). Interestingly, nothing of Claude's affair with Pilar, or Muriel's reaction to it, makes its way into Truffaut's adaptation.

Muriel is always aware of Claude's mother's potentially violent reaction to any relationship with Claude. Fascinated by Claude's relationship with Claire, and even Claire's relationship with her husband, Muriel comes to identify with Claire, with whom she shares the ideal of perpetual allegiance to a single man. At the same time, she is offended by Claire's hostility: "Your mother," she complains, "has invented a serial novel in which I am the siren and the bad fairy. She throws herself into this story, accuses me of being a flirt, a plotter, of setting a trap" (112).

Muriel is forced to recognize that Claire will do everything in her power to separate them. Claire even warns Anne that if Claude were to marry Muriel, she would refuse to see not only Muriel but also her own son and even any children that might result from the relationship. Muriel is especially disappointed because she had generously identified with Claire, projecting her as a romantic, idealistic, and monogamous person like herself. When Claude tells Muriel that his mother claimed to never have enjoyed love in physical terms, the puritanical Muriel responds that the fact "ennobles her in my eyes" (127). Muriel also speaks of her intense relationship with God and religion, a relation overlaid with sublimated sexual overtones. At thirteen she considers herself "possessed by God." She tells Him: "Lord, here I am. I am yours. Accept me. I will work for You" (185). Given her own ardent faith, she has difficulty accepting Claude's denial of the divinity of Christ.

At one point Claude conveys Claire's memories ("as she had recounted them so many times") transposed into the first person. Claire describes the *coup de foudre* between her husband-to-be Pierre and herself: "Pierre entered the room for the first time. He noticed me and thought: 'I will marry her.' I saw him and I thought exactly the same thing. [The next day], we exchanged a look which said: 'It's agreed'" (114).

Claire's erotic life with Pierre, we remember, was also mediated and nourished by art. Pierre courted Roché's mother "not with flowers, but with books."[9] Claire enlists artistic analogies even in relation to her way of bringing up her son: "I called you my monument and built you up, stone by stone" (137). One of Claire's stories evokes a genetic "artsiness" running in the family, a kind of painterly DNA. Claire reports that her husband Pierre loved painting and that he proposed to Claire that during her pregnancy they should visit the Louvre, so "their son would love painting" (115). In this sense Claude is cofathered, as it were, by Art.

But Claude is the son not only of his father and of Art but also of Oedipus. The mother reminds the son that at the age of four he had solemnly asked to marry her "when I [Claire] would be little and he (Claude) would be big" (116). Claude also recounts the incident, mentioned earlier, of the dream where his mother penetrates his sex with a needle, opening up the orifice and causing great pain, piercing "something deep within me." And he explains, that "after that dream, Claire no longer had any physical attraction for me. The link was broken. My filial love continued intact, but also a ferocious independence inhabited me, and the search for a woman, the opposite of Claire, but who also might resemble her" (11).

Muriel's response to Claude's report about Claire is to discern the strong triangular link connecting father, mother, and son: "Now, I understand. You are for Claire an extension of her husband Pierre, and that she cannot share" (119). But she also criticizes Claude from a very middle-class English perspective: "You were an only child, with a fragile infancy, like a little prince with no obligations, free to indulge his imagination. . . . [Y]ou were without sport, manual labor, which, for our English eyes, is a crime against childhood. You have little sense of realities, and you have a lively natural egoism, yet you also fight against that egoism, in your way, and thus go farther than me or Anne" (119).

Then Muriel speaks briefly of her own father, an element completely absent from the film. Speaking more generally, the characters bond, throughout the book, thanks to their fondness for art. Anne is delighted, for example, when Claude mentions one of her favorite paintings, *La Jeune fille aux yeux bandes.* (The title evokes again the leitmotif of blinkered vision.) Their conversation turns always around painting and sculpture; they get to know each other through their aesthetic responses to art. Their conversation is also laced with literary references of such writers as Nietzsche, Zola, Trollope, Laforgue, and Schopenhauer. Claude writes of Muriel that "she quotes the Bible and Anne Verlaine, and I quote Sancho Panza" (23). Muriel speaks of finding the bloody incidents in Zola's *Germinal* "hideous," but she is nonetheless grateful to the author for "rolling her in enormous and permanent misery" (122). When Anne hails Claude as "La France," Muriel reminds Anne of Claude's pan-European literary quality as symbolically "the continent," since he has also acquainted them with Cervantes, Dante, Schopenhauer, Ibsen, and Tolstoy.

The most innovative narrational feature of the Roché novel is its use of "split writing" in the chapter titled, appropriately enough, "La Séparation." Roché juxtaposes, in parallel columns, the diary entries of Muriel and Claude from the same day (May 29, 1902). Through the literary equivalent of a split-screen effect, one passage sets Muriel's dialogue with God alongside Claude's internal monologue with himself. Another passage offers Claude and Muriel's reflections on their feelings about being separated, with Muriel on the left and Claude on the right:

In the middle of tennis, which
Claude loves, after two sets,
had trouble seeing and had
to go in and lie on my bed. I
would love to be active, gay,
indefatigable!

you do not know this world.

Obedient to I know not what
I command. I put down my
rifle and came into all this
beauty, of which you were a
part,
Muriel. I think that
Should I start
taking siestas again. (161)

This unusual juxtaposition on the page of the words of separated lovers reminds us of certain filmic scenes—for example the magical reuniting of the yearning lovers in Vigo's *L'Atalante*—where specifically cinematic resources (split screen, superimposition, montage) magically overcome the diegetic separation of a couple by artfully reuniting them (in a transrealist chronotope of erotic fusion) within the space of the screen.

In her diary Muriel speaks about her own hallucinatory imagination. For her, every passing silhouette of a woman in black is Claire, and every tall man is Claude. But Claude is already distancing himself from Muriel and at one point imagines himself trading the gothically tormented Muriel for a simple, quiet, good, and robust woman. In an (unsent) letter to Claude, Muriel reflects on the treadmill of their impossible love: "Your response is no. Mine is yes. We have changed places, as in a game of musical chairs" (169). At times, Muriel's ambivalence takes rhyming, quasi-poetic form:

> *Aujourd'hui je suis prête.*
> *À force de m'attendre, il s'est fait ascète.*
> *(Today I am ready.*
> *But given all the waiting, he has become ascetic.)* (170)

The poetry in the novel includes the lines that Truffaut borrowed for the overture of *Jules and Jim*:

> *Tu m'as dit: "Je t'aime."*
> *Je t'ai dit: "Attends"*
> *J'allais dire: "Prends-moi."*

Tu m'as dit: "Va-t-en."
(You told me: "I love you."
I told you: "Wait"
I was going to say: "Take me."
And you told me: "Go away.") (172)

As these minipoems suggest, love in *Two English Girls* is almost always unrequited, nonsynchronous, out of step.

Muriel is also irritated by Claude's between-the-lines allusions to his affairs with other women, euphemistically evoked by his innocent-sounding phrase "des amies femmes" (women friends). She wonders how he has time to see other women and what he seeks in them. Muriel's love, for its part, is marked by flight and evasion. Embroidered with illusions and fantasies, it flees the here and now. Even before any real affair with Claude begins, Muriel is full of conjectures and Romanesque imaginings: "If you should leave for years at a time, like an explorer, or a pastor or a sailor, the spiritual presence of your wife will accompany you" (111). Although contradictory in the extreme, Muriel passionately believes, even if only momentarily, in her transitory convictions.

In her letter of June 1903 Muriel makes a "confession." After reading a rather puritanical sexual manual—"What a Young Woman Should Know"—Muriel recognizes with shock that she has been engaging in "bad habits" that "weaken both body and mind" (183) and ultimately lead to morbidity and disequilibrium, swollen eyes, and chronic fatigue. The "bad habit" in question is, of course, the "solitary vice" of masturbation. And here we must open a parenthesis for a background discussion of the views of masturbation in the period of the Roché novel. The rejection, even demonization, of masturbation was hardly a new phenomenon; in Europe it goes at least as far back as the anonymous eighteenth-century pamphlet *Onania*, whose subtitle read, in part, "The Heinous sin of Self Pollution, and all its Frightful Consequences, in both SEXES Considered, with Spiritual and Physical Advice to those who have already injured themselves by this abominable practice."[10] Masturbation was accused of causing palsies, distempers, fits, even death. But discourses about masturbation were particularly fevered and contradictory around the turn of the century. For the Victorians, as Thomas W. Laqueur points out in his encyclopedic study, masturbation fascinated because of its secrecy—it was not called "the secret vice" for nothing—for the ease with which it could be practiced, for its susceptibility to excess, and for its purely imaginary nature. In proto-Derridean language Rousseau had earlier called masturbation a "dangerous supplement," but at the time of the adolescence of the two sisters the discourses had become especially conflictual, to the point that masturbation became, in Laqueur's telling phrase, a veritable "doppelganger of modernity."[11] On the one hand, masturbation was pathologized as "self-pollution" and was accused of leading, especially in girls, to the collapse of the nervous system and even to an early grave. Richard von Krafft-Ebing, for example, linked masturbation to criminality and saw masturbation after childhood as prone to "contaminate" and even atrophy "all noble and ideal sentiments."[12] In *Scouting for Boys* (1908) the founder of the Boy Scouts, Lord Baden Powell, denounced the "beastliness" of masturbation, which led to healthy boys becoming feeble in body and mind and ending up in the insane asylum. Victorian inventors even devised penis switches that could activate an electric bell in the parents' bedroom if the son had an erection. Dr. Sturgess's book *Treatment of Masturbation*, published in 1900, exactly during the period of Roché's relationship with the Hart sisters, recommended a male "chastity belt."[13]

On the other hand, enlightened sexology declared that masturbation was neither a sickness nor a sin, although it might be a sign of an immature "merely clitoral" or pregenital sexuality. In a book published just six years before Muriel's anguished letter, Havelock Ellis argued that masturbation was a universal practice, at the very kernel of human sexuality. Yet still others argued that autoerotic excesses during adolescence could foster "false and high strung ideals," a phrase that in some ways would seem to characterize Muriel.[14] "Reading" her own feelings through the homiletic and pseudoscientific literature of the time, Muriel is convinced that she is "damaged," since Nature forgives nothing, and she is no longer to be numbered among "the pure." She thanks God, even, that she never married, since she would have been such an "unworthy" wife.

Muriel explains how she was initiated into masturbation by a childhood girlfriend, Clarisse, when she was eight years of age:

> When we were alone, she took off her nightgown, folded it and put it under the eiderdown. She removed mine as well, folded it and

placed it with hers. She spread the sheet over us and took me in her arms. I was all devotion for her. It was a night of the caresses of two little girls, one girl full of initiative, the other docile. . . . She taught me that it was enjoyable to touch certain parts of our bodies, especially one particular part. And we did it every night. At dawn, we would put on our nightgowns again. She persuaded me that it was our little secret and that I should never tell anyone. (184–185)

Here Muriel has ventured into doubly dangerous territory—masturbation and lesbianism—at a time when the medical and popular literature was often harsh and homophobic. In the work of Krafft-Ebing and Havelock Ellis, for example, lesbianism was associated with disease, perversion, and even paranoia.

In her struggle against "bad habits" Muriel relishes victories and laments defeats. At times masturbation becomes a soporific, a handy way of inducing sleep. At times, the encounter with "the thing"—the expression recalls Freud's "Id"—recalls some gothic struggle with the inextinguishable monsters of horror films: "When the Thing imperiously called me," Muriel writes, "I clenched my hands, and buried my face in the pillow, while imploring God. If I didn't manage to sleep, or to interest myself in something else, the horrible Beast returned until I would welcome it, quickly and fully, in order to get rid of it, to forget it. And I forbade myself to pray afterwards" (187).

For Muriel, the apparently simple act of self-pleasuring has become the equivalent of a world-historical tragedy. Her discourse in such passages forms a veritable symptomology of a repressed era when masturbation was assumed to stunt development, diminish powers of memory, and cause insanity, all maladies that were then transmitted to the innocent children of the self-abuser. After receiving a letter from the "League of Christian Women," Muriel points out that if she had known that the same body part that her girlfriend Clarisse touched also produced babies, she would have refused her friend's advances. She wonders if her migraines, her eye pains, and her depression are all a punishment for her "bad habits."

Throughout, the novel emphasizes the mental obstacles to sexual expression, obstacles at once invisible and real, rather like the invisible barriers that trap the aristocrats in Buñuel's *Exterminating Angel.*

At the same time, as MacKillop notes, Muriel's confession forms the solitary counterpart to Claude's relationship with Pilar, and it places them on the shared ground of sexuality.[15] Indeed, they both separately share, as it were, the solitary experience of an "oceanic" orgasm; she enjoys one at age seventeen, surrounded by swaying poppies (a word with opiate overtones), while Claude gives himself, Onan-like, to the rocky cliffs of the Alps.[16]

The next part of the book concerns Claude's relations with Anne, once the relationship with Muriel has come to seem impossible. In Anne's atelier in Paris, Claude observes her with desire and then seizes the initiative: "Once again I have the insane idea of touching her breast. Why not try it now? So I do it slowly, carefully, in the manner of someone feeling the weight of a fruit from a tree. Will she cry out? Slap me? Anne is bringing her right hand to remove mine . . . but no! Her hand lightly envelops mine and helps it hold her breast. . . . She unbuttons her blouse and slides my other hand onto her naked breast" (194–195). In response Anne tells him, "I wanted that and you sensed it," and she invites him to pass ten days at a lake.

In a letter written later Anne explains to Claude that her relationship with Muriel, whom she had always regarded as a dazzling and superior being, had been an obstacle to any relationship with him: "Her first prizes in everything, her capacity to beat me at all the games, all the sports, impressed me. She preferred my guitar to her piano, but her voice effaced mine. She wrote poetry, and she was the only actress on the stage of our town" (195).

With Anne, love is lighter and more reciprocal than with Muriel. Like Claude, she contemplates having multiple lovers, but she is afraid that he will leave her prematurely before the exact moment that she is ready to leave him. She tells Claude that she prefers sculpting statues to making babies and that she envies unmarried couples. Far from being jealous of Claude's affair with Pilar, she is hungry for more details. She says, "If the philosophy of a people is to be found, as you claim, in the way its women make love, then what clarity must characterize Spanish thought!"

When Claude makes love with Anne for the first time, he feels a light barrier give way, as she observes him with friendly eyes. After making love, she says that "it is intimate, but it is not yet us. . . . [I]t is

18. Anne and Claude. Source: Photofest.

as if you were playing alone" (205). But slowly Anne catches fire, and she writes, "Claude, Claude, I am too happy. My desires increase to the extent that you satisfy them. Do men calm down after making love? With me it's just the opposite. I had you to myself all day yesterday, but now I need you more. I don't know what to do. You fill me. When you go away, I'm empty. Who would have imagined . . . I am insatiable" (208).

Describing himself as a "newborn in love," Claude writes to Anne: "We build our love with our words and our gestures, rather like a statue created by both of us" (210). The statue simile demonstrates once again the symbiotic connection between sexual love and artistic creativity in the minds of this couple. But Anne ultimately decides that both she and Claude should love someone else. Anne ends up loving a man named Mouff, and Claude accepts the affair. As occurs in *Jules and Jim*, all the principals transcend possessiveness in a generous, amicable spirit. And throughout all the shifts and permutations of their relationships with Claude, the two sisters never stop loving each other, never lose their capacity to imagine everything from the other's point of view, never stop advancing the other's goals, no matter what those goals might be.

Once the liaison with Anne ends, Claude's attention returns to Muriel, who is now better disposed toward him. Their relation, too, is mediated through the arts: "I went to see Rodin's *The Kiss*. God made Claude entire, as he was, along with the attraction he felt for me. God also made me entire, as I was, and with some delays, made me love Claude" (228).

Meanwhile, Anne writes to Muriel about her multiple relationships and her philosophy of love: "Love is not an exclusive and definitive passion for a single being, but a feeling which plays freely, sometimes growing to the point of complete union, which can then be satiated and weaken, and then take off again, in its own time, for another. A warm friendship can remain. Each loved one is a separate treasure, the key to a different world. The wealthy, who divorce often, know it well. But divorce is too expensive for artists. So we only marry when we want children" (233).

But when Anne reveals to Muriel in person that she had been Claude's lover, Muriel reacts badly. She begins to tremble, falls, and hurts her head. Anne caresses and comforts her, and Muriel thinks, "And I, so much the mistress of myself, I who was so impermeable through all these years, I have given up my secret all of a sudden, and with such obviousness" (234). Muriel subsequently tells Claude of her shock at the news of the love between him and her sister but that she is now calm. Nevertheless, she says, in a strange construction that itself demonstrates internal conflict, "we is impossible." At the same time, she imagines, and then refuses, the idea of a ménage: "Imagine, Claude: Anne living sometimes with you, like these last years, when your work permits it, and me loving you equally, sharing you, receiving each in turn? And the impossibility for both Anne and myself to be happy if the other is not happy? Even if our minds find all that innocent, it would end up not being viable. I don't say I cannot see you again. I only say that I cannot kiss you" (236).

Subsequently, the usually reserved Muriel changes her perspective slightly, speculating about the possibility of a female-dominated equivalent for the kind of ménage Roché later wrote about in *Jules and Jim*: "Would you like to possess two women who are sisters? That Anne and I love the same man is tragic, but it's not extraordinary. I have lost nothing: what I hoped for could not be. I regret nothing, except that I didn't learn [about your affair with Anne] earlier. 'Thou shalt know the truth and the truth shall make you free'" (237–238).

And touching on a thematic leitmotif found both in *Jules and Jim* (novel and film) and in the diaries of Helen Hessel Grund, Muriel speaks regretfully of missed opportunities and specifically of the children she did not have with Claude: "My past includes the dead, the children I could have had with Claude. He doesn't know about it. I look at them. Here's a little one, bleeding, with cold hands . . . and the others. . . . How I would have loved them!" (241). (The final sentence was transferred to Truffaut's *Jules et Jim*.)

Once Anne marries, Muriel feels "available" and ready to love Claude. Their first clumsy sexual encounter is described in Claude's journal, in an account rich in metaphors and similes mingling geography with religiosity. As they undress, he glimpses "a little Nordic Venus" (271) comparable to "fresh snow which I grasp gently in my hands in order to make snowballs" (271). Claude recalls that he was always attracted to the nape of her neck, "the only part of her body that [he] could observe without being observed" (271). He thinks of kissing the nape but then decides that when she is nude, she is "toute nuque" (all nape). Comparing her to a "miracle after a long pilgrimage," Claude proceeds to "devour her, delicately" with his lips and teeth. Interestingly, the whole experience triggers memories of his own traumatic dream about his mother piercing his penis: "In this pre-natal memory, a whirlwind forms in me, a slow interior tide which carries a point, which pierces me as in the dream about Claire" (272).

In a kind of national-erotic allegory Claude compares his attempt at penetration to that of a voyager entering the "Great North," going into an "impassive country that is not hostile but where, having no landmarks, he feels lost" (272). We are given to understand between the lines that Claude has ejaculated on her body: "our children pour themselves out on her flank" (272).

A few days later Claude and Muriel make complete love for the first time. Claude describes what used to be called the "deflowering" in terms redolent of both geography and war: "Her ribbon explodes, after a resistance much stronger than was the case with Anne. I go to the bottom of the well, into the Grand North. It is not a question of happiness, or of delaying. It is a question of making Muriel a woman, against me. It's done. And then to beat a retreat" (277).

Summing up Muriel's bloody defloration in an understated yet graphic image, one that Truffaut picks up verbally and visualizes in his adaptation, Claude writes: "There was red on her gold." Although Muriel discovers that she and Claude are from "different tribes" with "different rituals," at times she nevertheless does love Claude. She writes: "Claude, cradle me. Envelop me. I place my forehead on your chin. Please, burn my letters. . . . Forget them. Forgive them. Love me. That's all I want. . . . My love is calm like a field of wheat" (283).

And anticipating a theme found later both in Helen's and Roché's letters and diaries, Muriel stresses the fusion of their two selves: "There is not even me, I am melted into you" (283). Describing herself as a "puritan in love," Muriel tells Claude that for her, "physical union" should be a "coronation, not a goal" (286). She is also sensitive to the interventionist role of both of their mothers in shaping, albeit in opposite ways, their relationship: "My mother forced you toward me. Your mother cut me off from you" (287). And picking up on his comparative geographical allegory, she proclaims, "I am your Great North. You are my continent" (288).

The novel ends with a double epilogue, successively entitled "Four Years Later" and "Thirteen Years Later." Ultimately, the two sisters both marry, while Claude, the bohemian, remains single. Yet once again we find the generous lack of possessiveness that is so affecting in Roché's work. Here is Claude's response to the news of Muriel's wedding to a certain Mr. Mitchell: "when I spoke to him of you and Anne, he said things about you which were so true that I felt like his friend" (294). After thirteen years Muriel, like Anne before her, has married and borne a number of children. And Claude notes in his diary (July 27, 1927) that in the metro he thinks he has seen Miriam, the daughter of Muriel Mitchell. As had occurred years earlier with Muriel herself, he thinks about taking the woman's hand. The book ends, in this volume where the figure of the mother has been a haunting, even dominating presence, with Claude's return to his maternal roots in the form of Claire, who asks him, with a hint of world-weariness: "What's wrong? You look old tonight" (297). While the sisters have moved on to marriage and children, Claude, we sense, will shift into a kind of Don Juanism reconcilable with his mother's unstated strictures and demands.

But what is it, finally, that moves us in Roché's novel? Despite the datedness of the attitudes, we are moved, first of all, by the incandescent sincerity of the two sisters. Although their situations and dilemmas are not terribly unusual, their ability to deal with them with such articulate sensitivity and flair does seem exceptional. Second, we are moved by their solidarity, their readiness to sacrifice their own interests in order to identify, even to the point of virtual fusion, with the other's needs and desires. Their sisterly relationship is never just a matter of duty; rather, it is a constantly evolving adventure in intimacy. The two sisters are always discovering new depths and resources in each other. At times their tenderness comes close to a kind of sibling lesbianism, when they speak of a desire to touch each other and wonder if Pierre/Claude might have wanted them to be "lesbiennes."[17] Third, we are moved by Claude/Pierre's courageous attempt to honestly render the experience of love and sexuality in the modern world, from what is unmistakably a male point of view. While we appreciate the sisters' sensitivity to romantic nuance, we also appreciate his sophisticated exactitude about the male experience of sexuality.

Fourth, the appeal of the novel, and later of the film, is deeply rooted in the liebestod tradition, the strong stream in Western literature that links love to death, to passion, to impossibility. The novel exposes a certain irrationality within love. Its narrative is replete with apparently unmotivated but calamitous separations, which have the effect of sabotaging love. Claude and Anne have no reason to separate after their island idyll, for example, yet they do separate. Muriel spends a night with Claude and then abruptly departs. It is as if true love can only be realized in writing (the journals) or in the absence of one of the partners. As in the liebestod tradition described by de Rougemont in *Love in the Western World*, love here is pathos, obstacles, ruptures, suffering. Margaret calls attention to the liebestod in a 1905 free-verse poem, where she speaks of "our dance of death and love / that dance of anguish, hopelessness, and love."[18]

Love in *Two English Girls* is also characterized by what René Girard calls "triangular" or "mediated" desire.[19] Here love is mediated not only by other people and especially by parental figures (Claude's mother, the sisters' mother) but also by art and writing. Since the relationship, given the geographical separation, was of necessity *only* epistolary, every erotic move is conjectured, contemplated, imagined, and interrogated before the fact and revisited and reevaluated after the fact. With exacerbated self-consciousness the characters watch themselves as they live and feel. Love is lived in the subjunctive—"if I were to take her hand"— or in the past modal—"I might have . . . perhaps I should have." The relationships are constantly redefined and reassessed through writing, refiltered through words, so that the discourse about love becomes just as important as love itself. We are reminded of Foucault's critique of the "repression hypothesis," his portrait of a modern world where sex is always discursivized, not as a release from repression but as a sublimation of sexuality itself. The real telos, for all of the young characters, seems to be writing itself. At times, writing substitutes for direct sexual contact. After any potential or real sexual encounter, they rush to get it down in their diaries; their sexual search is graphotelic.

CHAPTER TWENTY-ONE

TWO ENGLISH GIRLS
THE FILM

WHILE THE REAL-LIFE events on which *Two English Girls* was based occurred two decades before the events on which *Jules and Jim* was based, the chronology of the Roché novels (and the Truffaut films based on them) reversed their literal historical sequence. Interestingly, the circumstances of Truffaut's life at the time of the filming of *Two English Girls* in some aspects echoed the complex relationships in which Roché himself had been embroiled a half century earlier. At the time of the film Truffaut was in the process of breaking up with Catherine Deneuve over the very issue that ultimately separated Roché from Helen—whether or not to have a child. In short, Deneuve wanted children, and Truffaut did not. Interestingly, Truffaut sometimes called Deneuve "Kathe de Neuve," a name that evokes the Kate from the Roché novel.[1] ("Catherine" was also Helen Grund's middle name.) And like Helen Grund Hessel, Deneuve felt a veritable vocation for motherhood, saying, "The only moment in my life where I felt that everything, in myself and outside of myself, corresponded to my profoundest desire, was the period of my pregnancy."[2] The patient Griselda in this story, the real-life counterpart to the infinitely patient Gilberte in *Jules and Jim*, in this sense, was Truffaut's ex-wife Madeleine Morgenstern. A kind of caring and conscientious mother figure for Truffaut, Madeleine always nurtured her former husband through his losses and wounds and crises with other women.

But the events surrounding the production of *Two English Girls* also point back to other parallels between Truffaut and Roché. Just as Roché loved both of the Hart sisters, Truffaut also loved two sisters:

not only Catherine Deneuve but also her sister, the actress Françoise Dorléac. And in still another repetition with a difference, Truffaut ended up loving the same English actress (Kika Markham) who plays Roché's love Violet (Anne in the film).

Just as Truffaut "fell in love" with *Jules and Jim*—note the eroticized language to speak of art—he also adored the novel *Two English Girls*. Truffaut claimed to have read it every year, to the point that he knew it virtually by heart. Roché's novel was the only book that Truffaut had by his side when he suffered his nervous breakdown in 1971; its filming, in a sense, functioned as therapy. Truffaut claimed that he often spoke of himself in his films, "but not directly." Adapting literature, paradoxically, "authorized" Truffaut to be even more autobiographical but in an oblique manner. *Two English Girls* thus mirrored his own frustrated, quasi-tragic love affairs with two sisters but in a safe and refracted way, since, after all, it was "only an adaptation" of someone else's story.

Although based on the events involving the Hart sisters at the turn of the century, as well as on the various written accounts of those events, Roché completed the first draft of *Two English Girls* only many decades later in 1953, at a time when Truffaut was just beginning to dabble in film criticism. Thus the octogenarian novelist Roché was writing his first novels just as the young filmmaker Truffaut was beginning to think about making films. Roché's final draft in 1956 coincided with Truffaut's earliest short films. In fact, Roché had been rather slow in actually writing the novels based on his experiences, whether at the turn of the century (with the Hart sisters) or in the 1920s (the ménage with the Hessels), partially because so much of his literary energy was spent on his diaries (and art reviewing) rather than on his creative fiction. The diaries were a vital necessity for Roché, a kind of daily erotic pulse-taking. They existed in the somewhat inchoate form of notebooks, agendas, and scraps of paper. Since Roché tended to reveal his harsher side in the journals rather than in the novels, Truffaut's knowledge of the journals had the effect of making the film's character portraits somewhat more harsh, especially in terms of Roché/Claude. As Truffaut told Anne Gillain, in the novel Roché downplayed the women's' sufferings, but in the diaries "he is shameless, and recounts his own cruelty." At bottom, Truffaut told Gillain," I am for the two women, and against him [Claude]."[3]

Two English Girls was shot between May and July 1971. Truffaut at one point thought of casting two real-life sisters, but he settled in the end for two French-speaking English actresses. And as was his custom, he had an affair with one of them, namely Kika Markham. The set became the scene of what by now had become a familiar scenario of seduction: "Before me I find a girl, or a woman, moved and fearful and obedient, who places her confidence in me and who is ready to abandon herself. What happens then is always the same. Sometimes the love story [in English in the text] is synchronized with the shoot and ends with it; or sometimes it continues on because one of us or both wants it."[4]

Thus art imitates life, or more precisely, art (the film) imitates art (the novel), which imitates life (Truffaut's relationships), which imitates another life (Roché's relationships), which in its turn imitated art. Interestingly, Truffaut's Oedipally inflected family romance and search for surrogate fathers led him to bond with the parents—but especially the fathers—of the actresses he was dating and even to give the fathers roles in his films. During his affair with Kika Markham Truffaut gave her father David Markham a role in the film (and also in *La Nuit américaine* [1973], where he plays Jacqueline Bisset's doctor husband).

A crucial aspect of the art of film adaptation of novels is the multiplication and interbreeding of intertexts, largely facilitated by film's multitrack nature. As a composite and synesthetic medium, film "inherits" all the art forms associated with its diverse *maters* of expression. The image track, for example, can potentially incorporate the available visual archive (and the techniques) associated with photography and painting.[5] In perfect keeping with the adaptation of a novel written by an art collector, Truffaut and his director of photography, Nestor Almendros, looked at Victorian English and French impressionist paintings, both for aesthetic inspiration and for concrete information about the period. Turn-of-the-century costumes, furniture, and wallpaper, they noted, rarely feature pure, primary colors. The filmmakers therefore opted for intermediate shades like mauves and siennas. Almendros had harshly white fabrics like sheets dipped in tea to subdue their chromatic violence. Some artistically informed members of the audience noted that the French sequences were reminiscent in their colors and style of Monet and Renoir paintings, but that was less a result of technique than of the fact that the sets and props in the film resembled the kinds of objects portrayed by French impressionist painters.[6]

As was the case earlier with *Jules and Jim*, *Two English Girls* blends into its story a wide array of "alien" materials. For example, Truffaut infused material about another romantic set of sisters—the Brontës—as well as stories about Proust as a young man in love. (Proust was, after all, Roché's contemporary.) Gruault and Truffaut saw the film as a story, in their own words, "about Proust in love with Charlotte Brontë."[7] The fact that in the Truffaut version one of the sisters dies—and here Truffaut departs both from real life and from the Roché novel—has to do with Truffaut's fascination with the character and death of Emily Brontë. At the same time, Truffaut injects himself into the film in a highly personal manner, by himself providing the "impersonal" voice-over narration. Although Truffaut casts Jean-Pierre Léaud as Claude, we no longer find the intense personal identification that characterized the Truffaut-Léaud relationship in *The 400 Blows*, since Roché's Claude is rich, leisured, and cultivated, not an oppressed working-class adolescent like Truffaut/Léaud. "It's as if you were playing the role of Jim," Truffaut told Léaud, "if you had been born rich and tall."[8] Unlike both Léaud and Truffaut, Roché was a kind of dandy, an aesthete observing the world, cynical enough to exploit Muriel's personal letters about masturbation by publishing them.

Truffaut's life and work often betray a certain hostility to both male actors and male characters. *Two English Girls* was made "against" the Claude character, much as *The Soft Skin*, earlier, had been made "against" the philandering Lachenay character. Truffaut's knowledge of Roché's diaries, as we have noted, helped "darken" the image of the author/protagonist. At the same time, however, the experience of making the film renewed Truffaut's personal link to Roché, beyond the grave, as it were, in that it catalyzed an encounter with Roché's widow, Denise, who loved the adaptation, exulting that it was "as if Henri-Pierre had been sitting at [her] side."[9]

As suggested earlier, Truffaut had already borrowed and "used up," as it were, a lot of materials from *Two English Girls* in *Jules and Jim*. Countless phrases, formulations, and incidents had simply been transferred from *Two English Girls* into the adaptation of *Jules and*

Jim: Catherine's "catch me," the search for the vestiges of prehistoric civilizations, the footrace (actually Muriel's idea in the novel), the quotation of Albert Sorel on being "un curieux" and an "informateur," the bicycle rides, the character Thérèse, Catherine's line about "not suffering at the same time; when you stop, I'll start," and the opening "acousmatic" poem that begins *Jules and Jim*. Muriel's line about herself in the novel—"I'm not particularly beautiful or charming"—is transferred in *Jules and Jim* to Jules, who makes the same (rather unconvincing) claim about Catherine/Jeanne Moreau. Muriel's comment to Claude that "when you're forty you'll want a younger woman," meanwhile, is also transferred to Catherine.

At the same time, *Jules and Jim* and *Two English Girls* do share many themes and techniques. In thematic terms both feature mild-mannered and apparently un-macho men, an unusually generous erotic threesome attempting to transcend jealousy, and a mediating vision of art as a conduit for intense feelings between human beings. Both films reflect the pattern pointed out by Gillain, whereby the men's love object is first glimpsed as an image before being encountered in flesh and blood.[10] In *Jules and Jim*, for example, the two men first fall in love with the smile of a statue featured in a slide presentation and only later the flesh-and-blood Catherine. Symptomatically, after being rejected by the two sisters, Claude finds consolation through the collection of images, an avocation that confirms the view of Roché's biographers that collecting served as compensation for various lost loves. While collecting living beings inevitably ends in disappointment, the collecting of dead objects runs no such risks. Interestingly, Truffaut was a collector, *à sa façon*; he, too, as a teenager, compiled dossiers of press clippings concerning his favorite films and cinéastes.

Parallel cinematic techniques also figure in the two films: densely informative voice-over exposition; faces superimposed on moving landscapes; voice-overs that redundantly tell us what characters are saying even as we see them speaking; and rapid, deliberately "mise-dited," montages for sequences of falling (Claude falling from the swing, Catherine leaping into the Seine). Nevertheless, important differences also separate the two films. *Jules and Jim* offers a case of three people who often live together and only occasionally communicate through letters. *Two English Girls* offers the converse situation, of three people in different countries, who primarily communicate through letters and only occasionally see one another in the flesh. The amorous triangles, furthermore, are upside-down versions of each other; instead of the two men and one woman of *Jules and Jim*, we have the two women and one man of *Two English Girls*. While the former film is moving in its portrayal of male solidarity, the latter moves us through the solidarity of the two sisters. More pro-woman, less idealized and utopian, more critical of the Roché-based male character, *Two English Girls* in some ways constitutes a critique of *Jules and Jim*, much as *The Soft Skin*, a decade earlier, had critiqued *Jules and Jim* by replacing its tragic romanticism with a mundane portrait of the sordid underbelly of conventional adultery.

In terms of the actual processes of adaptation, Truffaut began, already in 1968, to negotiate for the rights to the novel. The publisher wanted 150,000 francs, but Truffaut reminded the publisher that it had been his own adaptation of *Jules and Jim* that had saved Roché from oblivion and thus increased the value of the literary "property" now being sold back to him. Jean Gruault then began to work on the screenplay on the basis of Roché's journals and Truffaut's annotated copy of the novel—shown in the opening shots. Gruault's first version of the script in 1969 consisted of 552 pages and 95 sequences. A few years later, Truffaut trimmed down the Gruault script to 200 pages.[11] Both Truffaut and Gruault also read biographies of the Brontë sisters, whom they saw as "puritanical, Romanesque and exalted" in the manner of the Hart sisters. Anne's last words in the film—"my mouth full of death"—are taken directly from Emily Brontë. Given the fact that Anne's real-life prototype actually had four children, one wonders if Anne's death is somehow symbolic "punishment" for her freedom, much as Catherine was "punished" for her sexually free actions and spirit in both the novel and in the Truffaut adaptation. Truffaut might also been have alluding to the untimely death of his own actress/lover Françoise Dorléac. In the novel, finally, Claude's mother does not die, while she does die in the Truffaut film. In this sense one wonders if Truffaut is not repeating the symbolic violence committed earlier against his own mother in *The 400 Blows*.

In terms of physical location, the "Wales" of the film is "played" by a geographical stand-in (France), and the city of Cherbourg doubles for

Calais. It was cinematographer Nestor Almendros's suggestion to film Claude and Muriel in front of the "vibrating light" of the Cherbourg harbor, as if their emotion were being projected into the shimmering visual quality of the image. Part of the literal darkness of the film derives from the fact that the film, and here it differs dramatically from the generally luminous *Jules and Jim*, strives to avoid including shots of the sky. Nothing in *Two English Girls* resembles the lyrical, aerial crane shots of *Jules and Jim*. Yet both films do share a favored Truffaut technique, the use of the "archaic" device of the iris-in, seen as appropriate to a period piece set in the time of the very beginnings of silent cinema.

The Truffaut version of *Two English Girls* opens, in a classically bookish gesture, with a shot of stacked-up piles of the Roché novel, followed by shots of the Roché text, "illuminated," as it were, by Truffaut's handwritten marginalia, a reflexive device that reveals Truffaut's own working methods. (One of the notations is a cross-reference to Roché's diaries.) The shots together evoke what I called earlier "the graphological trope": the notion of film and literature as two variant forms of writing. Roché's published written words, along with Truffaut's scrawled handwritten words, are seen simultaneously with Claude's spoken words about his decision to tell the story: "Last night I relived our story. Some day I'll write a book. Muriel thinks our story will help others." Moreover, we hear the voices both of the author/character (Roché/Claude) and that of the filmmaker, all within an overlay of temporalities: the past/present of reliving the past in the present, the future of "helping others." The sequence combines the image of Roché's text with the grain and sound of Truffaut's voice. The superimposed techniques evoke not only the real-life dialogue between Truffaut and Roché but also the transfer of affection, so typical of Truffaut, from literature to film, as well as the film itself as a hybrid discourse mingling both forms of authorship. *Two English Girls* is born, then, under the sign of the *livresque*. The constant presence of books and citations, and the literary discourse of the characters, helps shape this leitmotif. We have, then, both the story of a love and the story of its telling. And once again, through a compensatory mechanism, aesthetic success makes up for amorous failure.

Like *Jules and Jim*, *Two English Girls* performs many transformative operations on its literary source. The two sisters' male siblings, for example, are eliminated. The passages involving Claude's experiences as a soldier are also excised, along with the passages involving Claude and the sisters' sojourn in London. Anne is never seen at art school, nor is Muriel seen with her books. Claude, meanwhile, seems less bookish than in the novel. He becomes a writer, but the book he is writing is not about the two sisters but rather about the subject of another Roché novel—male friendship à la *Jules and Jim*—here thinly disguised as *"Jérome and Julien."* Claude's research into bordellos and prostitutes in the novel takes the form of his spoken reports to the two sisters in the film. In the novel the mother literally spies on and directly censors the letters between the young principals; in the film she is portrayed as a kind of puppeteer pulling the characters' strings from behind the scene. The film also downplays Muriel's disappointment that Claude has slept with Pilar. The novel's portrayal of Claude as spoiled in material terms, accustomed to the services of a maid, for example, is entirely ignored by the film. Claire's rather brutal threat to Anne—"If Claude marries Muriel, I will refuse to see him, her, or any children they might bear"—is eliminated. The character of the literary editor Chrub, barely mentioned in the novel, becomes a fully embodied character in the film. Truffaut also opts not to reproduce a key technical/stylistic procedure of the novel—the "split writing" juxtaposing Claude's and Muriel's diaries—avoiding conceivable equivalents such as a split-screen (à la Woody Allen's *Annie Hall*).

Truffaut skillfully deploys mise-en-scène to contrast the two sisters. The portrayal of Muriel is marked by absence and lack—first through the absence/presence of herself as a ten-year-old girl, then as an empty chair at mealtimes, then as the face with bandage-covered eyes. Muriel is the tragic figure whose amorous emotions are strong and vibrant yet blocked, a blockage "realized," as it were, through the relatively static camera and claustrophobic mise-en-scène associated with her appearances in the film. The frequent shots of her alone, and the "theatrical" technique of soliloquy, render her isolation. Anne's energy and dynamism, in contrast, are conveyed both through a restlessly moving camera and through her own movement in the shot. Her sexual initiation, unlike Muriel's, is calm and bloodless. Later she takes another lover, momentarily reproducing the two men/one woman situation of *Jules and Jim*. Whereas Muriel is usually framed

19. Claude and Muriel. Source: Photofest.

alone and still, writing letters or lost in thought, Anne is usually filmed with others and in motion. At ease with her body, she is shown as gregarious, sharing the frame with friends and acquaintances.

Truffaut associates the introspective Muriel, in contrast, with mirrors and interior, low-key lighting. Her dialogue is with herself. She confesses directly to the camera, which advances to frame her eyes only, in shots reminiscent of the opening shots of Jimmy Stewart's face in Hitchcock's *Vertigo*. Anne, meanwhile, is engaged with the world, associated with exteriors, and with brighter and more varied colors. Whereas Anne and Claude engage in direct face-to-face communication, Muriel's conversations with Claude are filmed with Muriel facing away. What, we wonder, is she afraid of? What is she looking for? She speaks in a voice-over or in soliloquy. Although she is clearly self-absorbed, her self-absorption does not amount to selfishness, since in a strange way she loves others even more than she loves herself. If she is narcissistic, her narcissism is strangely self-denying.

The two seduction sequences are handled very differently. Both sisters lose their virginity to Claude. But Muriel's deflowering is shown as a violent hemorrhaging, inundating the screen in a manner like the violent red of the subjective sequences in Hitchcock's *Marnie*, another film about a traumatized woman who freezes up during sexual intercourse. Close-ups of Muriel's face register her pain. Anne, meanwhile, is pleased with her sexual initiation yet also quite lucid: "It is not yet us." Truffaut seems to sympathize with both sisters, but he presents Anne's way of living as more flexible, coherent, and viable. The "deflowering" of Anne, for example, is treated with easy humor. Claude mocks her red flannel underwear, reminiscent for him of army-issue clothing. Their dialogue is light and calm. When Anne reveals her passion, we hear Truffaut's voice-over: "When the young English-woman took off her veil, Claude had the impression of a charming and modest nudity." As Gillain points out, "the proximity promised by the image is cancelled by the disturbance imposed by the text."[12]

Truffaut had always been circumspect in his approach to sexually explicit scenes, and his handling of the seduction scenes reflects his modesty and sexual *pudeur*. This shyness enters into contradiction with Truffaut's claims in a 1973 essay—"What Do Critics Dream About?"—written about a year and a half after the making of *Two English Girls*—where Truffaut argued that filmmakers must be more sexually explicit. Mentioning his admiration for Henry Miller—Truffaut's book *The Films in My Life* was modeled on Miller's *The Books in My Life*—Truffaut wrote:

> Erotic or pornographic films, without being a passionate fan, I believe . . . are in expiation, or at least in payment of a debt that we owe for sixty years of cinematographic lies about love. I am one of the thousands of his readers who was not only entranced, but helped through life by the work of Henry Miller, and I suffered at the idea that cinema lagged so far behind his books as well as behind reality. Unhappily, I still cannot cite an erotic film that is the equivalent of Henry Miller's writing.[13]

This passage is interesting in a number of regards. First, it is surprising that a sexually cautious filmmaker like Truffaut should pay such enthusiastic homage to a risqué, libidinous, and taboo-shattering writer like Henry Miller. Second, the passage displays again the affective transfer, in a move typical of Truffaut, from the medium of literature to the medium of film. Moreover, Truffaut's praise of Miller reverses the usual dichotomy contrasting puritanical America with sexually sophisticated France, in that Truffaut looks to an American writer, albeit an expatriate writer living in France, for his sexual education. (Coincidentally, Miller wrote about Place Clichy, for him the scene of orgiastic excess but for Truffaut the setting of his own repressed adolescence.) Truffaut explored romantic, sexualized emotions, but unlike Miller, he was not at all concerned with physical sexuality itself. Muriel's masturbation, and her childhood homoeroticism with Clarisse, for example, are treated in a delicate, indirect, and nonvoyeuristic manner. Although Truffaut portrayed an avant-garde and bohemian milieu in *Jules and Jim*, and to a much lesser extent in *Two English Girls*, in sum, he did not share the avant-garde penchant for breaking sexual taboos, at least not directly.

In Truffaut's work superpaternal, authoritarian father figures tend to provoke revulsion for their rigidity and dogmatism, within social worlds where male authority figures tend to be deficient or simply absent. *Two English Girls*, for its part, gives us a world largely without men. (The elimination of the two brothers from the novel is significant in this regard.) In a doubling structure taken from the novel, both mothers (Claire and Mrs. Brown) are widowed. The hero, Claude, is the son of a widowed mother who, from the very beginning, either dominates the screen space or hovers around its edges. In the opening sequence the mother reads while the children play. Encouraged by the girls, Claude plays at being an acrobat. (The children are played by Truffaut's own children.) But Claude falls, and his mother runs toward him. For Gillain, the falling camera marks a larger trajectory of fall and failure; the opening "Icarus" sequence metaphorically suggests that the mother's domineering ways have "crippled" him.

Speaking more generally, Claude is symbolically castrated, incapacitated for love. Claire, it seems, cannot allow any single woman to have Claude; only anonymous or uncommitted women are allowed provisional access to her beloved son. One has the impression that Claire, perhaps like Roché's own mother, is faithful to her dead husband but that she "cheats" vicariously and prosthetically through Claude's penis and affairs. Although the ineffectual Flint is the apparent agent of the enforced separation between Muriel and Claude, it is Claire's maternal authority, operating as if from offscreen, that really dictates the law. And after six months Claude has understood the rules of the game; he decides to give up Muriel. Don Juanism has in an uncanny way become a form of obedience to the mother. Thus we have the distorted mirror effect of the mother who loves only one (deceased) man and the son who cannot love any single woman, the man who loves many, paradoxically, in order to be faithful to one—the mother. "You have never been and never will be a husband," Muriel hurls at Claude as she leaves him, implying that his mother is his only real and lasting love.

Claire's domination of her son is brilliantly rendered not only through the plot but also through the staging and through the cinematic technique itself. Claude surrenders his right of erotic self-determination to his mother. Before mailing letters—for example, a letter communicating his decision to be alone and not to marry Muriel—Claude submits them to his mother for her stamp of approval. When Claire goes to Wales to check up on her son, her image is shown superimposed on shots of the train, while her voice on the sound track reads Claude's letter reporting his love for Muriel. (The mother seems to "hover" over the image, in a manner reminiscent of Woody Allen's ubiquitous "mother," hovering threateningly in the skies over New York in *Manhattan Stories*.) The superimposition shapes the impression of the mother rushing to the scene of an "emergency"—her son's possible marriage—generating in the spectator a feeling that she is "preventing" Claude (in the etymological sense of preventing or "coming before") from falling into what she sees as a catastrophe.

The Oedipal element, quite strong in the film, was even stronger in the novel. There, the mother reminds her son that at the age of four he had asked to marry her "when [she] was little and [he] was big." The novel also reports the horrifically Oedipal dream, mentioned earlier, about the mother piercing the son's penis with a needle. As a result of these traumas, a genealogy of impossibility is imprinted on Claude's search for love. While Muriel practices what might be called a paradoxical erotics of celibacy, Claude is embarked on an amorous mission impossible; he wants someone who simultaneously resembles his mother—such is his mother's phantasmatic power over him—and who at the same time is antithetical to her and thus represents an escape from her influence.

The relationship between Claude and Muriel seems not to work because both of them seem emotionally blocked in almost opposite ways. The imagery links love and death: the blood of his abortive suicide attempt rhymes with the blood of her deflowering. An incorrigible puritan, Muriel agonizes over masturbation, while Claude is much more cynical, as becomes clear with his decision to publish her personal revelations about "self-abuse." In some ways he regards Muriel the way a turn-of-the-century ethnologist might have regarded "his" tribe or an entomologist his insects. Muriel, for her part, is the polar opposite. She yearns for some absolute good, whether in the form of family, a man, or God. She wants an impossibly pure, unconditional, uncompromising love, with either the right man or with no man. In a Lacanian catch-22 she desires exactly the kind of love that Claude is constitutionally incapable of giving her.

In line with Truffaut's goal of making "not a film about physical love, but a physical film about love," the film has Muriel incarnate the suffering, vulnerable, overflowing body, racked by tears, fainting, vomiting, and bleeding.[14] Indeed, Truffaut's expressed goal was to show that love can literally "make people sick." Muriel swoons away in the manner of the Victorian heroines that she has read about. Literally hypersensitive—to light, for example—she suffers from viscerally felt mental and physical disturbances. She sees her own sex, otherized as "the thing," as a kind of enemy within. She writes passionate letters that she ends up not sending. She exhibits the pathologies and neuroses described in contemporaneous sex manuals and in the theoretical treatises of writers like Freud, Havelock Ellis, Kraft-Ebbing, and Otto Weininger. A figure of incessant contradiction, Muriel utters confident resolutions—"I cannot see you"—which she undoes in the next breath—"When you come." She tells Claude "I don't love you, Claude," yet when he asks if it's really true, she answers with an unconvincing "I hope so." Her imagination is so overpowering that she hallucinates Claude while playing tennis in the sunlight. Her hysterical body even suffers a false pregnancy. Within her psyche a religiously inflected asceticism wars with an equally powerful erotic passion.

The idea of vision literally haunts the film. Muriel's eye problems, and the specter of her eyes repeatedly framed in outsized close-ups, seem like a somatization, an acting out of metaphorical taboos on sight. Muriel repeatedly notes, "I have to take care of my eyes." Claude says that "once I've seen her eyes," but later she loses her normal vision. Eyes are referenced not only in the superimposed shots of Claire's eyes surveying the son's erotic entanglements but also in the love scene between Claude and Anne, where Anne places cloth over the statues' eyes. Muriel's masturbation, similarly, becomes linked to the idea that "self-abuse" renders its practitioners blind. Since Claude sees the two sisters as his own "soeurs," the relationship takes on incestuous overtones, and we remember that Oedipus blinds himself when he realizes that he has committed incest.

Truffaut's adaptation treats sexuality intensely but also gingerly. It starts with innocent games with erotic overtones, like the "squeezed lemon" game. Roché/Claude overlays the erotic story with cultural resonances. Referring to his own tumescence, the novel's Claude says, "the Mediterranean swells within me; I am aroused." But he is always shy, wondering, à la Julien Sorel in *The Red and the Black*, if he dares to take Muriel's hand. In a prudish Victorian period young people seem to lack even the proper names of sexual objects and activities. Perhaps influenced by her reading of the sexological literature of the time, according to which masturbation causes chronic fatigue, insanity, and worse, Muriel becomes ashamed about her "sin" of masturbation. She refers to the forbidden act as "the thing" and to love as "s.r.," short for sexual relations. And with Clarisse she practices a naïve and unnamed lesbianism—another love that "dare not say its name."

Repeatedly, the film enacts the tensions between desire and the law. In a game—as in *Jules and Jim*, here, too, games proliferate—Claude is to kiss Anne through a chair, against the backdrop of a hearth fire. The desire evoked both metonymically and metaphorically by the (somewhat clichéd) neighboring of the kiss and the fire is symbolically "contained" by the bars of the chair (the law). In a triangular configuration, Claude, before kissing Anne, looks at Muriel, whose eyes are hidden. Even the constantly reiterated motif that they are "all family," like brothers and sisters, both respects and violates the incest taboo.

In this sequence, as elsewhere, the law surrounds desire with a halo of tantalizing interdiction. The same conjugation of law and desire informs the "squeezed lemon" sequence. In a kind of childlike harem structure, Claude, the two sisters, and the chaperone all find themselves, during a storm, in a grotto, a site redolent of woman's sex and the camera obscura ("dark room") of sexuality. The movement of the game, which involves physical contact with both sisters, prefigures Claude's erotic involvement with the two of them. Here too the strong sexual overtones of grotto and storm and rocking touch are all circumscribed within the rules and limits of a game supervised, both directly and indirectly, by adults. As in the novel, we are clearly in the world delineated by de Rougemont, with its intermingling of Eros and Thanatos, where love thrives on obstacles, whether external (in the courtly tradition of marriage, the damsel's imprisonment in the castle, and here the parental constraints) or internal (the mores of the time, the internalized regulating mechanisms of the Anglo Puritanism of the two sisters). Thus the logic of the film is to both mobilize and immobilize desire, to nurture it but also to disrupt it, driving it underground.

In both novel and film, art plays a crucial role within this dynamic. Romance takes place almost always against an artistically connoted backdrop. Claude's love affair with Anne is conducted under the auspices of the visual arts, and especially of sculpture. They look at, and are silently watched over by, Rodin statues such as *The Kiss* or *Balzac*. We learn from Claude's mother that Claude's very physical conception and gestation was enveloped, womblike, in artistic purposiveness, designed to make the son "love painting." Claude's mother approves of his collecting both of paintings and of women. Art seems to simultaneously relay, mediate, and distance strong erotic emotions, keeping powerful feelings at an aesthetic remove. In the film Claude and his mother meet repeatedly in Renoir- and Monet-style outdoor settings, at cafés near the Seine, precisely the kind of festive, gregarious, and colorful scenes associated with the impressionist movement in painting. The first caresses shared by Claude and Anne take place in front of statues, whose eyes she covers as if the statues were peeping Toms. After her affair with Claude, Anne decides that she wants to produce statues instead of babies. During their island idyll, Claude sees Anne's hand as resembling that of a painting.

20. Love under the sign of mimesis. Jean-Pierre Leaud and Kika Markham in *Two English Girls*. Source: Photofest.

In both novel and film love thrives under the sign of mimesis. Gillain points out that in many Truffaut films—*Jules and Jim, La Sirène du Mississippi* (1969), among others—the ideal object of desire is first glimpsed as an image before being encountered in flesh and blood.[15] This tendency in his films, I would add, recapitulates Truffaut's own eroticized relation to the film image, as well as his habit of falling in love with film stars through their appearances in films, stars whom he subsequently cast in his films and whom he came to actually love. But *Two English Girls* specifically proliferates in doubles and doubling: the two sisters, the two seductions, the two deflowerings, the two separations (Claude and Anne on the island; Muriel and Claude at Calais), the two deaths (Claude's mother's and Anne's), and the two trips to Wales by two men (Claude and Dwirka). In both novel and film the love of art and the art of love become thoroughly commingled. The relation is both metonymic—lovers rendezvous in art museums next to admired statues—and metaphoric—love resembles art. Sculpture is a constant theme, as in the "statue game," a kind of "voguing" avant la lettre. Just as Claire claims to have built Claude "stone by stone, like a monument," Anne is literally a sculptor, while Muriel, when made love to, remains stiff and unmoved, like a statue.

The relation between art and love in *Two English Girls* is thus multifaceted. The artistic synergy between Claude and the sisters also helps engender more art, both verbal and visual. A Pygmalion motif informs both novel and film: Claude, like Roché himself, sees himself as giving life to women artists, both by bringing their dormant talents to fruition and by disseminating their work. And as a midwife for female stardom, Truffaut performed the filmic equivalent of Pygmalion's feat.

While *The 400 Blows* pays homage to Truffaut's artistic and intellectual mentors (Honoré de Balzac, Orson Welles, Ingmar Bergman, André Bazin), *Two English Girls* pays homage to a sculptured monument that combines the literary and the artistic, in the form of Rodin's statue of Balzac. As a filmmaker Truffaut had longed to render his homage to Balzac. His character Antoine worships at the novelist's shrine, and the protagonist of *The Soft Skin* lectures on Balzac's life and career. But here the Rodin reference is as important as the Balzac reference. As someone who, like Truffaut himself, received undeservedly bad reviews, Rodin becomes Truffaut's artistic precursor in suffering the slings and arrows of outrageous critics. Like Rodin's Balzac statue, Truffaut's *Two English Girls* was not at first well-received. (Rereleased in 1985, the film was still not a commercial success.) Yet a 1990 survey revealed that many critics thought *Two English Girls* one of Truffaut's best films. The secrets of this disconnect between critical prestige and popularity are not hard to find. Christian Metz pointed out in *The Imaginary Signifier* that pleasure and displeasure in filmic spectatorship are very complicated and overdetermined phenomena. When films frustrate our desire, we respond: "bad film"—much as the child says "bad breast" to the breast that refuses milk. We can reject films for reasons that have nothing to do with quality—because they frustrate our desire for a happy ending, for example, or because they provoke discomfort by reminding us of "unseemly" matters like menstruation. Therefore critics and spectators sometimes seek alibis to explain exactly why they did not like a film—it was too slow, or too old-fashioned, or too pretentious, or too avant-garde, or too anything—thus masking the psychic stakes in the emotional reception of filmic narratives.

A parallel to this process appears in the film itself. Along with showing the Rodin statue of Balzac, the film also speaks of its critical reception. Critics rejected the Balzac statue at the time and only later recognized it as a masterpiece whose originality consisted in showing Balzac in the process of "emerging from the stone." The voice-over mentions that the statue was refused by the "Société des Gens de Lettres," then the gatekeepers of the official art world. Yet now, the epilogue tells us, the "Balzac statue is admired by everyone." The whole trajectory from rejection to admiration clearly had highly personal echoes for Truffaut, who was himself both the subject and object of film criticism. It is as if Truffaut were addressing his critics: "You might not appreciate my film now," he seems to be saying, "but you will in the future, and then you will see it as a masterpiece."

CHAPTER TWENTY-TWO

THE (VARIOUS) MEN WHO LOVED (VARIOUS) WOMEN

THE GHOST OF Henri-Pierre Roché hovers over many Truffaut films, even those that were not adaptations of Roché novels. The Fergus (Charles Denner) character in *The Bride Wore Black*, for example, is portrayed as a collector of women not unlike Roché. The character describes himself as someone who is always looking for women, and he relates a nightmare in which he is surrounded only by men. He even compares himself—and here we are reminded of the convergence of religiosity and sexuality in Roché's Don Juan books—to a nun collecting alms: "I've collected from that one. That one, not yet. I'll have to try her." Truffaut's *Love on the Run*, meanwhile, encodes another side of Roché, his status as diarist. Antoine's lover Sabine gives him a complete set of Paul Léataud's *Diaries*, reminding us once again of Truffaut's fascination with Roché's diaries.[1] At the same time, Antoine's response to the gift underscores the link, in Truffaut's mind, between writing and sexual frustration: "Herein lies proof of the poor guy's trouble with women."[2]

Unlike *Jules and Jim* and *Two English Girls*, Truffaut's *L'Homme qui aimait les femmes* (1977) was not an adaptation, but it is nonetheless very much imbued with the memory of Roché's life and work. The story concerns the adventures and misadventures of an inveterate womanizer and writer named Bertrand, who careens from one amorous liaison to another until his untimely death. The film is framed, within a circular structure, by Bertrand's funeral, attended only by his former women lovers. The story configures the love/death nexus common in Truffaut's films, in novel ways. In the finale Bertrand is literally killed by desire, within a double movement of accidents. First, he is hit by a car just as he is tracking a pair of fascinating feminine legs. Then, after he has been hospitalized, he accidentally interrupts his own blood supply when he gropes at the legs of an attractive nurse. Literalizing the liebestod, he dies while in the throes of desire.

The Bertrand character was based on the experiences of three womanizing prototypes: Roché; Michel Fermaud, the coscreenwriter of the film; and, to a lesser extent, Truffaut himself. The director asked the screenwriter to compile tales of seduction, both Fermaud's own and those of his friends, which Truffaut would then interweave into the larger story. The links to Roché in the film are various and pervasive. First, the book that Bertrand is writing is modeled on Roché's diaries, which Truffaut had had in his personal possession as early as the time of *Jules and Jim* and which he had tried even then to publish. Indeed, the journals were originally typed up, to reiterate, only at Truffaut's request. The incident in the film where the typist refuses to type up Bertrand's diaries was modeled on the real-life incident, mentioned earlier, when Truffaut's secretary refused to type Roché's diaries because she was nauseated by the "unconscious cruelty" implicit in Roché's endless seductions of more or less interchangeable women. The links to Roché in the film are strengthened, further, by the film's portrayal of Bertrand as an obsessive diarist/writer. Indeed, many shots feature Bertrand pecking away at his *machine à écrire* (writing machine or typewriter), a phrase very evocative of the auteurist view of the cinema itself. Like Roché at the time of *Two English Girls*, Bertrand wants to write about contemporary sexual relations. The film also offers an echo of Roché's concept of "polyphonic writing," furthermore, in the fact that the woman/editor/lover character literally writes the last page of Bertrand's novel. Thus the writing itself, at least at the level of narration, becomes collaborative and multivoiced.

Other biographical connections also link Bertrand and Roché. Like Roché, and like Don Juan and Casanova, Bertrand is a collector, a seducer, and a writer of memoirs. In its portrait of a writer whose sensibility and sexuality are very much shaped by a dominant, eroticized mother, moreover, the film synthesizes Truffaut's and Roché's fraught relationship with the maternal figure. The writer and the filmmaker thus share a similar problem, even if the two mothers in

21. The wandering eye: Charles Denner in *The Man Who Loved Women*.
Source: Photofest.

question were in some ways polar opposites. Truffaut's sexuality was
shaped by a mother whom he saw as promiscuous and selfish, unin-
volved in his life. The story of the supposedly selfish mother is told,
in various degrees of obliqueness, in *The 400 Blows, Love on the Run*,
and *The Man Who Loved Women*. Roché's sexuality, in contrast, was
shaped by a mother who was *overly* involved in his life, whom he saw
as utterly faithful, not just to a husband but even more impressively
to the *memory* of a deceased husband. In Truffaut's case, a many-
man woman, at least in Truffaut's conception of her, gave birth to a
many-woman man. Maternal polygamy, in contrast, at least in Truffaut's imagination, engendered filial polygamy. In Roché's case a one-
man woman gave birth to a many-woman man. Maternal monogamy
engendered filial polygamy. The son becomes a Don Juan, in other
words, but with the mother's complicity. As we saw in *Two English Girls*,
the Roché mother, as exemplified in the Claire of the novel/film, sabo-
tages all serious relationships, thus encouraging the son (Claude/Henri-
Pierre) to have many lovers, as long as he does not become serious about

any one of them. Here Don Juanism gains a maternal seal of approval, as if the child operated as the "phallic mother's" surrogate in the world. Roché, Truffaut, and Bertrand all share another feature—the fate of not knowing their fathers, who either died when the child was very young (Roché's case) or was symbolically dead in the sense of literally not being known until late (Truffaut's case).

Like Roché, Bertrand publishes late, toward the end of his life. Like Roché, he is a shy (and sly) Don Juan, for whom seduction is a spiritual vocation. Bertrand is not the "macho man" who rushes to tell his male friends about his conquests. He is not the crude draguer who directly harasses women in the street. Nor does he dislike women. Indeed, his only friends are women, and only women come to his funeral. Like Roché, Bertrand has an aesthetic attitude toward women. He sees them as aesthetic products, simultaneously sex objects and "objets d'art." And as occurred with Roché, Bertrand uses risk and danger as a kind of aphrodisiac. In the film this fondness for risk is displaced onto the Delphine character, the lover who literally requires the danger of getting caught in flagrante to stoke the flames of her desire. Like Roché, Bertrand has to juggle an exhausting array of sexual relationships. The challenge for the real-life Roché had been even more daunting, of course, in that he "managed" an extraordinary number of wives, regular mistresses, and quick liaisons, sometimes hiding not only the relationships but also the fact that they had borne fruit in the form of children.

Some of the women characters recall Helen Grund and the portrayals of her in the various texts that speak of her. Helen courted danger like Delphine, and like her she was given to sudden emotional turnabouts. But in one sense both the novels and the Truffaut films idealize the reality of Roché's actual relationships. Thus *The Man Who Loved Women* is full of amicable separations, when we know that Roché's most serious lovers ended up hating him for his dishonesty, to the point that Helen Grund, for example, simply called him "the liar." Of that, in the film, there is little trace. But then, the film is a fiction, one not based exclusively on Roché.

The Man Who Loved Women features a very complex narrative and temporal structure. First, there is the frame narrative of Bertrand's funeral, where the voice-over is by Genevieve, who turns out to be the editor of Bertrand's book. Genevieve represents one narrative present, one point from which the story is told, after Bertrand's death. Second, there is the unfolding process by which Bertrand writes his book, furnishing another narrative present, the point at which he is looking back at his own life and tells that story in the present of his *écriture*. Third, there are the flashbacks, in black-and-white, related to Bertrand's childhood and his relationship with his mother. Fourth, there are the flashbacks, in color, recounting the various seductions. Fifth, there are the various subjectivized sequences, featuring dreams and hallucinations.

Many of the themes of the film come together in the five flashbacks concerning Bertrand's mother. Here the choice of a black-and-white format brings contradictory overtones. On the one hand, it suggests that we are getting the real story, since black-and-white was associated with documentary veracity and newsreel actuality. On the other hand, in the 1970s, black-and-white is no longer exclusively associated with those traditions but rather with the classic fiction film or with a black-and-white subgenre of the art film, and in this sense the sequences evoke a realm of fantasy and unreality. (In interviews Truffaut often expressed a dislike for color, which, for him, lacked the clear outlines of black-and-white and was too replete with extraneous detail.)

Many of the flashbacks recapitulate the idea of a boy unloved by his mother. The first flashback portrays a boy's initiation by a prostitute. (Both Roché and Truffaut, we recall, actually frequented prostitutes, and *The 400 Blows* has Antoine verbally recount his first sexual encounter with "professionals.") In the flashback sequence in *The Man Who Loved Women* a first prostitute tells the uninitiated Bertrand that she is too old for him and that she will look for a younger substitute. The unstated implication, perhaps, is that the older prostitute might remind the boy of his mother and thus indirectly trigger the fears attending the Oedipal taboo.

The second flashback literally compares the prostitute and the mother in terms of their similarly rapid manner of walking. The knees-down framing reminds us that Bertrand likes to watch women's legs as they walk. We are reminded not only of the adolescent Antoine admiring his mother's legs in *The 400 Blows* but also of Catherine as a tantalizing catalyst for movement in *Jules and Jim*. Women in movement, and specifically women's legs in movement, in other words, "move" Truffaut. But another moment in the sequence reverses the *voyeur vu* structure of *The 400 Blows*. In the earlier film a moment of reciprocal "gotcha" has Antoine "catch" his mother in the streets kissing her lover, but the mother, in that same exact moment, also "catches" the son playing hooky from school. In *The Man Who Loved Women*, in contrast, it is the mother who "catches" the son with a girlfriend, with the result that the son instantly leaves the girlfriend to follow the mother—much as Roché/Claude in *Two English Girls* abandons Muriel in the name of loyalty to the mother, whose castrating gaze orients the events of the film.

The third flashback portrays Bertrand with his girlfriend while she works as a babysitter. As Gillain points out, the symbolic mother—the babysitter—is here also a lover—thus suggesting an Oedipal configuration—but the mother, to be a lover, has to abandon the baby. The scene translates, in other words, Truffaut's simultaneous desire for, and resentment against, the mother. The scene conveys ambivalence; the girlfriend here is both a "bad mother" and the object of desire.

A fourth flashback portrays the mother's simultaneously stimulating and repressive role, thus recalling that other mother, at once sexy and repressive, from *The 400 Blows*. In the sequence the boy Bertrand reads a book as his mother walks around him in a flimsy nightgown. He is allowed to read, but he is forbidden to utter any sound. The structure, as Gillain points out, is both Oedipal and masochistic. Moreover, the sequence eroticizes reading. We are reminded again of the transfer of affect, seen in the movement, in *The 400 Blows*, from Antoine's love for Balzac to his love for Bergman and Welles. The joys of reading become transmuted into the erotics of spectatorship. Like the spectator in a movie theater, Bertrand remains immobile as he absorbs the moving spectacle of women who are literally in motion.

The Man Who Loved Women proliferates in images of perturbed sexuality. In this sense the press book for *The Man Who Loved Women* offers a key to interpreting the film. "If a sentence can serve as a common denominator for Bertrand's love affairs, it would be that of Bruno Bettelheim in *The Empty Fortress*: "It appeared that Joey had never had much success with his mother."[3] When Bertrand fails to seduce the owner of a lingerie shop, he dreams that she has him displayed in her store as a shop-window dummy. In the dream the proprietor runs her hands down the dummy's legs, then lifts one pant leg to reveal sock sus-

22. *The Man Who Loved Women*. Source: Photofest.

penders, just as a crowd, composed of Bertrand's lovers, looks intently to see the exposed leg. Bertrand, panic-stricken at this reversal of the voyeuristic gaze, wakes up in a cold sweat. Here scopophilia turns against the scopophiliac; the *voyeur* is *vu*. And in another reversal, unlike the case of Pygmalion, where the artist brings the dummy/statue to life, here, the writer/artist himself is turned into a dummy.

Truffaut said that what interested him in *The Man Who Loved Women* were the "detours" and "digressions" of love. Bertrand loves the meanders of the chase more than he prizes the actual capture of the quarry. In this context it is possible to think of the fetishism that characterizes both the film and the protagonist as an issue of "detours" and "digressions." Within fetishism the eye "detours" from the sight of the woman's sex, which, because of fears of castration, is imbued with anxiety, as the gaze slides to neighboring parts of the body and objects of apparel. The whole structure, as has been pointed out ad infinitum by psychoanalytic critics, is one of affirmation and denegation, that of "je sais, mais quand même" (I know, but still . . .). In *The Man Who Loved Women* the fetishism is quite literal, wrapped in lingerie, nightgowns, stockings, and high heels. But fetishism in the film also takes the displaced form of rhetoric and style.

Some rhetorical figures, it seems, have an elective affinity with fetishism. Thus *The Man Who Loved Women* is inordinately fond of synecdochic (part-for-whole) framing. The mise-en-scène emphasizes legs, detached from the torso, over faces. In the opening funeral sequence, male partialism structures the point-of-view shots, which presumably render Bertrand's postmortem view from the grave; the gaze proceeding from his dead body seems to look up at the women's legs. Here, love and death are configured together in the form of the loving/looking corpse. But what is interesting for our purposes here is that the gaze is arrested at the point just prior to the sight of the woman's sex. Many of the erotic episodes in the film involve objects, whether in terms of props and apparel, or in terms of technique, through displacement and partial obscuring. The "Aurora" character is just a voice, here "standing in" for her visual appearance. The usherette, in the dark of the cinema, is only partially glimpsed. Eroticism is triggered by the rustle of stockings, or it is displaced onto books and objets d'art. Even the fact that *The Man Who Loved Women* features very low levels of illumination contributes to an impression of hiding and obscuring. Truffaut chose the relatively anonymous and unrecognizable—for most viewers—parts of the city of Montpelier. Truffaut also prefers "detours" in the sense that he generally avoids nudity, preferring instead well-dressed eroticism.[4]

In the final flashback sequence Bertrand's mother asks the son to carry her letters—which turn out to be love letters—to the post office. Bertrand reads them and resentfully throws them into a sewer/gutter, as if they were just so much despicable garbage. In this sequence, too, the theme of writing becomes cathected with the theme of illicit sexuality. The spectator is reminded not only of the intertextual—in *The 400 Blows* Antoine's mother advises her son that he should study French because "you always have to write letters"—but also of the biographical (the fact that Truffaut himself literally discovered his mother's affairs *through* her letters).

Yet the idea of writing in *The Man Who Loved Women* cannot be reduced to sexuality. Writing in the film bears on a number of interconnected issues, notably authorship, auteurism, autobiography, and cinematic écriture. Bertrand brings up the issue of autobiography quite explicitly, for example, when he asks exactly how one can tell one's own story honestly. (The same question haunted Rousseau in his *Confessions*.) He poses the question haunting all autobiographers—how does one tell one's own story in an objective and nonnarcissistic manner? At times, Bertrand's statements about literary writing recall aspects of auteur theory as practiced by the New Wave, as when Bertrand quotes a friend's idea that "art is as personal as fingerprints," an echo of some of Alexandre Astruc's claims in his landmark 1948 "camera stylo" essay. As the film proceeds, we sense an equivalence between the film and the book written by Bertrand. Truffaut's own films, such as *The 400 Blows* and *Stolen Kisses*, we are reminded, are often literally autobiographical, and even his adaptations, such as *Jules and Jim* and *Two English Girls*, are also highly personal in their emotional thrust, although less directly autobiographical.

Subterranean currents, then, link the writer Roché, the filmmaker Truffaut, and the character Bertrand. For all of them art and writing are fired by a desire that is both sexual and more than sexual, at once metasexual and metatextual. Bertrand in this sense emulates his mother; like her, he writes love letters, and like Roché, he collects them. We know that Roché was an art collector, but we sometimes forget that Truffaut, too, was a collector *à sa façon*, albeit of clippings, stills, scripts, and other memorabilia. Collecting becomes a defense against severe emotional loss, linked to the loss of the mother's love. It is Bertrand's rejection by a woman, who tells him that she prefers younger men, we recall, that triggers his decision to write. Truffaut's artistry, too, was deeply connected to a sense of hurt over rejection, first by his mother and then by other women (even if only in his fevered imagination). We see this process whereby rejection nourishes art as a compensatory exercise already in the short film *Antoine and Collette* (1962), where the young Antoine is repeatedly rebuffed by Collette, and turns to the consolations of art. Writing, as Gide famously put it, can become a form of cheating, where one can always "correct" life by correcting the text, conforming it according to one's deepest desires or to the desires of others. We see this corrective process in the film itself, when Bertrand corrects the text—and Truffaut corrects the film—by changing the color of a child's dress from red to blue.

This same process of compensatory correction occurred with the real-life Roché, when he idealized his amorous life in his novels. Art became a form of solace, as well, with the project of polyphonic writing, which was to provide a "posthumous" writerly solution for an ill-resolved ménage. We are reminded, as well, of the ways that filming, for Truffaut, constituted a creative form of therapy, often serving to release him from the doldrums of depression. A man in frequent emotional and amorous crisis, Truffaut relied on the "happy family" of filmmaking, portrayed in *Day for Night,* for example, as a relief from the bad memories and resentments provoked by his actually existing family and relationships. In that reflexive study of filmmaking and the film milieu Truffaut presents a highly mediated version of Freud's family romance; the happy family of film production replaces the unhappy family of promiscuous mothers and absent fathers.

Feminist filmmaker Yvonne Rainer riffed on Truffaut's title in her film *The Man Who Envied Women,* and it is interesting that the film is deeply imprinted by male "womb envy"—the idea that whereas women procreate and thus create life, men can only create the simulacra of life in the form of art. In the film it is the elderly author/doctor (who has written a book on trout fishing), the man who diagnoses Bertrand's case of a sexually transmitted disease, ironically, who first provokes Bertrand into thinking of writing an autobiographical novel. And the doctor clearly expresses the umbilical link between childbearing, womb envy, and writing. "There is nothing more beautiful," the doctor tells Bertrand, "than seeing one's book published, except, perhaps, for experiencing the delivery of a baby that one has carried for nine months."

As Bertrand's editor, Genevieve, for her part, becomes a kind of "midwife" for Bertrand's creativity. The film's structure generates a kind of textual life-in-death; the character dies, but the book is born. Genevieve defends the manuscript to the publishers when the others—all men—reject it. Only women, it is implied, really appreciate Bertrand/Truffaut. (We are also reminded of the role of women such as Silvia Beach and Adrienne Monnier as the "midwives" of modernism.)[5] The collaboration of writer and editor in the film also recalls Truffaut's own collaborations with women editors and continuity persons and script doctors like Suzanne Schiffman. The editing of Bertrand's book, in this sense, recalls the editing of Truffaut's film, in that both entail an analogous process of selection and sequencing. Truffaut was famous for his endless up-to-the-last-minute modifications of his films, and Bertrand, like Truffaut himself, constantly reedits his text. Genevieve, for her part, gives birth to Bertrand's book, much as Truffaut, metaphorically speaking, facilitated the "delivery"—that is, the publication—of Roché's diaries, while also "midwifing" Roché's posthumous success. Genevieve provides the title for the book, and she is also the midwife in the sense that she tells Bertrand when he can no longer make revisions, which corresponds to the procreative moment when the contractions of labor give way to the actual delivery. We are reminded both of Roché's incapacity to stop writing and start publishing and of the flashback mother's admonition to Bertrand that he "cannot move" as he reads. The process of the film is to generate the film, which is both process and the product of that process. This mise-en-abîme procedure is, of course, already familiar from literature, as when *A la recherche du temps perdu* becomes itself the book that Marcel is writing, and also from the cinema, where Fellini's finished film *8½* is itself the film that the protagonist, Guido, is shown in the process of making.

The Man Who Loved Women exhibits a concern that typifies many Truffaut films: a concern with the actual process of production of art. As I noted earlier, the theme already marks Truffaut's overture film *The 400 Blows*, in the form of the references to writing, to printing presses, to handwriting, to typewriters, and so forth. The theme is also expressed in the shots of the pressing/printing on vinyl of musical albums in the short film *Love at Twenty*. *Day for Night*, similarly, lovingly delineates the stages in the production process of film. Truffaut spoke in interviews of his desire to make a film detailing the entire process of writing and producing and printing a book. (Truffaut's beloved Balzac had done precisely that, more than a century earlier, in his novel about the publishing industry: *Illusions Perdues*). Among the many symptoms of Truffaut's bibliophilia is the deep revulsion expressed by the characters in *Jules and Jim* at the sight of a newsreel showing Nazis burning books, and the destruction of books is, of course, the central theme of Truffaut's adaptation of the Ray Bradbury novel *Fahrenheit 451* (1966). Annette Insdorf has suggested that *The Man Who Loved Women* might as well have been entitled *The Man Who Loved Film*. It might have also

23. The midwife for art: Genevieve in *The Man Who Loved Women*. Source: Photofest.

been called, I would add, in a further architextual wrinkle, *The Man Who Loved Books*. The very last word in the film, significantly, is the word *book*: "On appèle ça un livre" (That's what's called a book).

The Truffaut film suggests a complex relationship between writing and seduction. On the one hand, writing is part of seduction and a compensation for failed seduction or failed relationships. In *The Man Who Loved Women* Bertrand seduces Genevieve (and vice versa) through the process of writing, much as Truffaut seduced many of his lovers through the process of filmmaking. On the other hand, the film offers a limited "happy end" for Genevieve, one of the few women in the Truffaut oeuvre who transcends the mother/whore dichotomy, in that she is both lover and symbolically at least, a "mother," if only of Bertrand's book. She is the only woman in the film not fetishized into eroticized body parts, the only one framed in her entirety. We remember the historical polarity, developed by Truffaut's mentor Bazin, between "bad" montage and "good" mise-en-scène, and in *The Man Who Loved Women* montage is on the side of fetishism and male partialism, while mise-en-scène is on the side of integrity and sexual maturity and a decent respect for women. Genevieve does not "cure" Bertrand of his restless womanizing, but at least she "watches over" the production of his child, the book, and thus serves as a "good enough mother." Anne Gillain notes that Bertrand dies as he is reaching out toward the motherlike nurse. The violation of the incest taboo, in a sense, kills him, as he cuts off his own blood supply. (We are reminded of the old joke that the blood that swells the penis in erection is drawn directly from the brain.) Bertrand is killed twice over by his obsession, first as he is in the process of—to use that wonderfully fetishistic phrase—"skirt-chasing" and second as he is "nurse-chasing." On another level, of course, the finale provides just one more example, so typical of Truffaut's films, of women, or at least of male desire for women, becoming dangerous to men's health.

The Man Who Loved Women also reveals Truffaut's highly fraught and problematic relation to feminism and the feminist movement. Truffaut provides the romantic-tragic art film counterpart to the comic-parodic version found in the Woody Allen films, that is, the portrayal of the plight of a bewildered man ideologically shaped by the phallocratic 1950s and now confronted by a resurgent feminist movement. That movement, in which Simone de Beauvoir's 1949 classic *The Second Sex* was a key text, challenged all the axiomatic gender assumptions of earlier eras. Reportedly, Truffaut was worried about how feminists might react to the film.[6] *The Man Who Loved Women* premiered, after all, just eight years after Nelly Kaplan's gyno-anarchistic *La Fiancée du pirate* and just one year after Agnes Varda's feminist *L'Une chante, l'autre pas*. And feminist critics did indeed find the film misogynistic, even while appreciating it in other ways. Truffaut's "worries" about the feminist reaction to the film suggest a parallel between two incarnations of denial: first, the mother in the film—as the woman who says "no," who tells Bertrand that he "cannot move"—and second, the feminists as those who "say no" to sexist representations by male artists and film directors, who say "no" to masculinist portrayals.

At the same time, the film hints at a not-very-persuasive baby-step version of feminist critique and the empowerment of women. Genevieve exercises sexual agency as a woman and intellectual agency as a critic/collaborator. At the same time, she exercises narrational power by providing the voice-over of the funeral frame story. Truffaut's own self-defense against the charge of misogyny was that women in his films were almost always stronger than the men. But one might object to this line of thinking, arguing instead that while his women characters are certainly strong, they are also lethal, phallic mothers who literally kill men, the case in *Jules and Jim*, *The Soft Skin*, *The Bride Wore Black*, and *The Woman Next Door*. (Indeed, Truffaut pointed out that *The Man Who Loved Women*, with its episodic structure, could as easily have concerned murders as seductions, in the manner of *The Bride Wore Black*). The more important point, perhaps, is that the women are seen fetishistically and even "solipsized," as Nabokov's Humbert Humbert says of Lolita. Furthermore, the film's "harem structure" grants one man access to many women. Like a pacha in his seraglio, Bertrand does not need to confront male rivals to his domain. That one of Bertrand's fantasies turns a pride of suited businessmen, at an airport, into a bevy of beautiful women betrays the polygamous fantasy at the kernel of the film's erotic utopia.

POSTLUDE

IN THIS VOLUME we have strolled like flâneurs through various lives and relationships and texts. We have disentangled the uncanny connections that link people and books and films across generations, across cultures, and across media. Many commentators have compared the relation between film and novel to that of a couple. For Gabriel García Márquez film and literature are like an incompatible couple whose members cannot live with, or without, each other. In this sense the cinematic adaptation resembles the "woman next door" of the Truffaut film, that is, the illicit, unacknowledged partner, the fatally attractive "other woman" who ultimately kills off the "original" husband or spouse.

Which brings us to a final question. What do these novels and memoirs and films, so obsessed with sexual "fidelity" and "infidelity," have to say about artistic fidelity in adaptation? Here I have tried to go beyond a one-on-one monogamous fidelity model in which we declare, thumbs up or thumbs down, the adaptation either faithful or unfaithful to the original. Rather, I have tried to place the novels and the films within a broader, ramifying transtext. In the end one can say of novels and their adaptations what Freud said of conjugal bedrooms: they are inhabited by many invisible participants. Or to put it differently, in the language of René Girard, the love involved in adaptations, like all forms of love, is triangular. For Girard, mimetic desire occurs when the subject desires an object because it is desired by another subject. Adaptation in this sense triggers a kind of mimetic amorous competition in relation to the source novel. As a postmodern boutade has it, any text that has slept with one text has inevitably slept with all the texts that the first text has slept with. Art, in this sense, is a textually transmitted dis-ease, a sexual/textual daisy chain of cross-media influence. In Truffaut's case it is as if the eroticized energies of the novels and memoirs catalyzed the eroticized energies of the films. Rather than a question of fidelity, we have a question of the new forms of energy coursing through various texts.

But adaptations are also triangular in the sense that they look backward and sideways, and even forward, at other texts. My goal here has been to pluralize perspectives on the actual prototypes and the characters drawn from them and thus to pluralize perspectives on the films. I have tried to "haunt" the Truffaut film with the ghosts of other texts and characters and persons lurking in the shadows and between the lines, not only with the biography of the real-life Helen Grund Hessel, for example, but also with the more spectral presences of the Helen of the various novels, of her own journals, or the Helen of Roché's journals, to reveal Helen/Catherine as she is seen polyperspectivally, by Franz Hessel, by Roché, by Charlotte Wolff, by her sons, and by Truffaut, in an infinite regress of refractions and reflections.[1] Both texts and selves, in this sense, are revealed as partial creations of the other's gaze.

TIME LINE

1878	Marriage of Pierre Roché and Clara Coquet
1879	Birth of Henri-Pierre Roché
1880	Birth of Franz Hessel
1886	Birth of Helen Grund
1889	Franz Hessel's family moves to Berlin
1894	Birth of Denise Renard
1895	Roché meets Violet and Margaret Hart
1897	Roché goes to England
1899	Franz moves to Munich
1902	Roché asks Margaret to marry him
	Roché meets Germaine Bonnard (longtime mistress and first wife)
1904	Birth of Charlotte Wolff
1907	Roché meets Franz Hessel in Paris
1909	Roché's affair with Margaret Hart
	Ménage à trois involving Roché, Franz Hessel, and "Lau"
1912	Roché meets Helen Grund in Paris
1913	Franz Hessel marries Helen Grund
	Helen's leap into the Seine
	Publication of Franz Hessel's novel *Der Kramladen des Glücks* (The Bazaar of Happiness)
	Helen and Franz return to Berlin
1914	Birth of Hessels' son Ulrich
1916–1919	Roché in New York, friendship with Marcel Duchamp
	Birth of Hessels' son Stéphane

1920   Publication of Roché's *Don Juan et . . .*

       Beginning of Roché's liaison with Helen Grund Hessel

       Publication of Hessel's *Pariser Romanze* (Parisian Romance)

1924   Franz Hessel first meets Walter Benjamin

1925   Franz/Roché/Helen ménage in Paris

1926   Franz Hessel and Walter Benjamin work on the Proust translation

1927   Roché's letter to Freud

       Roché's secret marriage to Germaine Bonnard

       Publication of Franz Hessel's novel *Heimliches Berlin* (Secret Berlin)

1928   Publication of Hessel's *Spazieren in Berlin*

1929   Death of Roché's mother

       Denise Renard becomes Roché's mistress in the "wake" of his mother's death

1931   Birth of Roché's son Jean-Claude from Roché's relationship with Denise Renard

1932   Birth of François Truffaut

1933   Both Germaine Bonnard and Helen Grund Hessel break with Roché (over revelation of the child with Renard)

       Franz Hessel is forbidden by the Nazi regime to publish in Germany

1934   Germaine Bonnard refuses to divorce Roché

1934   Helen lives with Charlotte Wolff in Paris

1936   Helen divorces Franz

1940   Hessel imprisoned near Aix-en-Provence

1941   Death of Franz Hessel

1943   First draft of *Jules et Jim*

       Roché writes two screenplays for Jean Renoir ("The Unique Man" and "The Unique Woman") based on Roché's friendship with the Hessels

1946   Roché submits a draft of *Jules et Jim* to Gallimard but without results

1947   Helen and her son Ulrich are naturalized French citizens

       Helen moves with her diplomat son Stéphane to New York (she stays until 1950)

1948   Death of Germaine Bonnard

       Marriage of Roché and Denise Renard

1953   Publication of *Jules et Jim* by Gallimard

1955   *Deux Anglaises* (Two English Girls) accepted for publication

1956   Truffaut mentions Roché's book *Jules et Jim* favorably in his review of Edgar Ulmer's western *The Naked Dawn* in *Arts*

       First contacts between Truffaut and Roché

1959   Death of Roché

       Truffaut's *The 400 Blows*

1961   Truffaut's *Jules and Jim*

1964   Truffaut's *The Soft Skin*

1971   Truffaut's *Two English Girls*

1977   Truffaut's *The Man Who Loved Women*

1977   Posthumous publication of Roché's *Victor*

1982   Death of Helen Grund Hessel in Paris; burial in Montparnasse cemetery

1984   Death of François Truffaut in Paris

1985   Release of Thomas Honickel's film *Der Schlüssel zu Jules und Jim* (The Key to Jules and Jim), which includes interviews with Ulrich and Stéphane Hessel and with Jean-Claude Roché, Henri-Pierre Roché's son with Denise Renard Roché

1986   Death of Charlotte Wolff

1989   Publication in Berlin of Manfred Flügge, ed., *Letzte Heimkehr nach Paris: Franz Hessel und die Seinen im Exil*

1990   Publication of Henri-Pierre Roché's *Carnets*

1991   Publication of Helen Hessel's *Journals*

1993   Publication in Berlin of Manfred Flügge's *Gesprungene Liebe: Die wahre Geschichte zu Jules und Jim*

Release of the film *Jules und Jim: Die wahre Geschichte* (Jules and Jim: The True Story) by Elisabeth Weyer

1998   Publication in Berlin of Ernest Wichner and Herbert Wiesner, eds., *Franz Hessel: Nur was uns anschaut, sehen wir* (catalogue for a Franz Hessel exposition)

1999   Publication of biography of Henri-Pierre Roché by Scarlett and Philippe Reliquet: *Henri-Pierre Roché: L'Enchanteur collectionneur*

2005   Release of the Criterion DVD of *Jules and Jim*, which includes edited excerpts from Thomas Honickel's film *Der Schlüssel zu Jules und Jim* (The Key to Jules and Jim), along with numerous interviews with François Truffaut concerning *Jules and Jim* and Truffaut's relationship with Henri-Pierre Roché, as well as interviews or audio commentaries by various collaborators such as cinematographer Raoul Coutard, screenwriter Jean Gruault, collaborator Suzanne Schiffman, editor Claudine Bouché, actress Jeanne Moreau, biographer Serge Toubiana, and film scholar Annette Insdorf.

This time line is culled from the various biographies and autobiographies mentioned earlier, those by Antoine de Baecque and Serge Toubiana; Manfred Flügge; Stéphane Hessel; Ulrich Hessel; Carlton Lake; Ian MacKillop; Scarlett and Philippe Reliquet; and Charlotte Wolff.

NOTES

PRELUDE

1 On "sexual modernism" see Christine Stansell, *American Moderns: Bohemian New York and the Creation of a New Century* (New York: Henry Holt, 2000), esp. 225–310.

2 Andrea Barnet, *All-Night Party: The Women of Bohemian Greenwich Village and Harlem, 1913–1930* (Chapel Hill, NC: Algonquin Books, 2004), 1.

3 See Carolyn Burke, *Becoming Modern: The Life of Mina Loy* (Berkeley: University of California Press, 1996), 191.

4 I would like to acknowledge my debt, in terms of biographical information, to the following books especially: Antoine de Baecque and Serge Toubiana, *François Truffaut* (Paris: Gallimard, 1996); Carlton Lake, *Confessions of a Literary Archaeologist* (New York: New Directions, 1990); Carlton Lake and Linda Ashton, *Henri-Pierre Roché: An Introduction* (Austin: Harry Ransom Humanities Research Center, University of Texas, 1991); Dudley Andrew, *André Bazin* (New York: Oxford University Press, 1978); Scarlett Reliquet and Philippe Reliquet, *Henri-Pierre Roché: L'Enchanteur collectionneur* (Paris: Ramsaye, 1999); Ian MacKillop, *Free Spirits: Henri-Pierre Roché, François Truffaut, and the Two English Girls* (London: Bloomsbury, 2000); Manfred Flügge, *Le Tourbillon de la vie: La Veritable histoire de "Jules et Jim,"* trans. Nicole Bary (Paris: Albin Michel, 1994); Stéphane Hessel, *Danse avec le siècle* (Paris: Seuil, 1997); Jean-Michel Palmier's preface to the French translation of Hessel's *Spazieren in Berlin*, translated as *Promenades dans Berlin* (Grenoble: Presses Universitaires de Grenoble, 1992); and Charlotte Wolff, *Hindsight: An Autobiography* (New York: Quartet, 1980). Flügge's *Le Tourbillon de la vie* also contains two informative autobiographies by Franz and Helen Hessel's sons: the elder son's "The Autobiography of Ulrich Hessel"; and Stéphane Hessel's "In Their Hands."

5 See Laura Kipnis, *Against Love* (New York: Pantheon, 2003).

6 See Robert Stam, *Literature through Film: Realism, Magic, and the Art of Adaptation* (Oxford: Blackwell, 2005); Robert Stam and Alessandra Raengo, eds., *Literature and Film* (Oxford: Blackwell, 2005); and Robert Stam and Alessandra Raengo, eds., *Companion to Literature and Film* (Oxford: Blackwell, 2004).

7 Quoted in Carlton Lake, *Confessions of a Literary Archaeologist*, 38. I would like to thank Richard Sieburth for prodding me to look, however briefly and inadequately, into these literary antecedents for the writing of the Hessels.

CHAPTER 1. THE ORIGINS OF TRUFFAUT'S *JULES AND JIM*

1 François Truffaut, *Le Plaisir des yeux* (Paris: Cahiers du Cinema, 1987), 163 (translation mine).

2 From the archives of Truffaut's film production company (Films du Carosse), quoted in de Baecque and Toubiana, *François Truffaut*, 91 (translation mine).

3 See Andrew, *André Bazin*, 151, 195–196.

4 Letter cited in ibid., 208.

5 Truffaut, *Plaisir des yeux*, 146–155.

6 Michael Hollington suggests a less savory link between Truffaut and Roché, to wit, their roots in Vichy, which Hollington suggests, without giving evidence, that Truffaut supported, and which Roché clearly did support, going so far as to write a Vichyist replacement for the "Marseillaise." Roché's Germanophilia, as Hollington puts it, "admirable in the 20s, when there was near-total aversion in France to all things German, [had] clearly taken a more unattractive turn." See Michael Hollington, "About Some Figures of Matriarchy from Bachofen to Truffaut via Benjamin, Roché, and Hessel." (I thank Dudley Andrew for sending me this apparently unpublished manuscript.)

7 In practical terms Truffaut worked with screenwriter Jean Gruault to annotate the novel, choose key passages, and reduce the treatment to a manageable size. Truffaut had the idea of alternating voice-over narration and direct enactment. He added some anecdotes and quotations (e.g., from Apollinaire) not in the novel. According to Carole Le Berre the adaptation went through four distinct stages after Truffaut's initial treatment: (1) the Gruault version, based on Truffaut's notes, which had a more political ending: Jules and Gilberte go to Germany, where the couple is distressed by the triumph of the Nazis; (2) a second version, in which Catherine takes on more importance, with heightened emphasis on the First World War; (3) a third version (never filmed), which includes Jim's escape from a German prison camp; and (4) the shoot itself, where Truffaut added certain sequences such as the bicycle rides and Thérèse's cigarette locomotive. See Carole Le Berre, *Jules et Jim: François Truffaut: étude critique* (Paris: Nathan, 1995).

8. Anne Gillain, *François Truffaut: Le Secret perdu* (Paris: Hatier, 1991), 19.

9. Ibid.

10. The story of Truffaut's search for his real father is also told in the Michel Pascal and Serge Toubiana documentary *Portraits volés* (1993).

11. See de Baecque and Toubiana, *François Truffaut*, 361.

12. See Truffaut, *Le Plaisir des yeux*, 247.

13. This question of the mother's exclusive knowledge of the "real father" is reminiscent of an old joke. A young adolescent begins to date girls from his own town but discovers that every girl he courts has already slept with his father. Distraught, he seeks companions farther afield, in neighboring cities, yet even there he discovers the same thing—all the women have slept with his

father. Becoming more and more desperate, he goes abroad, only to discover exactly the same situation. In despair he finally goes back to tell his mother. Her response: "Don't worry. He's not really your father."

14. See Anne Gillain, *Le Cinéma selon François Truffaut* (Paris: Flammarion, 1988), 386.

15. François Truffaut, interview by Anne de Gasperi, *Le Quotidian de Paris*, May 2, 1975.

16. Francois Truffaut, *Arts*, quoted in De Baecque and Toubiana, *François Truffaut*, 163.

17. In Genevieve Sellier's words the New Wave "claims legitimacy from a male-singular point of view, over against the collective patriarchal instance undergirding the 'popular' cinema of the preceding period" (Sellier, "La Nouvelle vague: Un cinema à la premiere personne du masculin singulier," *Iris*, no. 24 [1997]: 78).

CHAPTER 2. THE NEW WAVE AND ADAPTATION

1. Astruc's essay was first published in *Ecran Français*, no. 144 (1948). It is included in *The New Wave*, ed. Peter Graham (London: Secker and Warburg, 1969), 17–23.

2. See Maria Tortajada, "From Libertinage to Eric Rohmer: Transcending 'Adaptation,'" in *A Companion to Literature and Film*, ed. Robert Stam and Alessandra Raengo (Oxford: Blackwell, 2004).

3. Andre Bazin, *What Is Cinema?* trans. Hugh Gray (Berkeley: University of California Press, 1967), 1:75.

4. André Bazin, "Adaptation, or the Cinema as Digest," in *Bazin at Work: Major Essays and Reviews from the Forties and Fifties*, trans. Alain Piette, ed. Bert Cardullo (New York: Routledge, 1997), 48–49.

5. Ibid.

6. See Antonio de Baecque, *Histoire d'une Revue: 1951–1959* (Paris: Cahiers du Cinema, 1991), 1:107–109. For an extended discussion of these polemics, see Richard Neupert, *A History of the French New Wave Cinema* (Madison: University of Wisconsin Press, 2002)

7. Bazin, "Adaptation, or the Cinema as Digest," 46.

8. Ibid., 49.

9. See François Truffaut, *Le Plaisir des yeux*.

10. Ibid., 233.

11. See *Cahiers du Cinema: The 1950s, Neo Realism, Hollywood, New Wave*, ed. Jim Hillier (Cambridge, MA: Harvard University Press, 1985).

CHAPTER 3. THE PROTOTYPE FOR JIM

1. Quoted in Lake, *Confessions of a Literary Archaeologist*, 37.

2. Ibid., 41.

3. Ibid., 31.

4. For informed speculation on this point see Reliquet and Reliquet, *Henri-Pierre Roché*.

5. Ibid., 283.

6. Quoted in MacKillop, *Free Spirits*, 69.

7. Quoted in ibid., 136.

8. Henri-Pierre Roché, *Carnets: Les Années Jules et Jim* (Marseille: Andre Dimanche, 1990), xxxii. Subsequent references to this work will be given as *Carnets* in the text. All translations are mine.

9. See MacKillop, *Free Spirits*, 12.

10. Ibid.

CHAPTER 4. NEW YORK INTERLUDE

1. Annie Cohen-Solal, *Painting American: The Rise of American Artists* (New York: Knopf, 2001), 204.

2. Ibid., 153.

3. For one portrait of modernism and collecting in this period see Marius de Zayas, *How, When, and Why Modern Art Came to New York*, ed. Francis M. Naivan (Cambridge, MA: MIT Press, 1996).

4. See Mabel Dodge Luhan, *Intimate Memories* (Albuquerque: University of New Mexico Press, 1999), 119.

5. Quoted in John Leland, *Hip: The History* (New York: HarperCollins, 2004), 246.

6. Quoted in Jonathan Margolis, *O: The Intimate History of the Orgasm* (New York: Grove Press, 2004), 315.

7. See Stansell, *American Moderns*, 274–275.

8. Ibid., 225.

9. See Shari Benstock, *Women of the Left Bank: Paris, 1900–1940* (Austin: University of Texas Press, 1986).

10. Cohen-Solal, *Painting American*, 86.

11. From an unpublished piece called "How New York Did Strike M," cited in Reliquet and Reliquet, *Henri-Pierre Roché*, 81.

12. Ibid.

13. Quoted in MacKillop, *Free Spirits*, 143–144.

14. See Barnet, *All-Night Party*, 40.

15. See Robert Motherwell, ed., *The Dada Painters and Poets* (New York: George Wittenborn, 1951), 259 (cited in Barnet, *All-Night Party*, 31).

16. Cited in Barnet, *All-Night Party*, 32.

17. Quoted in ibid., 34.

18. Quoted in Ruth Brandon, *Surreal Lives: The Surrealists, 1917–1945* (New York: Grove Press, 1999), 69.

19. Beatrice Wood, quoted in Brandon, *Surreal Lives*, 65.

CHAPTER 5. THE DON JUAN BOOKS

1. See MacKillop, *Free Spirits*, 135.

2. Shoshana Felman, *The Scandal of the Speaking Body: Don Juan with J. L. Austin, or Seduction in Two Languages* (Stanford, CA: Stanford University Press, 1983), 17.

3. Henri-Pierre Roché, *Don Juan et . . .* (Marseille: Andre Dimanche, 1994), 3.

4. Manfred Flügge, *Gesprungene Liebe: Die wahre Geschichte zu "Jules und Jim"* (Berlin: Aufbau-Verlag, 1993). See Flügge, *Le Tourbillon de la vie*, 209.

5. Roché, *Don Juan et . . .*, 3.

6. See the interview with Carlos Fuentes in *The World of Luis Buñuel*, ed. Joan Mellen (New York: Oxford, 1978), 69–70.

7. de Baecque and Toubiana, *François Truffaut*, 78.

8. François Truffaut, *Les Films de ma vie* (Paris: Flammarion, 1975), 14.

9. Helen Hessel, *Journal d'Helen: Lettres à Henri-Pierre Roché* (Marseille: Andre Dimanche, 1991), 454. Subsequent references to this source will be cited as *Journal* in the text.

10. Henri-Pierre Roché, *Jules and Jim*, trans. Patrick Evans (London: Marion Boyar, 1992), 216. All references are to this translation.

11. Henri-Pierre Roché, *Deux Anglaises et le Continent* (Paris: Gallimard, 1956), 58, 136 (all translations mine).

12. *Two English Girls*, 136, quoted in Reliquet and Reliquet, *Henri-Pierre Roché*, 30.

13. Quoted in MacKillop, *Free Spirits*, 40.

14. Ibid., 48.

15. Quoted in Reliquet and Reliquet, *Henri-Pierre Roché*, 248.

16. See Robert Greene, *The Art of Seduction* (New York: Viking, 2001), 45.

17. Quoted in Flügge, *Le Tourbillon de la vie*, 60.

18. "The Nude-Descending-a-Staircase-Man Surveys Us," *New York Tribune*, Sep. 12, 1915, quoted in Reliquet and Reliquet, *Henri-Pierre Roché*, 84.

CHAPTER 6. THE PROTOTYPE FOR JULES

1. See Hessel, *Danse avec le siècle*, 12.

2. Ibid., 13.

3. Hollington, "About Some Figures of Matriarchy" (see chap. 1, n. 7).

4. Ibid.

5. Palmier, preface, 14–15 (see above Prelude, n. 4).

6. Hollington, "About Some Figures of Matriarchy," points out that Benjamin also read at least two books by Roché—the 1921 *Don Juan* and *Six semaines a la conciergerie pendant la bataille de la Marne*.

7. Quoted in Susan Buck-Morss, *The Dialectics of Seeing: Walter Benjamin and the Arcades Project* (Cambridge, MA: MIT Press, 1991), 38.

8. Ibid.

9. Cited in Momme Broderson, *Walter Benjamin: A Biography*, trans. Malcolm R. Green and Ingrida Ligers (London: Verso, 1996), 165.

10. Quoted in Flügge, *Le Tourbillon de la vie*, 209.

11. Michael Hollington speculates that Benjamin initially declined the invitation to live with the Hessels because he suspected that Helen might "be enlisting him as a pawn in her struggle with Roché, which consisted in part . . . in outdoing her lover in the art of seduction" (Hollington, "About Some Figures of Matriarchy" [see chap. 1, n. 7]).

12. Broderson, *Walter Benjamin*, 166.

13. Cited in ibid., 169.

14. Quoted in ibid.

15. Gillain, *François Truffaut*, 18.

16. See Anne Friedberg's *Window Shopping: Cinema and the Postmodern* (Berkeley: University of California Press, 1993).

17. See Manuela Ribeiro Sanches, "Franz Hessel ou a Provocacao da Insolencia," *Revista Portuguesa de Estudos Germanisticos*, no. 13–14 (1990).

18. Ibid., 409.

19. From Franz Hessel, *Ermunterungen zum Genuss*, quoted in Ribeiro Sanches, "Franz Hessel," 408.

20. Anke Gleber, *The Art of Taking a Walk: Flânerie, Literature, and Film in Weimar Culture* (Princeton, NJ: Princeton University Press, 1999), viii.

21. From *Ein Flaneur in Berlin*, quoted in ibid., 66.

22. See Walter Benjamin, "Paris of the Second Empire in Baudelaire," in *Charles Baudelaire: A Lyric Poet in the Era of High Capitalism*, trans. Harry Zohn (London: Verso, 1983), 37.

23. On the Brazilian modernists see my *Subversive Pleasures: Bakhtin, Cultural Criticism, and Film* (Baltimore: Johns Hopkins University Press, 1989). For more on the key role of flânerie, as both concept and practice, in the literature of modernity, see also Buck-Morss, *Dialectics of Seeing*; Guiliana Bruno, *Streetwalking on a Ruined Map: Cultural Theory and the City Films of Elvira Nartori* (Princeton, NJ: Princeton University Press, 1993); and Friedberg, *Window Shopping*.

24. Gleber, *Art of Taking a Walk*, 77.

25. See Ron Shields, "Fancy Footwork: Walter Benjamin's Notes on Flânerie," in *The Flâneur*, ed. Keith Tester (London: Routledge, 1994), 77.

26. Quoted in Gleber, *Art of Taking a Walk*, 93.

27. Ibid.

28. Sellier, "La Nouvelle vague."

29. Ibid., 78–79.

30. Ginette Vincendeau, *Stars and Stardom in French Cinema* (London: Routledge, 2000), 120.

31. The essay is included in Truffaut, *Le Plaisir des yeux*.

CHAPTER 7. HESSEL AS NOVELIST

1. Hessel, *Danse avec le siècle*, 26–27.

2. Although Henri-Pierre Roché had many Jewish friends, he was disturbingly acquiescent in demonstrations of anti-Semitism, both before and during Vichy. As his "American friend," the art dealer John Quinn became more and more pathologically anti-Semitic, Roché never disputed his ideas. When Quinn wrote in a letter that a Jewish man, Charles Sheeler, was a crook and that, furthermore, "Jews look like pigs," Roché responds only that he "didn't know Sheerer was Jewish." See Reliquet and Reliquet, *Henri-Pierre Roché*, 144.

3. Ribeiro Sanches, "Franz Hessel ou a Provocacao da Insolencia," 410 (see chap. 6, n. 16).

4. Flügge, *Le Tourbillon de la vie*, 220.

5. Quoted in Gleber, *Art of Taking a Walk*, 79.

6. Cited in Palmier, preface, 28 (see above Prelude, n. 4).

7. Hessel, *Danse avec le siècle*, 58.

8. Palmier, preface, 28.

9. Hessel, *Danse avec le siècle*, 65.

10. See Reliquet and Reliquet, *Henri-Pierre Roché*, 143, 215–216.

11. Quoted in MacKillop, *Free Spirits*, 152.

12. See ibid.

CHAPTER 8. HESSEL'S *PARISIAN ROMANCE*

1. Franz Hessel, *Le Bazar du Bonheir/Romance Parisienne* (Paris: 10/18, 1990).

2. Ibid., 263 (all translations are mine).

3. After having largely disappeared from public consciousness, Hessel was "rediscovered" because of the 1961 film and rediscovered again when his principal texts began to be published in Germany (through publishers such as Suhrkamp and Das Arsenal) and translated in France (beginning in 1989).

CHAPTER 9. THE PROTOTYPE FOR CATHERINE

1. A personal communication from Ulrich Hessel reported by Jean-Michel Palmier, in Palmier, preface, 17n (see above Prelude, n. 4).

2. Stéphane Hessel to Jean-Michel Palmier, reported in ibid.

3. See MacKillop, *Free Spirits*, 149.

4. Quoted in Flügge, *Le Tourbillon de la vie*, 203 (translation mine).

5. Quoted in Karin Grund's preface to Hessel, *Journal d'Helen: Lettres à Henri-Pierre Roché* (Marseille: Andre Dimanche, 1991), x.

6. Vincendeau, *Stars and Stardom*, 126.

7. Ibid., 128.

8. See MacKillop, *Free Spirits*, 150.

9. The very minor figure of Thérèse, in Truffaut's film, finally, was borrowed from a character in Roché's *Two English Girls*, a provincial circus performer who migrated to the urban bohemia of Montparnasse.

CHAPTER 10. L'AMOUR LIVRESQUE

1. For Anne Friedberg the flâneuse emerges simultaneously with the department store and the emergence of the woman as prototypical consumer. See Friedberg, *Window Shopping*, 32–37.

2. From Charlotte Wolff, *Augenblicke verandern uns mehr als die Zeit* (Weinheim: Basel und Beltz, 1983), 123, quoted in Hessel, *Danse avec le siècle*, 34.

3. Charlotte Wolff, *Hindsight*, 69.

4. Ibid., 71.

5. Ibid., 96.

6. Ibid., 112–113.

7. Hessel, *Danse avec le siècle*, 33–34.

8. Wolff, *Hindsight*, 122.

9. Ibid., 135.

10. Quoted in Gleber, *Art of Taking a Walk*, 114.

11. See Flügge, *Le Tourbillon de la vie*, 229.

12. Franz Hessel, *Le Dernier voyage* (Paris: Le Promeneur, 1997), 47.

CHAPTER 11. THE POLYPHONIC PROJECT

1. Laura Kipnis, "Adultery," *Critical Inquiry* 24, no. 2 (winter 1998): 312.

2. Roché, *Jules and Jim*, 91. Subsequent quotations from this source are cited parenthetically in the text.

CHAPTER 12. *JULES AND JIM*: THE NOVEL

1. Reliquet and Reliquet, *Henri-Pierre Roché*, 292.

CHAPTER 13. FROM NOVEL TO FILM

1. Lake, *Confessions of a Literary Archaeologist*, 42.

2. François Truffaut, preface to Henri-Pierre Roché, *Carnets: Les Années Jules et Jim* (Marseille: Andre Dimanche, 1990), x (translation mine).

3. From *Arts*, March 14, 1956, quoted in de Baecque and Toubiana, *François Truffaut*, 154–155.

4. Truffaut, *Le Plaisir des yeux*, 144.

5. See Gillain, *Le Cinéma selon François Truffaut*, 132.

6. Ibid.

7. Roché, *Jules and Jim*, 79.

8. Ironically, Truffaut's adaptation in the 1960s is less mainstream and conventional than the 1980 Mazursky remake, *Willie and Phil*.

9. See Le Berre, *Jules et Jim*, 17. Le Berre's book provides a meticulous analysis of the film in all its aspects.

10. See my essay "Introduction: The Theory and Practice of Adaptation," in *Literature and Film*, ed. Robert Stam and Alessandra Raengo (Oxford: Blackwell, 2005).

11. See Le Berre, *Jules et Jim*, 32. While checking proofs for this book, I became aware of Le Berre's marvelous recent book *François Truffaut au Travail* (Paris: Cahiers du Cinéma, 2004). Le Berre offers a detailed analysis of the process of creation of all of Truffaut's films.

12. Ibid., 42.

13. Ibid.

CHAPTER 14. DISARMING THE SPECTATOR

1. See David Davidson, *"Jules and Jim,"* unpublished essay submitted to my French New Wave class.

2. Roché, *Jules and Jim*, 9.

3. Here Truffaut picks up an important theme in the work of the New Wave directors when they were film critics and theorists: film's relation to the other arts.

4. Truffaut, preface to *Jules and Jim*, by Henri-Pierre Roché, trans. Patrick Evans (London: Marion Boyars, 1992), pages not numbered.

5. See Truffaut, *Le Plaisir des yeux*, 172.

6. Quoted in Lake and Ashton, *Henri-Pierre Roché*, 154.

7. See de Baecque and Toubiana, *François Truffaut*.

8. From the "Dossier Godard" at the Films du Carosse archive (cited in ibid., 275).

9. Quoted in Gillain, *Le Cinéma selon François Truffaut*, 143.

10. Harold Bloom, *Yeats* (New York: Oxford University Press, 1970), 485.

11. Cited in Flügge, *Le Tourbillon de la vie*, 307.

12. See Reliquet and Reliquet, *Henri-Pierre Roché*, 219.

13. Roché, *Carnets*, 38.

14. For a detailed analysis of the style of *Jules and Jim* see Le Berre, *Jules and Jim*.

15. Quoted from Truffaut's correspondence in de Baecque and Toubiana, *François Truffaut*, 255.

16. Quoted in Reliquet and Reliquet, *Henri-Pierre Roché*, 255.

17. Cited in de Baecque and Toubiana, *François Truffaut*, 264 (translation mine).

CHAPTER 15. POLYPHONIC EROTICISM

1. See Lake, *Confessions of a Literary Archaeologist*, 35.

2. See Reliquet and Reliquet, *Henri-Pierre Roché*, 52–53.

3. The previous entries are quoted in Lake, *Confessions of a Literary Archaeologist*, 45–48. For a discussion of Hessel's relations with Walter Benjamin see Dudley Andrew, "Jules, Jim, and Walter Benjamin," in *The Image in Dispute: Art and Cinema in the Age of Photography*, ed. Dudley Andrew (Austin: University of Texas Press, 1997), 33–54.

CHAPTER 16. SEXPERIMENTAL WRITING

1. Kipnis, *Against Love*, 18–19.

2. See Wyatt Phillips, "François Truffaut: Two Specific Intertextual Discourses" (Dec. 2003), unpublished paper for my French New Wave class.

CHAPTER 17. SEXUALITY/TEXTUALITY

1. Roland Barthes, *A Lover's Discourse: Fragments* (New York: Hill and Wang, 1978), 142, 173.

2. Ibid., 73.

3. Quoted in MacKillop, *Free Spirits*, 95.

4. Barthes, *A Lover's Discourse*, 32.

5. On this tradition in painting see Walter Laqueur, *Solitary Sex: A Cultural History of Masturbation* (New York: Zone, 2003).

6. For a Bakhtinian analysis of the languages of eroticism see my *Subversive Pleasures*.

7. Quoted in Greene, *The Art of Seduction*, 73.

8. Interestingly, neither Franz nor Helen Hessel passed on all their knowledge about sex to their children. In his autobiography Ulrich Hessel writes that "neither my father nor mother gave me the slightest sexual education, with the result that I had all sorts of fantastic ideas. Thus for a long time I believed that the woman's sexual organ was placed horizontally, parallel to the mouth, and could be kissed in an endless kiss. Women for me were noble and unattainable creatures. Furthermore, I thought that my mother had no sex, and therefore

had a special status. The same was true for my father, in a less absolute kind of way." The autobiography is included as part of Manfred Flügge's *Le Tourbillon de la vie*. See Flügge, *Le Tourbillon de la vie*, 146 (translation mine).

9. See ibid.

CHAPTER 18. THE GENDERED POLITICS OF FLÂNERIE

1. From Adrienne Rich, "Compulsory Heterosexuality and Lesbian Existence," quoted in Gleber, *Art of Taking a Walk*, 177.

2. Ibid., 175.

3. Quoted in ibid., 184.

4. Gleber, *Art of Taking a Walk*, 177. One of the surprises for women who join cross-dressing experiments in cities like New York is to discover that they, in their incarnations as men, can actually inspire fear in the women they happen to cross.

5. Wolff, from *Hindsight*, quoted in Gleber, *Art of Taking a Walk*, 179.

CHAPTER 19. COMPARATIVE ÉCRITURE

1. Cited in Flügge, *Le Tourbillon de la vie*, 69.

2. See Mikhail Bakhtin, "Art and Responsibility," in *Art and Answerability*, ed. Michael Holquist and Vadim Liapunov, trans. Vadim Liapunov (Austin: University of Texas Press, 1990).

3. Quoted in M. F. Hans and G. Lapouge, eds., *Les Femmes, la pornographie, l'erotisme* (Paris: Seuil, 1978), 50.

4. See Stephen Heath, *The Sexual Fix* (London: Macmillan, 1982).

5. See Mikhail Bakhtin, *Rabelais and His World*, trans. Helene Iswolsky (Cambridge, MA: MIT Press, 1968).

6. Interestingly, whereas the two Hessel sons speak adoringly of both their parents, Roché's son, Jean-Claude, describes Roché as a very unloving father. In an interview included in the film *The Key to Jules and Jim* Jean-Claude Roché complains that his father gave little either to his wife (Denise Renard) or to his son. "He never paid attention to me as a child or took me in his arms. . . . He never took the time to raise his children." Jean-Claude reports that he only learned at age twenty-one, when his parents married, that he was, in legal terms, an "illegitimate child."

7. See Flügge, *Le Tourbillon de la vie*, 128.

CHAPTER 20. *TWO ENGLISH GIRLS*: THE NOVEL

1. See MacKillop, *Free Spirits*, 156.

2. Quoted in ibid., 73.

3. Roché, *Deux Anglaises et le Continent*, 14. Subsequent page notations for this novel will be included in parentheses in the text.

4. Quoted in MacKillop, *Free Spirits*, 69.

5. Ibid., 20.

6. Ibid., 155.

7. MacKillop, *Free Spirits*, 65.

8. Ibid.

9. See Reliquet and Reliquet, *Henri-Pierre Roché*, 25.

10. See Laqueur, *Solitary Sex*.

11. Ibid., 419.

12. Quoted in ibid., 380.

13. See Margolis, *O*, 287–288.

14. Quoted in Laqueur, *Solitary Sex*, 378.

15. MacKillop points out that the letter from the League of Christian Women, with its Gothic type, "is the one most likely to have been fabricated by Roché" and that is a strand powerfully used in the Truffaut film. See MacKillop, *Free Spirits*, 60.

16. See ibid., 84–85.

17. See ibid., 122.

18. Ibid., 99.

19. René Girard, *Deceit, Desire, and the Novel* (Baltimore: Johns Hopkins University Press, 1965).

CHAPTER 21. *TWO ENGLISH GIRLS*: THE FILM

1. See de Baecque and Toubiana, *François Truffaut*, 376.

2. *Life*, Jan. 24, 1969 (cited in ibid., 410).

3. Gillain, *Le Cinéma selon François Truffaut*, 284.

4. Letter to Lilian David, cited in de Baecque and Toubiana, *François Truffaut*, 422.

5. I elaborate on these points in Stam, "Theory and Practice of Adaptation."

6. See Almendros's account of this process in Nestor Almendros, *A Man with a Camera* (New York: Farrar, Straus, and Giroux, 1984), 101–105.

7. MacKillop, *Free Spirits*, 176.

8. *Telerama*, Aug. 14, 1971 (cited in de Baecque and Toubiana, *François Truffaut*, 420).

9. de Baecque and Toubiana, *François Truffaut*, 423.

10. See Gillain, *François Truffaut*, 137.

11. For a thorough account of Truffaut's working methods, in this film and in others, see Carole Le Berre, *François Truffaut* (Paris: Cahiers du Cinema, 1993).

12. Gillain, *François Truffaut*, 132.

13. Quoted in MacKillop, *Free Spirits*, 194.

14. Quoted in ibid., 195.

15. See Gillain, *François Truffaut*, 137.

CHAPTER 22. THE (VARIOUS) MEN WHO LOVED (VARIOUS) WOMEN

1. In an interview with Anne Gillain, Truffaut points out that Léataud's diaries had the same volume as Roché's, and that like Roché, and like his own father, Léataud was an inveterate womanizer. See Gillain, *Le Cinéma selon François Truffaut*, 356.

2. I am grateful to Wyatt Phillips, a graduate student at NYU, for calling attention to this point.

3. Reprinted in *Truffaut by Truffaut: Texts and Documents Compiled by Dominique Rabourdin*, trans. Robert Erich Wolf (New York: Abrams, 1987), 155. My thanks to Wyatt Phillips for calling my attention to this quote.

4. In an interview Truffaut told Anne Gillain that nudity in Henry Miller novels remained abstract, whereas nudity in the cinema "becomes anecdotal or too picturesque, which hurts the story; the spectator begins to think about the form of the breasts, the various skin spots, the hair etc." (Gillain, *Le Cinéma selon François Truffaut*, 356).

5. See Benstock, *Women of the Left Bank*, 20.

6. Advising his actor Charles Denner on how to answer potential press questions from the "ladies of the M. L. F. [Women's Liberation Movement]," Truffaut suggested, "I favor replying that we haven't tried to soft-soap the M. L. F. but the female characters, numerous and episodic as they are, are strong enough to stand up to Bertrand Morane" (*Truffaut by Truffaut*, 156).

POSTLUDE

1. *Willie and Phil* begins with the two male leads meeting each other at a screening of the Truffaut film at the Bleeker Street Cinema in New York. We watch the audience as we hear the final lines of the original: "Everyone called them Don Quixote and Sancho Panza. Jules wanted to spread their ashes, but it wasn't allowed." From that fairly interesting beginning, the film goes downhill almost immediately. First, Mazursky, unlike Truffaut, is mainly preoccupied with the sexual aspect of the triad. He is not interested in the utopian dimension or, for that matter, in cinematic experimentation. The female lead lacks the dangerous edge and charm of Jeanne Moreau, and the two men are macho and, unlike their real-life and their intertextual prototypes, obsessed with not being gay. While Roché and Truffaut stressed the internationalism of the relationship, Mazursky stresses the ethnic tensions between the Jewish American and the Italian American, at one point reaching the low of having the two curse each other with ethnic slurs. Mazursky adds moralizing parent characters who constantly ask the young people why they haven't gotten married. The commentary is hyperexplicit and moralistic, completely lacking in poetry. In the end the film conveys no sense of either passion or friendship.

INDEX

ABOUT THE AUTHOR

Robert Stam is a professor at New York University. He is the author of more than fifteen books on literature, cinema, and cultural studies, including *Reflexivity in Film and Literature: From Don Quixote to Jean-Luc Godard, Subversive Pleasures: Bakhtin, Cultural Criticism, and Film,* and *Film Theory: An Introduction.* Most recently, he published (together with Alessandra Raengo) a trilogy of books on the subject of literature and film: *Literature through Film: Realism, Magic, and the Art of Adaptation, Literature and Film,* and *Companion to Literature and Film.* He has lived and taught in Tunisia and France and has studied both literature and film theory at the Sorbonne and at Paris III (Censier). He regularly teaches the course on the French New Wave in the Cinema Studies Department at New York University. An interview with him is featured on the Criterion DVD of *Jules and Jim.*

A NOTE ON THE TYPE

This book was set in the OpenType version of Adobe Warnock.
Begun as a personal typeface for the co-founder of Adobe Systems, John
Warnock, by noted type designer Robert Slimbach, the project gradually grew
to include an italic and multiple weights, and it was decided to release the
typeface to the general public. A full-featured modern composition family
designed for versatility in a variety of mediums and printing situations,
Warnock synergizes classically derived letterforms of old style types
with elements of transitional and modern type design.

Book designed and composed by Kevin Hanek

Printed and bound by Sheridan Books,
Ann Arbor, Michigan